Reading and the curriculum

Proceedings of the seventh annual study conference
of the United Kingdom Reading Association
Durham 1970

Editor   John E. Merritt

Ward Lock Educational

ISBN 0 7062 3330 1

First published 1971

Set in 10 on 12 point Press Roman
by David Ashley Limited
for Ward Lock Educational
116 Baker Street, London W1M 2BB
Printed in England

Contents

Introduction

As knowledge proliferates understanding tends to disintegrate. It is more important, therefore, to help students to identify critical relationships than to 'top them up' with information.

If we ourselves cannot perceive the critical relationships within the content we purvey how can we in all conscience expect it of our pupils — either now or later?

If we choose to persist in our teaching, the least we can do is to help our pupils to discover these critical relationships within the field of our knowledge that our own education should have helped us to understand in the first place. If we step off our pedestals to do this, and thus stop pretending to be that which we are not, we shall render our pupils the greatest service we can ever offer — our humility in the face of our own relative ignorance and their potential which we may unloose. They may then value our counsel instead of merely accepting, or reacting against, our brittle example.

The teacher of reading is not exempt from these strictures. On the contrary, the reading situation is one in which these considerations should be central in our thinking and our practice. This is the theme of these proceedings.

John E. Merritt

Part one
Reading and the curriculum

Reading and the curriculum

John E. Merritt

Professor of Educational Studies
Open University

Introduction

The title of my paper this morning is 'Reading and the curriculum'. And I propose to begin with some resounding cliches in terms of the state of man and of society. Cliches are statements which are so beautiful, or impelling, or important that they are universally taken up and repeated so often that they lose their impact. This is a phenomenon like saying a word over and over again until it loses its meaning and becomes a mere jumble of sounds. So, in an age of mass communication, we are exposed daily to the frightful problems of our age until we come to regard them with glazed eyes and dulled sense of responsibility. But these problems are the essential core around which educational thinking must revolve and therefore I make no apology for beginning my remarks with reference to facts with which you are all too familiar.

Man can now grow ten ears of corn where one grew before. He can create his own atmosphere and carry it with him to the ocean bed, or to the moon — tomorrow, perhaps, to the boundaries of our solar system. He can control the climate of his home and place of work. Tomorrow, he may manipulate the climate of the open spaces. He can hear over distances far beyond the range of any ear and see events taking place far beyond the range of human vision. He can move mountains and create great lakes. He can erect buildings that rival nature in their grandeur and design machines whose action is more precise and powerful than that of muscle — animal or man. He can travel at a speed that mind can scarcely comprehend and calculate with computers at a speed far beyond the capability of the human brain. In addition, he can manipulate the minds of his fellows with a degree of sophistication that is not yet fully realized.

7

Against all this, millions of human beings starve in the midst of plenty, millions die early because of our polluted atmosphere, many are cold and lack the elementary comforts essential to human decency, millions of people live and die in ignorance of the world beyond their neighbourhood, and even on our own doorstep people persecute and kill each other with little regard for that tolerance and compassion which is the very basis of the religions they profess.

How extraordinary it is that man is so magnificent in all except the practical expression of his humanity beyond his immediate reference group — that with so much power at his disposal his behaviour as an organized social animal is such that a pessimist would be tempted to classify him as 'ineducable'.

In setting the theme for this Study Congress as 'Reading and the curriculum' I am taking the view that man is in fact educable. If he were not, he could never have learned how to achieve such mastery of the physical universe, nor could so many have learned how to dominate the minds of their fellows for their own advantage. If men can be educated to do all this, where is the educationist who will suggest that man cannot be taught two simple lessons that are common, with rare exceptions, to the lowliest animals — not to foul his own nest, and not to persecute his own kind? To put it more positively, who will say that man cannot be taught to think constructively about himself and his fellows?

In teaching constructive thinking our failure as educators is, in my view, a simple one. It is simple to diagnose and, in principle, perfectly simple to remedy. In practice it is somewhat harder, as we ourselves are the product of our education system and find it hard to break the shackles of our own inheritance. It is hard, too, because we are so insulated from the consequences of our failures. The teacher in the infant school is far removed from the 'bovver boy' — skin-head and white collar variety — whom she helps to produce. The teacher at the secondary stage is insulated by an examination system which makes almost as slight a contribution to the child's broader educational needs as the degrees on which his 'successful' pupils will dissipate the majestic years of their youth. Not for us the rapid descent into bankruptcy that is the fate of the business man who fails to satisfy the demands of his market. Not for us the inglorious defeat of the soldier who has fought the wrong battle at the wrong time and in the wrong way. In the midst of our failure we can sail sublimely on, fortified each day by the reinforcement we receive from our favoured pupils as they vie for our esteem; fortified also by our feeling of virtue, as we succeed in getting some of the less favoured to achieve that limited array of educational tricks with which the more able so readily give us satisfaction.

The supreme tragedy is that the 'good' teachers are often the worst offenders. Their satisfaction with the fantasy world of the classroom is complete. They can close their classroom door, blot out the world and bask in the love they feel for their children – and their children's love for them.

But love, alas, is not enough. Love can make a man whip his children to rid them of the devil, or burn the heretic at the stake. Nor is it enough for us to teach children the tricks required to manipulate the forces of nature.

What we must do is to help children to understand their own immediate and long term needs and to appreciate the legitimate needs of others. That is what the syllabus is about. We must help children to learn to satisfy those needs, whilst respecting the reasonable needs of others. That is what the curriculum is about. We must help children to determine their own life course with due regard for others. That is what education is about.

And this is the point at which we singularly fail. We are content to be teachers of subjects, or teachers of tool skills such as mathematics or reading. We are not prepared to be educators and consider whether the knowledge we purvey is adequate in range and relevance. We are not prepared to tie tool skills sufficiently closely to their applications. We are not prepared to do either within a context which ensures that children develop all those abilities necessary to self-determination and humanitarian consideration. We train them instead as manual or intellectual labourers.

Education in self-determination

I have said that the solution is simple. It is so simple and so obvious that you will listen, agree, assume you already do it, and forget it. And so you do. But you do not do it well enough.

In order to do what is required well enough you must analyze what you do and do it consciously and deliberately at all times – not fittingly as the mood takes you, and sometimes not at all.

But what is this 'it' that I am talking about, which is so commonly practised, yet so neglected? 'It' is simply that logical sequence of events which is essential to the efficient making of decisions and the taking of effective actions. I propose to describe this sequence so that you can see how essential it is to self-determination. I shall then use this same sequence in tackling the problem of the relationship between reading and the curriculum.

Let us first look at the simple sequence which may be observed in any complete action – Motivation Plan Implementation Review. We may remember the initials – MPIR. There is no action without motivation, no satisfaction without a plan that is then implemented, no satisfactory profit from experience without review.

But this is a simple descriptive account of what naturally happens. Our job is to be prescriptive. It is our job to analyze this process and see whether we can help children to control their own actions in accordance with an adequate appraisal of their own needs and the dictates of humanity and responsibility. Let us therefore take each stage separately and consider the implications for the teacher.

Motivation

It is not enough that a child should have knowledge of his needs, he must be able to weigh one need against another and determine his priorities. To do this, he must first distinguish between his *aims* and his *objectives*. His aims are those states of body or mind which he wishes to attain. His objectives are the environmental correlates of those aims. Thus, the satisfaction of hunger may be an aim. A plate of steak might be the correlated objective.

An academic distinction you may say. But Alexander was frustrated because he ran out of objectives. There were no countries left to conquer. He had failed to recognize life's essential paradox — that it is the material objectives which prove ephemeral to the mind and the intangibles, i.e. the aims, that alone have substance. How many millionaires — and headmasters — are frustrated because they have reached the pinnacle of their ambitions. Having achieved their objectives they are left without the aims that would make them worthy custodians of their fortunes.

I must ask you, is this the first consideration in each segment of your teaching? Do you really help the child to survey all his needs, define his aims and set his own objectives? Or do you cunningly limit his choice, if you give him any, to that which is convenient to you? Or again, do you hasten through this process quickly so that you can get down to 'brass tacks', mistaking the shadow — reading age perhaps, or examination marks — for the substance of educational progress?

Plan

This subdivides into *strategies* and *tactics*. Strategies are the theoretically possible ways of achieving an objective; tactics are the ways in which actual resources are to be deployed. An academic distinction? But how often do we narrow a child's horizon by imposing aims, objectives and strategies, then praise him to our colleagues for his ingenuity in seeing how to carry out the task we set. We might as well praise a lemming for its ingenuity in overcoming obstacles on its route to self-destruction in the sea. Surely, if a child has so much ingenuity he can be educated to operate at the higher levels and not merely at the lower, for this calls on no greater powers of intellect.

Implementation

This subdivides into *method* and *technique* and I will not elaborate on these distinctions at this point. This is the area on which the vast bulk of what passes for education is concentrated. We spend millions of man hours teaching children what and how to do. All we forget is to spend sufficient time helping them to discover why they need to do it in the first place. Of course we can tell them it is for their own good, but a method is only as good as the results it produces, and telling children things is not the most effective of our methods.

Review

This resolves into *evaluation* and *consolidation*. Evaluation is the assessment of each phase of an action in terms of the extent to which it helped in the achievement of aims. How can we expect children to develop the habit of evaluating aims if in the first place they knew little of them and cared less?

Again, how much useless activity do we ourselves continue to indulge in simply because we do not take the trouble to evaluate what we are doing in terms of aims? Like Alexander, we are too 'hooked' on objectives. If our children show progress on a word recognition test or get the 'right' number of O levels we are quite content that we are doing our job. But if we do not look beyond these objectives and evaluate in terms of aims we are are neglecting our professional responsibility. If we do not systematically ensure that children evaluate each action they carry out in terms of aims we are neglecting our educational responsibility.

Consolidation is the final stage. Here, we allow children to labour for years then consign the products of their endeavours to the waste-paper basket. Little wonder that so many children have as much contempt for school work as we have — and see little point in providing fodder for our litter bins. If work is worth doing it is surely worth storing for future reference. If it is to be discarded it should only be because it is replaced by something better. The child needs to consolidate his educational endeavours by storing the products of his labours so that he can refer back to them at any time. He must learn to select what is of lasting value, to edit and to update. If he spends the bulk of his time discarding the products of his endeavours then we, and he, must question the validity of the original exercise.

You will see from this analysis that educating children towards responsible autonomy is not some high flown aim to which we may merely pay lip-service, nor is it something that can be achieved by well-meaning but woolly minded 'progressives'. Neither can it be achieved by limiting a child's educational diet to subject teaching and skill training. Instead, it is a curriculum component which requires the most meticulous analysis and assiduous effort on the part of the teacher. The aim of personal autonomy must be converted into precise educational objectives, and the above analysis is the first stage in that process.

This cannot be left to any single teacher but must be developed at all times and in every curriculum activity by every member of a school staff acting as a member of a team. This team must devise strategies and tactics to achieve these objectives and devise new methods, or adapt existing methods, in order to implement these plans and evaluate and consolidate each gain. Now the question is how may we marry the teaching of reading to this curriculum requirement?

Education in reading
What is sauce for the goose is sauce for the gander. Let us go through our own personal autonomy routine with regard to education in reading.

Aims in teaching reading
The aim of reading is to profit from the experiences of others in seeking to satisfy our own needs.

Different needs call for us to think in different ways. We do not think in precisely the same way about food as we think about personal relationships. We do not think in the same way about science as we do about art. But reading is thinking in the context of print, therefore reading in relation to one need is often very different from reading in relation to another need. If, then, we wish to develop an overall competence in reading we must develop reading in the context of those needs which are immediately significant to the child and which will be significant to him as an adult. We must, as our American colleagues say, teach reading in the content areas — but this must be a need-content and not merely a subject-content.

This does of course mean that teachers must have a comprehensive understanding of human needs — a theme I propose to develop elsewhere (Merritt and Cohen — in preparation).

Still within the context of aims we must consider the nature of the media which must be read in order to gain information to satisfy our various needs — newspapers and magazines, private and official letters, forms and instructions, and so on. Anyone who has made any serious study of reading skills knows that the skills required in reading vary according to the medium. An income tax form is very different from a love letter and must be read for somewhat different kinds of implication! Again, a publicity brochure or advertisement calls for skills rather different from those required when reading an authoritative textbook on a well established subject.

Finally, in considering our aims in teaching reading we must consider the mode of approach in reading. From what I have said earlier it should be quite clear what this should be. Reading entails a motive, requires a plan, must be implemented and must be followed by review — again MPIR or motivation, plan, implementation, review. Let us spell this out in a little more detail.

Motivation
The reader's aims
These must be defined following an analysis of needs, the kinds of resource materials to which he may have recourse, and priorities to be observed in selection of material.

The reader's objectives
These must be specified in terms of the particular questions to which answers are required, and the specific materials to be accessed for each question, bearing in mind the suitability and availability of each unit of material.

Plan
The reader's strategies
These must be designed to ensure that the reader selects materials which are suitable in terms of his criteria and which are feasible from the point of convenience of access.

The reader's tactics
These must satisfy the criteria of economy of time and his own capabilities in selecting each specific source or section of material within each source.

Implementation
The reader's methods
This is the process of identifying sequences and perceiving main ideas. It includes gambits such as locating key words and noting factual detail, gaining impressions and scrutinizing assumptions, identifying arguments and evaluating conclusions.

The reader's techniques
These are the hierarchies of learning sets relating to linguistic competence which I have referred to elsewhere (Merritt 1970a) as the intermediate skills, and those more elementary recognition skills which we may call the primary skills. They are manifested in the flexible use of scanning, skimming and processing habits which are deployed according to the objectives to be achieved in successive units of material.

Critical as these skills are, note how low down they come in our list. This is because they are not what reading is about. Like the data tape or the filmstrip, they are merely the medium through which we get the message.

The reader's evaluation
This entails checking the answers against the questions in a systematic

fashion and checking back on any discrepancies. It includes evaluation of performance in each phase of the reading sequence as well as evaluation of the results.

The reader's consolidation

This entails committing to memory the key concepts, relating each item to every relevant area of personal knowledge, storing useful material in the resource unit with appropriate cross references, and communicating significant information to those who want it and will make good use of it. This is the critical phase of the action and it is clear that we are as inadequate in this as we are in the preparatory stages. This is the point at which the reader's subjective schema must be modified and his horizons enlarged.

These then are the aims of the teacher: to develop reading in the context of the child's needs, to develop the ability to read the particular kinds of material which must be processed if those needs are to be understood, and to develop the child's autonomy as a reader. Our aims for the reader are simply a facet of our curriculum aims.

Objectives in teaching reading

Our objectives in teaching reading must be defined in terms of the competence which we think our children should attain and they must be limited to those we need to teach. In this day and age, when presidents, business executives and academics are taking courses in efficient reading it is alarming that so many teachers think that learning to read is something that happens in the infant school and determine their objectives accordingly. They equate reading with that essential but minute area which I briefly mentioned under the title of primary skills.

No doubt many of those present today would reject such a view, but how. many have worked through the analysis made above and gone on to define the whole range of objectives which are essential if their pupils are to make satisfactory progress? Alas, not many!

This, of course, is an exacting demand. But no one entering the profession was ever given a certificate stating that the job was easy. Only those who have failed to work through the implications of the foregoing analysis systematically can jog along complacently, assuring themselves that they do 'that sort of thing'.

Strategies in teaching reading

There are four principal strategies which we may adopt in teaching reading and these, not surprisingly, are the four principal curriculum strategies:

1 reality situations

2 simulations
3 practical investigations
4 theoretical studies.

1 Reality situations

When I speak of a reality situation I refer to a situation in which whatever actions occur are directly related to someone's immediate needs. Thus, if children from a primary school run errands for an infirm adult or relieve the loneliness of a senior citizen, that is a reality situation. If pupils in a secondary school relieve the anxiety of an overanxious parent by looking after her children for periods in the school flat, that is a reality situation. If they research the holiday resorts in Britain and abroad so that parents can use the school as a resource unit, that is a reality situation. If they research the leisure facilities available in their own neighbourhood, that is a reality situation. One could go on for ever giving examples, but I would suggest to you that it is convenient to consider reality situations under five headings: Home and Family; The Community; The Consumer; Employment; Leisure.

Through the exploitation of reality situations in each of these areas, children can learn about their own needs as well as the needs of others, and how both may best be satisfied.

Such activities provide excellent opportunities for children to define their own aims, establish objectives, devise strategies, and so on. In other words, putting children in reality situations provides the teacher automatically with opportunities to help children to develop personal autonomy — provided, that is, that the teacher has taken the trouble to master the routines I have described above. If not, the product will simply be a lot of busy-looking children, working like ants to create a display of work that looks marvellous to the visitor but is fully understood only by the teacher — not the children.

The reality situation, like any other, only works for the children if the teacher is concerned to see that they do their thing, not his. How many exhibitions are simply products of the teacher's professional ego rather than the children's understanding? This occurs when the teacher has set the wrong objectives. The only antidote to self-deception of this kind is for the teacher to undertake the somewhat tortuous task of working through his own personal autonomy routine using the model exemplified in the structure of this lecture.

Given the reality situation and full pupil participation, the reading routines fit in as one of the many varieties of the autonomy routine that children may adopt. If and when you read this lecture in its published form you should, at this point, go back and check through the MPIR sequence which I spelled out in terms of reading, and think of this in relation to a variety of realistic situations.

Returning however to our own strategies in teaching reading, our next consideration is that of media. The reality situation demands realistic media. In the case of the resource unit on leisure facilities, for example, one might well consult brochures, guide books and newspaper articles. However these often provide a somewhat biased picture, or fail to give information which is of direct concern to child or parent.

The people who may be in the best position to fill in the picture are children in the areas concerned. They can readily provide information about, for example, what is really a 'stone's throw' from the beach, oil on the foreshore, exorbitant prices, tatty amusement arcades, and so on.

Information obtained from other children provides an extra dimension to a child's understanding. On the one hand, such information provides a check on his other sources and makes him appreciate how careful he must be about what to rely upon as evidence. On the other hand, it provides him with a viewpoint that is more likely to coincide with his own, and which is therefore more significant to him.

2 Simulations

This is the world of make believe. Children love make believe and can learn a great deal from simulation. One example is the commercial department in the comprehensive school which sets up a number of 'firms', each 'doing business' with each other. Experiences that would take months or years in reality can thus be telescoped into weeks or days. This approach can be infinitely more satisfying and meaningful than the dreary routine of book-keeping exercises.

There are, of course, many kinds of simulation exercise, varying from the games children play in the nursery school – doctors, schools, mummies and daddies – to the harsher economic games of the business school or the war games of the Pentagon. It is not in my brief today to examine and evaluate all the possible applications. For a useful introduction Tansey and Unwin (1969) and Walford (1969) might be consulted.

In simulations, as in reality situations, there are numerous opportunities for children to work systematically through the personal autonomy routine – defining aims, specifying objectives, defining strategies, devising tactics etc. Indeed, these situations have minimal value if they do not. In addition, there will be many occasions when this routine will automatically convert to a reading routine. If simulations are conducted with more than one school taking part, then once again we have opportunities for developing communication skills with children using material prepared by other children to add an extra dimension to their understanding.

3 Practical investigations

These are the present favourite for the 'progressive' teachers, and the investigations carried out are often monumental in their pointlessness.

Their greatest value lies in their use for developing personal autonomy and the ability to perceive relevance. Too often they become exercises for converting children into mines of useless information. If there is some real point in a practical investigation, and if it is clearly perceived as relevant by the child, then it is most likely that children will benefit by sharing their experiences. Thus, once again, communication between schools may be seen as an important educational strategy and one which provides suitable materials for reading.

4   Theoretical studies

As this form of education is the norm rather than the exception, I do not propose to dwell upon this theme. It is unfortunate that theoretical studies are associated, in the minds of many teachers, with formal teaching. I would affirm, on the contrary, that in helping a child to undertake formal studies our aim should be to help him towards independence, not teacher dependence. The teacher must be only one of many sources which the child can use. This means that every subject teacher should be concerned, first and foremost, to develop the child's ability to go through the routines referred to throughout this paper and described, albeit briefly, in an earlier section.

Children pursuing theoretical studies may work independently or in small or larger groups. Like investigators at college or university they should be capable of communicating with others pursuing studies in the same field. Thus the exchange of experiences between children is as vital in theoretical studies as in those which have a severely practical basis.

Now, let me draw together some general points about experience exchange (Merritt 1964) as a strategy for teaching reading.

First, in the four curriculum strategies described above there can be no doubt that the development of personal autonomy must be central. Reading routines are one particular form a personal autonomy routine may take and must be accorded commensurate priority in devising curriculum strategies. Experience exchange provides a situation *par excellence* for the teacher to help children to see the need for developing those habitual routines which are the essential basis for the exercise of personal autonomy.

Second, experience exchange has other, more specific values.

1   Vocabulary: The vocabulary of children is ever changing. Using children's material the vocabulary is always up to date. As this material is always to be contrasted with other sources, motivation increases the likelihood of vocabulary enrichment.

2   Sentence structure: The more closely sentence structures match our expectations the more fluently we read (Merritt 1970b). The use of children's material ensures that children have adequate opportunities for developing fluency. This will tend to transfer to published material. Being

able to read the more familiar structures with greater fluency, the child will cope more readily with the residual problems.

3   A further point on sentence structure: The more closely sentence structures resemble those used by the child in his own speech the greater his comprehension (Ruddell 1965). Experience exchange material, being for this reason easier to comprehend, encourages the habit of reading to comprehend rather than the sterile habit of 'reading' single words, or reading to produce what our American colleagues call the 'spit back' in response to so called comprehension exercises.

4   Experiential content: The more divorced the content of our reading from our own experience, the less we understand it. The writer may use familiar words, write in a familiar style and adopt a simple structure in his presentation. However, unless we have some sort of experience relating to the content our comprehension is seriously limited.

The adult writer, I propose, has very great difficulty in bridging the gap between his experience and that of the child. In terms of promoting real understanding, as opposed to the ability to produce in the child uncomprehending paraphrasing, many textbooks are as much use as the person of whom we ask the way in a strange town. The better he knows the way, the less likely it is that he will remember to tell us of those critical features which are so familiar to him and so unfamiliar to us. Little wonder that the child gets lost!

Few textbook writers possess both the requisite knowledge of their own subject and the ability to communicate to the child what he needs to know in language he can understand. The products of experience exchange however, are the products of a comparable experience. A significantly deeper level of comprehension is therefore to be expected. Moreover, any deficiencies in communication may speedily be remedied in the course of a second exchange. This in itself provides a salutary discipline and brings the sender up sharply in his appreciation of the requirements of effective communication. The direct experience the child thus gains, and the materials received in the exchange, serve then to help the child in his efforts to profit from the experience of the more knowledgeable writer of the textbook.

I do not intend now to proceed to an examination of the teacher's tactics, methods and techniques in organizing experience exchange. This will be done by subsequent speakers who are actively organizing this kind of work in their own schools. I will, however, conclude by commenting on the review phase.

Evaluation in teaching reading
This stage, like each other stage, has its own discipline, and I am very

conscious of the fact that hitherto I have given you the main headings but not the subheadings which guided my exposition. For this stage it is essential that I should spell them out. In fact, they follow obviously from what I have already said.

First, one must look back at the aims and reappraise them in the light of experience. Next one must compare the aims with the objectives achieved and consider the discrepancies. One must review the strategies and consider how effective they were as procedures for achieving objectives. One must also check that they were entirely consistent with the aims. For example, the strategy of stealing money might be excellent in terms of some financial objective but it is hardly consistent with what I hope would be included in our aims. Similarly, one must check tactics against strategies and against aims, methods against tactics and against aims, and techniques against methods and against aims. The formula for this may be set down as follows: A—AO; OS—AS; ST—AT; TM—AM; MT—AT.

The evaluation may be subjective or objective. That is, you may rely on personal judgment, or on some sort of measures, or on tests. Either way, the evaluation must be systematic and lead to a clear recognition of what still needs to be done.

Consolidation in teaching reading

Just as the pupils need to store what is of value, so must the teacher. Much of our failure in our work, our inability to make sufficient progress, springs from the fact that we do not organize ourselves so that we can profit adequately from experience. How many exciting things have you done in the past that are not now included in your repertoire? How many of you can readily put your hands on that article that so stimulated your imagination and which would now serve to fire the imagination of a colleague? How many of you can now find that pamphlet which is just what this child now needs? How many of you can lay your hands on the essential details of that project which you must now plan again from scratch? Or if you can find all these things, how long will it take you? Are they all stored neatly and indexed for convenient retrieval? Or are they piled up amongst a heap of miscellaneous items whose only relationship is that achieved by the frantic random search you made last time you wanted to look something up?

I'm afraid that most of our consolidation falls in the latter category. Worse, like the farmyard hog wallowing smugly in its sty, we tend to be proud of it. This sentimental, self-indulgent, self-protective attachment to inefficiency from which we all suffer may be good enough for managing our private affairs — although I personally do not believe this. It is certainly not good enough for the work we have to do.

Again, we are stuck in the implementation rut. We spend so much time being busy we don't stop to think what it is we are being busy about. In order to do thinking of this kind, and to make steady progress in developing our teaching skill, we need to be able to draw readily upon our previous experiences, and those of our colleagues. Our need for a resource unit is just the same as that of the child. We can use his resource unit to help him to evaluate his progress. We can use our resource unit to evaluate our own and to use previous experiences as a springboard for further action.

Perhaps I should reverse the argument. Once we have learned how valuable it is to practise efficient consolidation in our own work, we may realize how important this is for the child. As we develop consolidation skills ourselves — collating, analyzing, summarizing, editing, storing, referencing and retrieving — we realize how invaluable this process is in the development of critical and evaluative reading skills in children.

Now, let me review experience exchange in relation to the total process of reading. As I have shown, the manner in which children's material can be handled provides opportunities for development in each aspect:

1 The children can establish their own aims, determining their own needs and specifying their own objectives.
2 The children can devise their own strategies and their own tactics.
3 The children can assume complete responsibility for the operation and this creates, in them, an understanding of the need to develop their methods and techniques, their work-attack skills, and scanning, skimming and processing skills.
4 After any exchange of material the children are highly motivated to evaluate what has been achieved. They are highly critical of their own work and that of others. They are ready to indulge in surprisingly perceptive analyses of what is and is not worth doing, and how things should be done. They have opportunities when consolidating to relate each aspect to each previous experience and to previous knowledge. In so doing, the aim is not to blur important distinctions but to note important relationships and so develop their understanding of the world and of themselves. For an account of how this approach works with less able children at the secondary stage, the reader should refer to Laybourn (1970).

Conclusion

And here I return to my opening remarks. No one can be sure that we can, through education, ensure that growth of tolerance and concern for others which man needs if he is to survive. What we do know is that without opportunities for studying the needs of other people in other areas and other lands we cannot escape from the stultifying effects of parochialism which let us tolerate the suffering of others with such fortitude. The growth of regular contact between children in different schools and in different countries is, I believe, of vital importance as a means of achieving education in social responsibility. I believe this is the most important factor in human development. That is why I believe we should encourage the forms of communication I have described not as an occasional expedient but as a major educational principle.

This morning I have taken you through a rigorously analyzed and rigorously argued examination of the relationship between reading and the curriculum. I have also presented you with a framework within which to examine your own role in relation to both. If you ask yourselves now how much you can remember, the answer, I'm afraid, will be 'not very much'. You will be tempted, as I said at the outset, to agree with what I have said, assume you already do it, and forget it. Such is the inadequacy of the lecture as a means of communicating. Only if you have had the experience of debating at length the implications of each separate point and working through to actual implementation and review, would you begin to appreciate the full significance of what I have been saying. However, we can at least indulge ourselves in an experience exchange, for some of my colleagues who will be speaking today have begun the process of working these ideas out and following them through to the classroom floor. If they can succeed in putting flesh on the bare bones of educational structure that I have exposed then I shall not have made my point – but they they will have made it for me.

Reading to some purpose: Schedule for the development of effective reading routines

Need: Deciding what information is needed and where it may be found
Aims

Modules:	What are the major units within which the information obtained is to be organized for the particular purpose for which it is required?
Media:	What classes of printed material may be accessed in order to obtain this information?
Mode:	Will the material be subjected to overview, reference or systematic study?

Formulate aims, in terms of priorities, indicating mode to be adopted in relation to each class of medium.
Objectives

Modules:	What are the specific units of information that can be obtained from each kind of medium?
Media:	In the case of each unit of information, what class of source will provide answers?

Mode: What questions may be posed in the case of each specific kind of source material?

Specify objectives in terms of the questions to be answered by reference to each kind of source material taking into account utility of the sources for the purpose and their availability.

Plan: Deciding how to find and how to select the most likely sources of information

Strategies

Modules: What are the resources which might be accessed for each class of source materials? (e.g. libraries, firms, associations)

Media: What or who are the media which may be utilized in order to locate and obtain these sources? (e.g. information services, tutor librarians, personal contacts etc)

Mode: In each case, how may these media best be utilized in order to obtain appropriate sources?

Design feasible strategies for obtaining access to the most suitable sources.

Tactics

Modules: What are the best sources among those located? (e.g. which book, index, pamphlet, newspaper, journal etc)

Media: What are the parts of each source which provide information which can be used in evaluation?

Mode: What criteria may be adopted for the purpose of arriving at an evaluation?

Devise tactics for making an efficient selection of sources which are within your capability.

Implementation: The reading process

Methods

Modules: What kinds of item must I identify in respect of each question?

Media: How are these items dispersed throughout the medium?

Mode: How may I locate each item?

Apply economical and convenient routines and gambits in locating each item.

Technique

Modules: What relevant facts or ideas are to be found in this passage?

Media: How are these facts or ideas expressed?

Mode: How can I ensure that I have read this passage sufficiently accurately for my purpose?

Deploy those habits and skills which require least effort but which are most effective in decoding.

22

Review: Getting maximum benefit from reading

Evaluation

  Modules: What must be evaluated?

  Media: What materials may be used in evaluation?

  Mode: What kinds of procedure may be adopted in evaluation?

Evaluate achievements systematically in terms of aims.

Consolidation

  Modules: What are the categories to be used in consolidating?

  Media: What resources may be used in consolidating?

  Mode: What are the essential considerations?

Consolidate achievements comprehensively and constructively, storing material required for future reference in appropriate sections of personal resource unit, cross-referencing where necessary and communicating information to others when this is necessary or desirable.

References

Laybourn, M. (1970) 'An experiment in experience exchange' in *ACE Forum 4: Teaching Reading in Junior and Secondary Schools* London: Ginn

Merritt, J. E. (1966) 'Developing competence in reading comprehension' in *Reading Instruction: An International Forum* Newark, Delaware: International Reading Association

Merritt, J. E. (1970a) 'Reading skills re-examined' in *Readings in Educational Psychology* Stone, E. (ed.) London:Methuen

Merritt, J. E. (1970b) 'The intermediate skills' in *Reading Skills: Theory and Practice* Gardner, K. (ed.) London: Ward Lock Educational

Merritt, J. E. and Cohen, A. (in preparation) *Priorities in Education* London: Ward Lock Educational

Ruddell, R. B. (1965) 'The effect of oral and written patterns of language structure on reading comprehension' *The Reading Teacher* no. 18

Tansey, P. J. and Unwin, D. (1969) *Simulation and gaming in education* London: Methuen

Walford, R. (1969) *Games in Geography* London: Longmans

Literature and the curriculum – A teacher's confession

Frazer Thompson

Deputy Headmaster
Newtownbreda Primary School, Belfast

> Alice was beginning to get very tired of sitting by her sister on the bank, and of having nothing to do; once or twice she had peeped into the book her sister was reading, but it had no pictures or conversations in it, 'and what is the use of a book,' thought Alice, 'without pictures or conversation?'

To begin with I'd like to sympathize with Alice. It was just over 100 years ago and Lorina, Alice's sister, was reading what seems to have been a very 'improving' book. She undoubtedly would not have been allowed to read anything of a frivolous or romantic nature. Small wonder that Alice made her escape from that rather overbearing literary environment by diving down a convenient rabbit hole.

I suppose we all have our personal ideas as to what constitutes literature. We each create for ourselves our own literary environment. For my small daughter it means anything which she is able to read. It's 'Peter and Jane are on the swing' and 'Halt major road ahead' and 'Guinness is good for you'. It's also the stories read to her at bedtime and the tales she tells about her adventures at nursery school. To all these aspects of her literary environment she attaches value; and I think of literature as being that body of literary composition with which I have contact and to which I attach value.

I must then, in coming into the environment of my classroom, consider the value of the literature pertaining to that environment. My values have some validity here but so too have the values of the children – that is possibly thirty or forty different valuations of that specific body of literary composition.

In general terms the literary environment in the classroom can usefully be divided into two main parts: firstly other people's work, secondly our own work.

I should like to say a little about how I deal with other people's work – that is work produced outside the classroom. I feel a strong duty to control very carefully the literary environment of my children but in order to do this I must work out my criteria for acting as a type of censor. I must do this in the face of a huge quantity of available material and a small amount of cash. My use of those slim resources must satisfy the values and tastes of as many of the individuals in the class as possible.

What criteria do I use?

1   Readability: The children must be able to read the book.

2   Suitable maturity of subject matter: Often I find it very difficult to find material that is easy to read and yet that appeals. Young Keith may find the Ladybird *Cinderella* readable but he is so much more likely to enjoy reading the Ladybird *Adventures of Columbus*. Again the range of maturity among the children means that whereas Elizabeth is tackling and appreciating *The Wool Pack* by Cynthia Harnett, Leslie has a large enough challenge in reading *The Fox That Went Hunting* by John Burningham. I feel too that we need to give in more often to children in the sense of allowing them access to material of a level which they have long since passed. I found Peter and Ann engrossed in some infant library books which had been delivered to my room for allocation. Subsequently we all·had a most enjoyable morning reading the books, commenting on content, layout and style in a 'whole book' way that was so much more difficult with more advanced books. We ought not always to tell a child that a certain book is too childish.

3   Suitability for sex: I seem to be able to discover lots of well composed books for boys but a woefully inadequate supply for girls. Some books are much less sex-specific in this way.

4   Social implication: We need to be aware of the social environment in order to respect the feelings of the children. This might appear more of a problem in some areas than in others. In Belfast I think deeply before reading Paul Gallico's *The Small Miracle* to a Protestant class. Here I am saying no more than that as in many areas of the class environment there exist sensitive spots where the teacher needs to tread softly. It was pointed out to me by an inspector that a book in the school library contained a poem which spoke of glorious King William as 'that bastard Billy'. This description would clearly be quite in order in some areas. In others it is not.

5   The children's tastes: The overriding check on all these criteria is provided by the children. They either like it or they don't. If you're lucky and have reckoned their tastes correctly they·will like most of the books provided. In any case I have always suggested a change for any boy or girl who is not enjoying a book with the proviso that they read enough of it to give the book a fair chance.

The greatest difficulty in creating a literary environment in the classroom is to translate the above criteria into literature by providing a rich and varied selection of books and accepting only those books to which I attach literary value. Rubbish is commonplace and there is no room for it in a classroom. But how do I tell the difference? I'd like to read you some rubbish and then some work to which I attach value but I have to stress that this is only my opinion.

This is an extract from a book about Thelma who has 'adventures' at boarding school:

'It's no use to talk, Dad,' said Thelma. 'I hate the idea of school.' Mr Relson sighed as he put down his painting brush and palette, turning sadly to his fifteen year old daughter, who sat perched cross-legged on a pile of crimson silk curtains which lay on the studio sofa.

'I'm sure I hate it quite as much as you do, Mia,' he replied dismally; 'but it is for — '

Thelma bounced up, and was in time to place a small, sunburnt hand over her father's lips before the hateful word was spoken.

'It is not for my good, you dearest, most worried of dads,' she urged. 'But don't be afraid. I'm going to Polgrath Manor School tomorrow; I'm going to work like a Briton; and I'm going to 'finish' and turn up my hair on my seventeenth birthday. After which, beware! for I shall rule you with a rod of iron, and not even allow Sarah to interfere on your behalf.'

They laughed joyously over the picture and the happy future when schooldays should be done with. There were only the two of them — Thelma and her father — since the bright-haired young wife and mother had died when Thelma was three years old, and Thelma never remembered any care but that of her father, who idolized her, and old Sarah the housekeeper. Sarah ruled the house at Hampstead with a rod of iron, and alternately scolded and spoilt Thelma, who, she was wont to say, 'was too masterful by half, but with that way of coming over a body with her wheedling there was no resisting it.'

It had been a bitter blow to poor Thelma when, three months ago, an unexpected aunt had returned from India, and swooped down on the happy little household in Bohemia.

This miserable shallow tale finally reaches its climax on page 299.

But Thelma only laughed, and spread her toast even more recklessly.

'Nothing matters at this moment,' she retorted, 'because we're as happy as can be. And next week you shall see Treloan's Cave for yourself. I wonder if Bertie will still be there. I hope he won't have gone to France.'

'Ah, Bertie,' smiled Mr Relson. 'I had forgotten him on the list of attractions.'

But Thelma had not.

I found this book in my classroom. I may say it is no longer there.

If I am forced to try to define why this tale is unworthy of a place in my classroom I have to say that it lacks richness of language, ideas and characters.

In my view it does not compare with a story like Leon Garfield's *Jack Holborn* (1964). At this point in the story the smugglers are about to land on an apparently deserted beach:

A very breathless night with no moon and a black blanket of a sky; mighty close, it seemed — as though we were shut away from Heaven for some purpose or other . . . .A sheet, hanging loose from the mainyard, began to smack gently against the mast: and such was the quiet that it sounded like a man being flogged. Then the distant sound of the longboat touching on shingle. . . .

I think it must have been when the boat was not quite beached — secured, I mean — that there was disaster. Another minute might have accomplished more.

In the woods and undergrowth, an ambush had been waiting! Very quiet and deadly they'd lain there: watchful: eyes along musket-barrels: observing the little beach: breathing deep when the longboat came: counting footfalls on the shingle: patient: under cold orders — till one man, either from fright or eagerness, fired off his charge!

So they'd no choice but to abandon caution and burst out of hiding before the panic-struck men of the Charming Molly could scramble back into their boat! Those of them who'd been engaged in hauling, hopped and lay flat in the scuppers till the musket-fire was volleyed out. The others — the better half — were midway up the beach, so the onrush of the ambush cut them off. But for that too soon shot, not a soul would have got back to the boat.

Now began hand to hand fighting of the utmost fierceness and confusion. Cutlasses, knives, swords, nails and even teeth all set to work at once. The lost part of the crew scattered and fought ferociously to regain the longboat and, scratched, bitten, kicked and hacked-at, the ambushers pursued them in the tangled dark. Strange desperate duels were engaged, broken off, re-engaged with a shout, carried on across the tumbling pebbles and finished off in some squalid patch of black.

Then the ambushers re-formed and our men fought among themselves for a few seconds before they realized they'd got a slender chance. Those who could, fled: those who could not, lay like black starfish on the beach. One or two who lay close enough were dragged aboard the longboat, but the rest were past caring for, and with their last eyes watched all hope of salvation float panting

and desperate out to sea. At last, the longboat scraped alongside
and the shore party crept back aboard the amazed and silent ship.

It seems to me that even in this short extract one can feel the richness
with which Leon Garfield has endowed his story.

It would be impossible in a short space to catalogue the best of
available children's literature. I have to say that in selecting there is no
substitute for personal knowledge. 'How so?' I hear you cry. Am I
suggesting that any teacher could possibly cope with even ten percent of
the current output to say nothing of the still extant volumes of the past?
Of course it is not possible. However I think we need to try to manage
one book a week in order to keep in touch with what is new. It really is
no hardship to read a fine book like Joan Aiken's *The Wolves of
Willoughby Chase*. Indeed I have found it impossible on one or two
occasions to put a book on the shelves of the class library until my wife
has finished it.

There are reliable guides to children's literature which cut down the
quantity under serious consideration, and discussion with one's colleagues
can save unnecessary wastage of time and resources.

I would appeal for variety in the books on the class library shelves. I
make categories for myself and try to plan on building up these categories
in proportion. I introduce some historical novels if these are absent,
attempt to keep a fair balance between the books for the boys and girls,
try not to forget that humorous work has a valid place in literature for
children as well as adults. This extract is from *The Small Adventures of
Dog* by David Buck (1968).

'Well,' said Dog, 'I'm a leather-coloured pig.'
'Pigs are pink,' said the blackbird, 'not leather-coloured.'
'Pink?' said Dog. 'What's pink?'
'Well-er,' said the blackbird, 'pink is a colour halfway to red.'
'Halfway from where?' asked Dog.
'That's not important,' said the bird, 'what is important is that you
become pink as quickly as possible. And stop floating.'
'Why?' asked Dog.
'You'll get arrested,' said the bird.
Dog wasn't really quite sure what arrested meant.
'Locked up,' explained the bird, 'put in prison.'
'Why?' asked Dog.
'Because they don't like pigs just floating around,' said the blackbird.
'Especially leather-coloured pigs. It's not allowed.'
'Not allowed?' queried Dog.
'An awful lot of things aren't allowed down there,' said the blackbird,

'and I'm sure that's one of them.'

'I see,' said Dog, but he didn't.

'How do I become pink?' asked Dog.

'I don't know,' said the bird, 'I don't understand anything about you.'

'Oh,' said Dog.

'You could think pink,' suggested the blackbird.

'I beg your pardon?' asked Dog.

'Think pink,' repeated the blackbird. 'If you can float by thinking
float, it should be a simple matter to think yourself pink.'

'I don't know what pink is,' said Dog.

'I'll help you,' said the blackbird. 'Do just as I say.'

'Certainly,' said Dog. 'I'll try.'

'Think white first,' said the bird.

Dog thought white.

And changed into a beautiful glossy white all over.

'Splendid,' said the blackbird. 'You're halfway there. Now think red.'

Dog started to think red.

'Stop!' cried the blackbird, but too late.

Dog was a bright pillar box red, from snout to tail.

Perhaps I have appeared to overstress the importance of a well considered
collection of fiction in the literary environment of my classroom. I feel,
however, that such a collection very much sets the tone of literary
achievement among the children and must influence their own literary
work while also providing a standard against which they can measure the
literature which they come across elsewhere.

I do not wish to dwell on the collection of reference material which is
also available, for many of the same criteria apply equally here. The most
outstanding difficulty which I have encountered in satisfying the needs of
the children in this direction is making available books which are accurate
and up to date. Again I have found it more worthwhile to shop around
rather than decide prematurely on a book which may be wanting in
accuracy, detail or illustration. Most of the reference books which my
children use belong to the central school library, and clearly each teacher
must feel that he or she influences the content of that collection by
suggesting to the librarian volumes which will be of value. My children
make frequent use of the public library during and after school hours, and
again I believe that it is valuable for me to have contact with the local
librarian, whom I have always found to be very helpful and cooperative.

It would be a mistake to leave the topic of other people's literature in
my classroom environment without mentioning the work of other children.
Largely due to the efforts of John Merritt, more and more teachers are

putting into practice the idea of experience exchange. I have not had the opportunity to put such a scheme into operation although I hope to do so in the coming year.

The quantity, quality and variety of literature stimulated by such an exchange is quite staggering. It must be seen as forming an ever increasing part of the literary environment of the children. Work arriving from other children is read avidly and criticized in a knowledgeable and very humane manner, for the reader is well aware of the problems of the author since he himself is an author involved in the composition of a parallel type of literature.

Since there is a large output of potentially valuable material within the classroom, the question of preserving it arises. Every literature has its archives — no less so should that of my children. Their enquiries, research, feelings and experiences may provide a valuable museum of thought for the future. I decided last November to try to work out a way of creating such an archive, only to find myself baffled by the amount and variety of material which the children were producing. Perhaps someone has devised a cheap and simple system, perhaps someone had developed ways of deciding what is valuable and what must be thrown out for lack of space. So far I have failed.

Hence we come to the second aspect of the literary environment of my children — the literature which we produce. Our writings have a personal significance which at times makes them of greater value than the combined works of the Garfields, the Aikens and the Sutcliffs of national and international literary repute. It is right that this should be so since no Lewis Carroll can express Carolyn's feelings as she watches a flower wither from beauty to decay, and only Brian can say what he feels about the death of his uncle. I can think of no other area of the curriculum where I must choose each word I say to a child with such care. If we are lucky my children may be prepared to unlock their souls so that together we will add their thoughts and experiences to our literature.

I have to stress the fact that this is something which we do together. I have no interest in competitions which call for the unaided work of children, although I have occasionally come across outstanding examples of children's literature produced with no assistance whatsoever. I see it as my function to help — not I may say to try to stamp my personality on the work but to encourage a dialogue which will create an awareness of the problems which the child is facing in expressing himself in a manner which has literary value, and which may also produce in the child the solution to some of his problems.

It's a lonely, frustrating and discouraging thing trying to put thoughts on paper. It's fraught with the uncertainty of what other people will think. It deserves the most understanding support which we can give. By 'we' in this case I mean not the teaching profession, but the author's colleagues who may be aware of a current problem and may be able to suggest possible solutions.

The subjects chosen by the children for their writing vary tremendously. Sometimes a chance remark may spark off a discussion resulting in a spate of writing. Other equally lively discussions have no such consequence. This we have to accept. Gone are the days of the weekly composition so far as I am concerned. My approach needs to accept that if Gary is not in a writing mood then no amount of cajoling or forcing will do either of us any good. I feel a great temptation to expect of the children an output which I know in moments of honesty to be beyond them. There is great satisfaction in looking at the results of a session which has produced something of literary value. It is equally difficult to write off a stimulating discussion without a concrete endproduct. If I cannot resist the temptation and press ahead I may indeed be able to read with pleasure the results of the sessions — I may also have had a severely discouraging effect on the future literary activities of that child.

It is difficult to see any specific subject areas which stimulated a high degree of literary activity. Some people have suggested that adversity produces a reaction in the children. Here is an example of such work.

Illness
It was a warm night,
               stuffy.
And I have a headache.
Stars and the dark,
Make me feel as if I want to faint.
I see buildings,
But they are blurred.
There is no moon
But the stars make silhouttes.
Everyone is asleep,
I can smell a faint smell of fags
Some writing is on the wall.
            It says
Maureen loves Jonathan,
            And
Agnes loves Tommy.
I see an upturned bin.
            I feel ill.

            Agnes Brown

Perhaps this poem about Christ also comes into this category.

Father, Son and Holy Ghost
He was Lord,
I was a servant,
He was born in a stable
I was born in a hospital
He was a son of Jesus
I was not
I love Him
He died for us;
He was born to save us
People cried;
Bound to the tree
He died on the cross for us
His love,
His love,
His gracious love on us
Blood poured down from Him
Father, Son and Holy Ghost.   Amen

Malcolm Beers

Religion plays a large part in the lives of most of my children. This piece seems to me to show a highly personal view of the place of Christ's birth.

The Stable
The sweet smelling hay.
The small manger full of feed.
The fence cutting animals off from
the freedom of earth.
The mother and foal resting
happily among the thick layer of straw.
A cow sitting on its own
in one little corner.
A harness hung on the wall by a nail.
Whitewashed walls and ceiling glowing
with rebounding light.
The oil lamp turning with a flicker.
This is the stable
where he was born.

Timothy Harbinson

Politics too make their impact on the literature of children in a piece that was written about seven years ago.

Wet Street
Cold and hard was the long wet street,
Clicking heels, shuffling feet,
My own echo made me afraid,
At the shadow behind me, behind the gate,
As I tore along, I was suddenly stopped,
By a body all bleeding and cut.
It was all because of the tricolour
And Paisley, and policemen fighting there.

Lynn Mason

These pieces about animals seem to indicate the many viewpoints which children develop. Note the realistic approach of Rosemary writing about alley cats.

Alley Cats
Their world is of alleys, dustbins and rats,
In their man made jungle there live the cats.
Silhouetted against the sky, on the back yard wall,
can be heard at night their feline call.
From the upstairs window the old boot thrown down,
sends one off to prowl the town.
He has no name his home is nowhere.
He's just a wanderer and who could care.

Rosemary Hay

This one reflects brutality tinged with fascination. Animal instinct was very close to the surface when this was written by Elaine, a very feminine ten year old.

A Poor Little Birdie
Poor little birdie
Hops up the path
With a broken wing.
A frightened little birdie
Is what Mum catches
And it pecks her hand,
But she puts it in the shed.

Goodbye little birdie!
Dad is home with
A great heavy stick,
Two big 'thumps'
And birdie is dead
Poor little birdie.

Elaine Harris

Gordon was shocked by his own cannibalism almost when he wrote this.

Flesh Dinner
At home,
Yesterday we ate flesh
Cows flesh
Cooked in the oven
All cut in bits.

Mum brought it in on a plate,
Slices of flesh,
With turnip, peas and potatoes,
Lying in the pools,
Of flesh juice.

I stuck the fork
Into the flesh,
And out came flesh juice,
I couldn't believe
It was walking about yesterday.

Gordon Kennedy

Hazel's piece is quite different, written for an audience, to be read to other children.

Jam
Every summer Puck picks gooseberries and blackberries and makes jam. Well Puck one summer was just out in his garden putting labels on his pots when down swooped a big eagle and carried Puck and all the jam pots off. Puck kicked and shouted for help but he just went on and on until he came to a huge nest on the hillside. Then the eagle told Puck he was going to give Puck over to Frank who would

make him work double harder than usual. Then the eagle flew over to Frank's house bringing Puck but not the pots of jam.

Frank took Puck and told him to make some jam. Suddenly Puck had an idea how to get out. When he had made the jam it was almost teatime and so he made the tea and found three hairy spiders which he put in the jam. When Frank opened the pot he said, 'Ugh! spiders' and told Puck to get another pot. Meanwhile Puck had put more spiders in the next pot and Frank took it away and soon there were no pots left and Frank was feeling sick. 'Puck,' he said, 'Take those spiders away and put me to bed.' So Puck threw the jam away and ran to his house as quickly as he could. As for Frank, he was so angry he gave himself chickenpox and did not get out of his house for a month.

Hazel Lamberton

As you can see, styles and subject matter vary infinitely among the children. I suggest that their work has to be regarded in its own terms. I view it as an accurate reflection of their lives and not as a poor attempt to do something which adults do much better. I believe that if we interfere with their literary processes we will destroy something which Picasso, in the world of art, has found it well nigh impossible to recapture. These last two poems represent that something.

My Grandmother's Hat 1968
My Grandmother's hat was too big for her head
So it hung from the wall to carry
Newspapers and odds and ends.
So loose, So thin, So weak,
Every time a page goes in
Crack! Crack! Crack!
But when empty
Squeak! Squeak! Squeak!
My Grandmother took ill and very ill she
Was yet there was not a movement
Only her heart saying
Plump! Plump! Plump!
Everytime granda heard this
Gulp! Gulp! Gulp!
And he sighed
And lay back
And dozed into a sleep and a trance;
When granny died the hat broke.

Malcolm Beers

This poem defied all the rules of a free curriculum by being written in twenty minutes as an end of term test.

A Walk in a Graveyard at Night
It was half past nine and it was pitch black,
The sun was down long, long ago,
The noise I heard gave me a fright that sounded
like an owl.
My very own footsteps sound like a bang.
The white grave stones appear like stones in a heap
On a grave. In a graveyard. In the night.

The light shines on the gravestones,
White black and mossy,
The fear that lies beside me,
And the golden white light moon,
Makes fear turn away.

The growl of the dog makes fear come back,
The silence and fear once again.
The murmur of hungry tummies,
The rumble of owls landing on dead leaves
Yet still I've got the sudden fear of death.

The graves mean death,
Sorrow and grief,
My Granda's grave lies at my feet
The fun is gone now he is gone
And the flowers of love are gone.

The graveyard is darker
Night black and frighting.
Love has gone from dead bodies
All is left is skeletons
In an old coffin —
The graveyard.

Richard Clarke

In looking at the two aspects of my children's literary environment, I have omitted in either case to create any distinction between prose and poetry. So far as I am concerned there is no need to say that this is prose and that poetry. I don't believe the children need the complication of that distinction.

Is it possible to say with value how all this literature comes together in the children's curriculum? Are there any objectives which I have at the beginning of a year's contact with the children?

Firstly I would like to give them a glimpse of the life of the past as reflected in its literature. Again I must try to suggest to them values of behaviour and thought which are appropriate. Since childhood is a limited period all this needs to be balanced with other activities — I have seen children so involved with literature that they become 'bookish' and dangerously inward looking.

If I am forced to reduce my attitude to the relationship between children's literature and the curriculum to a few words, I have to say that the availability of a rich literature written by others within their environment is as essential to children's development as the respect which is due to their own literature.

I hope that the Alices of my world will flee in disgust from anything trivial or dull which I may offer. I hope too the rabbit hole at the other side of the room into which they dive is charged with variety and excitement and interest.

References

Buck, David (1968) *The Small Adventures of Dog* London: Heinemann
Garfield, Leon (1964) *Jack Holborn* London: Constable

Experience exchange —
The infant school

C. W. Deininger

Senior Lecturer in Education
Sunderland College of Education

Experience exchange

To us, as educationists, experience is a key word. We all benefit one way
and another from new experiences and these are particularly vital in the
life of the developing child. We must stimulate the child by new experience.
The good infant teacher, and it is with the infant age range that I am
particularly concerned, cannot just wait for interesting subjects to arise by
accident, but must actively create situations and provide experiences which
the children will want to question. The teacher who successfully implants
this attitude of lively enquiry into a young child's mind, gives him something
which will act as an aid to learning throughout his life.

> Each new experience reorganizes, however slightly, the structure of
> the mind and contributes to the child's world picture. (Plowden 1967)

In this particular project we have been attempting to stimulate children
by exchanging experiences. We have been giving to the child the experience
of another's environment — in many cases an environment which is vastly
different from his own. The idea of course is not new. Many schools
exchange experiences with others in different parts of the country, some
even to the extent of living in the exchange area for a few days in order
to give first hand experience of another environment. But of course the
infant stage does impose its own limitations.

A group of primary headteachers in Sunderland were invited to a
preliminary meeting and asked to think about the possibility of pairing
off with another school, preferably one with a contrasting environment.
They were asked to consider the feasibility of exchanging written work,
art and craft, visits etc with their infant counterparts over a term, and
then to evaluate the results for this conference. All were willing to
participate, but one must be perfectly honest and say that the very
nature of the rather impressive sounding title 'experience exchange',
and the mention of exhibition or display at this conference, caused some
degree of scepticism. If there was to be any suggestion of a gimmick then
the whole venture was unacceptable.

The entire content and conduct of the exchange was left to the individual schools. Once the idea was sown the mechanics were left to the teachers. The river in Sunderland formed a very convenient dividing line in some cases, although one or two schools selected an exchange from outside the area. One school had already made contact with schools in Hull. Some of the groups decided to exchange with two or even three schools.

The exchanges began with preliminary meetings of teachers in order to formulate plans of work. The early pieces of work from the children generally contained information about themselves, later extending to their families, homes, school and neighbourhood. The tremendous amount of interest which has been stimulated can easily be seen by looking at the display with its variety of work which includes news, views and opinions, stories, poems, graphs, maps and models.

A map and a model coming from a beautiful new school in middle class suburbia provided a tremendous challenge to children from one of our oldest school buildings surrounded by old single storey terraced cottages, which are so familiar on Wearside. The school building is close to the docks and even closer to Roker Park Football Club — a fact which puts this school in a very enviable position, so of course there were interviews and film from the Football Club and an excellent map of dockland all included in the next folder of work for exchange.

The school exchanging with Hull found that the distance was too great for the young children to sustain any real interest. On taking another exchange with an old local school from across the river, the interest was really rekindled and sustained. Here the experience reached its peak with a visit of children from the old school to the new for a picnic in the head's 'secret place' — a beautifully secluded square of lawn reached only by passing through a huge store cupboard, which none of the children had explored in the five years the school had been in existence.

Not all the schools were able to exchange actual visits by children during the term which has been given to this project. In one case where a visit was possible, the children came from a small rural school in County Durham to one of our oldest and largest school buildings, a real 'beacon of enlightenment' housing infant, junior and secondary children.

Again there is variety in the ages and number of children participating from any one school. Some schools are family grouped and work from the youngest children has been included because they 'did not want to be left out of the parcel'. Some schools have confined the exchange to the top age group, some to two or more classes. In one case four classes out of six have been involved. There was obviously some advantage to be gained from exchange with more than one school for, as one head commented, 'having more than one school reduced the period of waiting, more children were involved and there was always work coming in'.

Interest has been stimulated in many directions. Interest in language arose when children from a mining area wrote about their fathers eating 'bait' for their lunch. Now 'bait' to children from the exchange school could only be associated with lug worm and rag worm which are used for fishing. One could visualize the stimulation of further interest in language if recordings of good Wearside dialect were played to children from the village school in south Durham.

Interest in traffic was stimulated in another pair of schools which compared the volume of traffic passing their respective buildings and translated this onto graphs. The new experience stimulated one of the children to conduct his own traffic survey from his bedroom window, hidden behind his curtains in his pyjamas when mother thought he was asleep! His story is included in some of the work on display. Some children have had interesting interviews with the lollipop lady whom they brought into school to talk about her job. Some have made up their own reading books which the head has had typed so that they can be preserved for posterity. I think one would agree that books made by teachers and children about the activities of the class or individuals in it figure prominently among the books which children enjoy. They help children to see meaning in reading and to appreciate the purpose of written records.

The amount of time which has been devoted to this work has obviously varied with the school. In some cases it has been concentrated into a week or so, with a break whilst awaiting the arrival of an exchange parcel. In others this work has been taking place for most of the time over the last term. Some schools have managed two exchanges of work in the term, others more.

What then has been achieved? How do the teachers view the project? The major criticism has been concerned with the time factor. Due to circumstances beyond our control we were a little late in getting the scheme off the ground, with the result that schools have only had about twelve weeks from first deciding on pairings. One is unable at this stage therefore to observe any long term effects. Having to meet a deadline was to some extent inhibiting. Then again this is possibly not the most convenient term for beginning a project such as this. There are 'breaks' in the term for one thing or another — occasional holidays, Open Days, sports etc. The summer term in particular is fraught with interruptions. Some schools have had students on teaching practice for five weeks and again this can bring its problems.

Distance can prove to be a drawback. There is little value to be gained at infant level by having school contacts which are too remote. Hull, one hundred and twenty miles from Sunderland, without the prospect of an actual visit, was far too distant. Hull created another problem in that it has recently reorganized into first and middle schools with first schools encompassing the five to nine age range.

The need for frequent meetings between teachers from contributing schools to talk over common problems and exchange ideas has been stressed generally. The team of participating teachers have no doubt about the educational value of a project such as this. It has been exciting, interesting, and a challenge to both teachers and children. It has stimulated ideas. Standards of work, and the display of work, have been raised after only one term. Possibly the greatest benefit of all has been gained by the backward children, who, to quote one headteacher, 'seem to have found their identities'.

This project is a welcome step in further attempting to break down the barriers of the classroom. It makes us widen our horizons and helps us to compare our standards and evaluate what we are seeking to achieve. It can be seen to be of tremendous value to the diffident teacher and the teacher lacking in confidence.

It has been stressed generally that the work displayed should be the child's own efforts with only the minimum of correction in order to facilitate easy communication. Teachers must realize that they are not being judged on their results. As one headteacher remarked, 'If we stood on our heads the results would be no better, so we put everything in'. Surely this is the right attitude. Many teachers worry lest their efforts compare unfavourably with those of other schools. What must be realized is that there are wide discrepancies in the quality of environment and this can be clearly seen from some of the work on display. What should be our prime concern is that the child has done the best of which he is capable. It is by seeing the efforts of others that our own standards may be improved.

Older children will probably gain more from use of tape recorders etc. Infants may, for instance, find the technique of interviewing difficult, but this is something to be explored.

The majority felt that there should be the minimum of interference from the teacher and that as far as possible the children should arrange their own display.

One interesting side effect was spotlighted by a headteacher who claimed that it was only after visiting his exchange school that he was able to see a particular reading scheme in a new light. This surely emphasizes again the need for closer cooperation with our colleagues.

The team feel that this project has provided an incentive. It has been a breath of fresh air. Lack of time has proved to be the biggest drawback but we have established a starting point for the future. This is only a beginning and the real value of experience exchange will be seen in another year. All the infant display material is to be placed in a centre in Sunderland next term, when it is hoped that all teachers will be invited to discuss the project, common problems and ways of extending the scheme. It is hoped that this will be the first of a series of regular meetings. This particular exercise has been but a modest beginning.

Plowden suggests that the amount and quality of children's writing could well be the most dramatic of all the revolutions in English teaching over recent years. Projects such as this will keep this revolution alive.

References

Department of Education and Science (1967) *Children and Their Primary Schools* (The Plowden Report) London: HMSO

Experience exchange —
The junior school

R. T. Bloomfield

Headmaster
Elmfield Junior School, Newton Aycliffe

Experience exchange

I am sure no member of this audience would contest that whatever activity
is carried out in a school should be a result of the ethos of the school. At
the school where I work, we try, as do lots of teachers, to discover the needs
of the individual child and, so far as we are capable, to satisfy them.

It was logical for me therefore, when I was privileged to be appointed
headmaster of the new Elmfield Junior School in Newton Aycliffe in June
1968, to plan educational activities based on the principles of the
integrated day. It seems to me that within this framework opportunities
exist for children to be involved in activities which are stimulating whether
the children be bright or dull and which allow them to pursue individual
interests relevant to their needs — interests which are not stifled by the
artificial classifications of a rigid timetable.

One of these opportunities is experience exchange. Shortly after the
school was opened, arrangements were made to exchange work between
a vertically grouped third and fourth year class at Elmfield and a fourth
year class at Harding Memorial Primary School in Belfast. The Elmfield
children were enthusiastic at the idea of making contact with children in
another school. Even in the pre-riot era, there was an excitement about
communicating with children in what to our children was a 'foreign'
country because it is cut off from the mainland.

It was impressed upon the Elmfield children that their work would need
to be the very best of which they were capable because it would be assessed,
critically, by the Harding children. As it happened, teacher's finger-wagging
exhortations turned out to be superflous. The Elmfield children were,
for a number of reasons, mostly low average and below average achievers.
The first consignment of work from Harding gave every indication of
being produced by high achievers. The Elmfield children were initially
awe-struck by the standard of the work received. The consequence of
this was that the Elmfield children recognized out of a sense of self-respect
that their work must be their very best. They were extremely self-critical
and rejected on their own initiative any work which they considered

unsatisfactory. Their own self-imposed standards turned out to be higher than those that would have been considered adequate by their teachers. Work was done again without it being suggested by the teacher and there was no evidence that the children regarded repetition of work as a chore.

The environment has been used as source material for much of the work which has been produced by individual, group and class efforts. Environmental studies can be purposeful and stimulating. The sense of purpose and stimulation in this case were enhanced because the children understood that all their efforts were directed towards communicating information about their own environment to others who were quite ignorant of it. Their individual efforts were, they were told in simple terms, entirely devoted to the purpose for which language is taught – the communication of facts and ideas to others. I suggest that there is much more point to this educational activity than that which directs a large proportion of children's efforts into the waste-paper basket via the exercise filled notebooks. Now that the majority of teachers in junior schools no longer have to hiss '11 plus' down the necks of their pupils, it is possible to climb out of the exercise book-orientated rut. Experience exchange is only one of several alternatives which we may now adopt to make work in junior schools more meaningful.

Early exchanges of work between Elmfield and Harding were in the form of handwritten booklets and sheets of writing paper mounted on sugar paper for wall display. Such methods of presentation have value and will continue to be used. However other methods have developed which are rather more sophisticated and, I believe, more effective. A significant development is that the Elmfield children are now having much of their written work converted into typescript. The self-imposed discipline that work must be the best of which the children are capable because it will be read and assessed by other children still exists. The children understand that their work must continue to be legible and attractively presented for the benefit of the typist to whom it will be presented.

The teacher of commercial subjects in a secondary school was approached and her cooperation was invited by asking if our children's work could be typed by pupils on the commercial course. The invitation was accepted and some of the children's work was typed in this way. Another agency has also been used. A parent offered to do typing and her services have proved to be extremely valuable.

Having the work of the children typed seems to have two advantages. First, it gives the less able child considerable satisfaction to see his work given the dignity of the professional appearance of typescript. Secondly, the poor reader has less of a hurdle to surmount when he is faced, not with the diversity of manuscripted letter formations, but with the comparatively standardized form of typescript. The fluent reader also benefits. It is reasonable to assume that he, like you and me, prefers to read type rather than manuscript. Typewritten work with its professional look, if simply bound into book form, has a permanence that wallcharts lack.

On educational visits beyond the immediate school environment — and these visits are an integral part of our school life — the use of audio and visual aids has been introduced. A camera loaded with 35 mm colour film is taken on every visit. When the coloured slides are shown, they help the children to recapitulate the events of the visit and act as a direct stimulus to written work. Children produce notes to accompany the slides and these are 'sound tracked' by means of a tape recorder.

A start has been made on recording experiences on 8 mm colour film with accompanying tape recorded sound track. A portable tape recorder has been used to capture experiences that would defy recording in any other way. Recently, a video TV tape recording was made in Elmfield school by the television unit of Bede College. You were to have seen this recording but I understand that gremlins got into the apparatus when somebody wasn't looking. However it will be available for another occasion.

The use of all these audio-visual aids is symbolic of the widespread activities which can take place within the framework of experience exchange.

Every story should have a climax and our experience exchange story is no exception. Following early examples of how children worked with interest and purpose in their exchange activities, the idea developed that an exchange visit had obvious advantages. My deputy head (who was the teacher of the class involved) and I visited Belfast during the Whitsuntide holiday in 1969. We had the double pleasure of taking part in a UKRA Study Congress and of meeting the staff and children of Harding Memorial Primary School.

An invitation was extended to Harding to visit Newton Aycliffe. There was very little of the term left in the Belfast schools — they start their summer holidays at the end of June — but with organizational dexterity worthy of a conquering general, a party of Harding children accompanied by teachers Yvonne McKay and Frazer Thompson (both of the Belfast Branch of UKRA) came to Newton Aycliffe before the end of their term and were installed in the homes of the Elmfield children and parents.

In the comparatively short time that the Harding party were with us, they became involved in the life of the school and saw some of the sights we in the north-east sometimes boast about — this city with its lovely cathedral and the glorious Northumberland countryside with its unique Roman monuments.

A visit by an Elmfield party to Belfast was an inevitable sequel. This took place as recently as last May. We flew to Belfast on a Friday and spent seven days in the province, seven days full of happy and memorable activities. The accommodation pattern, established at Newton Aycliffe, was repeated in Belfast. Our children were well and truly integrated into the family atmosphere of their hosts' homes.

How much more has this type of educational visit to commend itself than its traditional counterpart which consists of conducting a party of children to an alien place, where they visit and view the sights but, cocooned in their school group, staying in a hostel or hotel with others of their ilk, they learn their lot from the official guide and little from any personal relationships with the inhabitants of that country. If more educational journeys were made on the same basis as the Elmfield and Harding visits, I am sure that they would be both more valuable and memorable than many of them seem to be at present.

After their return to Newton Aycliffe, our children naturally did some followup work — some of which you will see on display. However only a part of the experiences enjoyed by our children have found their way into verbal or pictorial records. Not all experiences are capable of being recorded by an immature mind.

There was the boy who was very nervous before he left home because he was going to live in the home of a stranger. Within hours of his arrival, the strangers were friends and a hurdle which had existed in his mind had disappeared. I doubt whether it will reappear.

There was the quiet boy who learned the skills of language and mathematics slowly and laboriously. When we went climbing in the Mournes he was always first to the top of a mountain. 'Well done Paul!' was enough to give his already pink face an extra glow.

Billy's speech is very limited. It's an event when he speaks two or three sentences with an identifiable sequence. The experiences which he shared with his friends encouraged him to talk much more than was his usual habit. On a cliff walk along the Antrim coast towards the Giant's Causeway we came across a notice which recorded the wrecking of a Spanish galleon in 1588. Billy couldn't read the notice but was fascinated by the story of the Spanish Armada. I don't believe in miracles in education so it came as no surprise that this experience did not unleash Billy's tongue to a frenzy of verbal activity. All that happened was that he spoke appreciably more than he had done before — six sentences is appreciably more than three sentences. There are lots of Billys and Pauls in our schools and they are more likely to develop *their* full potential in a situation which sparks their interest and enthusiasm whilst at the same time permitting it an outlet.

Recently there was an article in *The Guardian* (1970) about Barry Hines who wrote a book about an educational failure — a failure that is by the standards of examinations and marks. It was Hines's book that provided the script for the highly praised film *Kes*. Hines, who was described in the article as a survivor of an educational system that has no time for academic runts, argues that non-academic children can do all kinds of things, if only they are given the opportunities. 'The function of a school,' he says, 'is to realize the potential that all kids have, and to make them happy. To fit the curriculum to them instead of the other way round.'

Sir Alec Clegg seems to hold similar views. He wrote recently about the developments of our 100 year old State educational system. He reminds us that vessel filling is the traditional concept of education and from the educators' point of view this is the easy way because it is relatively simple to measure just how much the vessel has taken in. And it's also easy to blame the vessel if the contents are at a low level. Easy it may be but totally illogical. In any school where children are assessed solely by what they can reproduce from the facts that have been fed to them there will be, as Clegg says, duds that don't matter and for whom nothing is done to arouse in them a love of learning. Whatever the methods or the ploys we use in schools, they should surely help all Billys and Pauls to realize their potential. Sir Alec writes enthusiatically about the immense progress that has been made in schools where one sees gay colourful classrooms, attractive displays and children getting on with their chosen work with an application, energy and self-discipline at which he marvels. The achievements which he has witnessed and has written about have been produced by a variety of methods. Experience exchange is one method. There is no attempt to suggest that it washes whiter than someone else's brand X. I cannot claim, for example, that the achievements of our children are greater than those in Sybil Marshall's village school which she described so vividly in *An Experiment in Education* (1963). Mrs Marshall used Beethoven while we used Belfast. Different methods, different achievements, but both practised, I think, with the same long term objectives in mind. These objectives, as I suggested initially, are largely concerned with discovering the needs of individual children and then attempting to satisfy them. Experience exchange has helped us at Elmfield to achieve this.

However there is another aspect of experience exchange which ought to be of particular interest to this Conference of the United Kingdom Reading Association and that is the extent, if any, to which it assists a child in achieving reading skills.

John Merritt has written about competence in reading on a number of occasions and has argued that experience exchange is an activity through which it may be developed. Merritt has quite rightly reminded us that the learning of primary reading skills, i.e. the decoding of each printed word, is still considered by many teachers to be the only mastery which the child needs, and that having achieved this skill his subsequent development in reading ability will be determined by his individual linguistic skill and his intelligence. If teachers are to help children develop higher order reading skills, i.e. those that go beyond simple decoding to analyzing what is read, then they must develop additional techniques. The traditional favourite for this purpose is the comprehension exercise. Unfortunately many comprehension exercises are of limited value. Even if they are performed with dexterity, like the accurate repetition of multiplication tables, there is no certainty that these limited skills will transfer to situations outside the specific learning situation. John Merritt has analyzed the sophisticated skills which the truly competent reader must possess and suggests experience exchange as one means by which they may be achieved. After two years of activity is there any evidence that the children of Elmfield Junior School have developed any of the more sophisticated reading skills?

First I must state that no objective analysis or assessment has been made of the children's intermediate reading skills and higher order skills. *Can* they be adequately assessed, I wonder? Subjective impressions are that as a direct result of corresponding with their peers, our children did not hesitate to challenge statements which they would have uncritically accepted had they been the work of superior adults. I believe that the encouragement of *critical* reading is an essential part of what John Merritt has described as the 'higher order' reading skills. Children share broadly similar language structures whether they live in Newton Aycliffe or Belfast, and when these structures are read by peer groups the content is easily assimilated. Slow readers appeared to enjoy reading exchange material and this must surely be an incentive to more skilful reading.

I have perhaps given an impression that exchange work is particularly beneficial to the slow learner and this may suggest that the able child has less to gain from participating in this activity then from following formal academic pursuits. I am quite certain that the able child can derive just as much benefit as the less able. The able child will discover for himself, in the flexible organization of an investigation and subsequent exchange, a rich variety of opportunities for developing his talents. If we have an obligation to help those who will never achieve significant academic success, then we have an equal obligation to help those who can.

It is the scope which experience exchange presents to the able and less able alike which makes it, to me, a most worthwhile educational activity and a valuable addition to the teacher's existing repertoire.

References

The Guardian (1970) 'Dick Hines' Lad' *The Guardian* July 18th
Marshall, Sybil (1963) *An Experiment in Education* London: Cambridge University Press

Experience exchange –
The special school

T. N. Parkin

Headmaster
Hare Law Day School, Annfield Plain

Our school admits children from many different home environments and,
possibly more relevant to the problem of the reading experience, from
many different primary schools, with varied approaches in their infant
departments to pre-reading activities and reading teaching.

The children, with extremely few exceptions, have only one thing in
common when they are admitted – the label of failure. The depth of
failure, with its consequent condition of fear or apathy, or reluctance to try
for fear of failing again, depends on the age of the child and his previous
experiences in the reading situation to which he has been exposed. This
will vary from two to as many as seven, eight or nine years in the more
intractable cases. This conditioning to expect failure has various
manifestations. They range from the state of acute awareness, which can
usually be overcome in the non-pressurized environment of the special
school, to the chronic condition when, in self-defence, the child has
rationalized failure by cultivating an attitude to reading which defies
for years the efforts of skilled teachers.

It is said that the most difficult children to teach are the deaf and those
with hearing problems. Many of our children could almost be grouped in
the same category, for they share a similar handicap. Whilst they do not
suffer from hearing difficulties, there is so little communication within the
home environment that their experiences of language are minimal.

There are children whose only experience of the spoken word for long
periods is that which comes from the ubiquitous television set. This is
particularly so when they cannot play out of doors, either because they
are refused permission to do so by overprotective parents, or because they
have no one who will play with them, or because the weather confines them
to the home. In the home, especially where the parents are also illiterate
or dull and unimaginative, experience in communicating is limited to crude
essentials.

In effect this means that there are children who come into school with
so little experience in communicating that the teacher must often start by
teaching them to play and talk. It takes some time before such children

can appreciate that communication is a two way process of give and take. For such children, the immediate, concrete experience is the most valuable in stimulating the flow of words. Unfortunately, when they do begin to talk, they still have the problem of relating the speech of the teacher to the local dialect to which they are accustomed.

Formal reading methods are not much use with such children as the environment with which they are familiar is far removed from that depicted in the orthodox reading scheme. Indeed, faced with a typical reading scheme they find themselves struggling with what virtually amounts to a foreign culture.

Another problem stemming from the home is the attitudes of the parents to reading and writing. In defence against their own failure or relative failure to achieve literacy, the parents come to accept that they are different and rationalize their difference by indifference — after all, they have managed without it. And while there are non-reading parents who actively want their children to learn to read, there are those who pass on their own indifference and expect their children to get along without reading.

The children in the special school bring with them a varied pattern of inability to read, or a failure to come to terms with and accept the need to learn this difficult trick of interpreting the symbols we use in reading. Success on the school's part can spell the difference for many children between a successful integration into adult life and that isolation which can be the cause of social ills both in school life and, more important, later life.

A consideration of the ability of many slow learners to observe, discriminate and use appropriate language provides an interesting insight into their disabilities and capabilities. One or two examples may serve to illustrate this aspect of the problem.

A ten year old, a non-reader who had lived all his life almost in the shadow of the local TV mast, on being asked what it was replied quite readily that it was a telepole graph. An eleven year old, who had almost achieved literacy, on being asked the name of a particular flower emphatically declared it a daisy. It was in fact a daffodil. When responding to illustrations in books it is not unusual to find everything with four legs is called a dog, or a horse or whatever animal happens to be familiar to the child. One could give many such examples.

On the other hand, a non-reader aged twelve described for me how to tickle trout, talked of 'sheep in a field where the Roman Camp is', but where 'nobody goes that I know of'; and knew about rabbits and hares in the fields and woods. He also knew about animals that would not go into the auctioneer's ring, and about them getting holes punched in their ears when they were sold. He could 'feed the beast on hay and barley' and knew you had 'to be careful with the bull' for 'he would horn you if he could'.

A boy of very limited reading ability gave me information sufficient to create two books on keeping pigeons, and the fact that this was a branch of knowledge in which he could show that he knew more than I did, certainly did his confidence no harm.

The problem of dialect creates an added difficulty. For example, a few weeks ago I was walking across the school field when I was accosted by an eight year old. 'Paul oyed an arfy it the gallawa,' he informed me. My request for the result of this action yielded the information that 'the gallawa upped and off'. Translation: Paul threw a stone (a half brick) at the horse which got up and ran away. This was a perfectly good piece of reporting by the child who was anxious to communicate, and who did so in the only way he knew. At his own level this was an experience which he was only too anxious to exchange with me. The fact that this same child was eight, and had therefore been exposed for three years to the teaching of reading, is surely significant.

Another case worth mentioning to illustrate the need for an oral pattern in teaching reading concerns a thirteen year old. He had made some small progress in reading but still had many problems. One such was with the letters h and n. This was highlighted when I asked him to pass me the hammer he had just put down. He replied that he didn't have one. When I pointed to it he said, 'Oh, you mean a nammer'. From this it emerged that words which started with a vowel or h, were to be pronounced with n in the initial position.

These few examples are an indication, if one were needed, of the inadequacy of so many reading schemes and reading devices for children of below average ability. The best device for teaching reading comes on two legs, and much of the paraphernalia that has been developed for teaching reading could be dispensed with if there were enough teachers to tackle the problems.

The school environment should give the child enough stimulation to encourage him to experiment, and from his experiments both on his own and, more important, with his peers, he must gain the urge to communicate his experiences. This permits the teacher to dip into the well of another child's experiences, as Sylvia Ashton-Warner puts it in *The Teacher* (1963), from there draw the material to create his own reading scheme, made to meet his needs.

My first experience in this vein centred round a group of older boys of thirteen to fifteen who arrived at a new school as an initial intake. Their collective reading attainment was negligible. For most of them, books were of little importance. It was decided, as a matter of policy, that the problems required an approach other than that with which they had already failed. Consequently I decided to rely solely on material drawn from practical experience in my teaching of reading and writing.

An attempt was made at this stage, now over ten years ago, to reproduce the reading matter in a form which would help in the transition from imperial sheets and writing books to orthodox reading material. As books had little appeal a transition stage appeared necessary and various methods were used. These included the use of rubber printing sets, hand scripting and typing. In each case there was little resemblance in fact to the endproduct in mind. Nevertheless, the wealth of varied experience put into the production of the material did have the desired effect of improving reading skill. Further experiments in the production of reading matter based on experience continued, and experiments with various layouts were done both in school and at the Newcastle Institute of Education.

Most of the typewriters in current use were tried and finally an electric model with variable spacing was selected. This could produce an original of the required standard but had the real disadvantage of producing only one copy. Had the machine been available in school with the typist on hand to print as required this would not have mattered. Unfortunately each 'book' had to be typed in Newcastle. By the time a book came back in typed form the memory of it had receded and the value from the child's point of view was much reduced. It was apparent that unless more copies could be printed, and to order as it were, we were no further forward.

The case for printing school reading matter was put to my LEA (Durham) and finally the production of our books in this way was agreed. An electric typewriter was used, the material was duplicated for use, collated, and then bound in the library department at County Hall. Alternate pages were left blank and then illustrated by the children.

Various methods were used to elicit suitable subject matter. In the case of a child who is struggling with the beginnings of reading, an oral approach is essential. With children who have gained some skill the approach can be varied. I have found that students from the local grammar school can help by talking to children and writing material based essentially upon their ideas.

No matter what approach is used, the situation must contain a need to communicate. In the oral situation, the valuable give and take of conversation helps in gaining the confidence which comes from speaking one's thoughts and having someone listen to them.

I think the production of books which resemble those produced commercially should be within the capacity of every school. Maybe one day this will come.

Ideally, one would like to have the means to produce reading material in different sizes of print. However, most important is the need for the child to see and be directly involved in the production process. Of course, this need not stop at the special school level. Think of the help an accessible printing press could be in any school!

I have said little about the exchange aspect of experience exchange as it applies to this method of teaching reading. This is a relatively recent development as a systematic teaching strategy and it has yet to be evaluated. Books produced in the method outlined above have, however, been used elsewhere, and the reports which follow may give some indication of the value of this kind of exchange.

Within the school there is a natural exchange as the books are printed in sufficient numbers for them to be available to all groups. If the acceptance of reading based on individual and group experience is to be assessed on the acceptance or rejection by children in the same school, then there is no doubt that children like them and find them interesting. Most interest centres on what local newspaper makers have long known — names sell papers. Similarly, the names of other children who are familiar to the children reading the books sell the books.

References

Ashton-Warner, Sylvia (1963) *The Teacher* London: Secker and Warburg

Reading as a thought-getting process *

Amelia Melnik

Professor of Education
University of Arizona

A basic concept of reading, which should underlie instruction at all levels,
is that reading is a thought-getting process and as a thought-getting process,
reading involves comprehension. To comprehend, the reader must
judiciously select, organize, and relate the author's pattern of thought. To
be selective, the reader must raise significant and appropriate questions
relevant to the material as a basis for establishing a purpose for reading.
His questions determine what he reads, how he reads, and what he gets out
of his reading. In short, questions underlie and guide the reader's quest for
understanding as he engages in a dialogue with the author. In this sense,
then, reading is inquiry.

What is the role of questions? And how are they formulated to serve
their multiple purposes?

The role of questions

Questions function in both reading and teaching situations. In reading,
questions establish a basis for identifying and clarifying a reader's purpose
which influences his method of reading, the degree of comprehension, rate
of reading and the skills employed in reading. More than anything else, a
reader's purpose influences what he reads and how he reads.

In instructional situations, the role of questions is by far the most
influential single teaching act. According to Taba

> A focus set by the teacher's questions circumscribes the mental
> operations which students can perform, determine what points
> they can explore, and what modes of thought they can learn.
> (Taba 1964)

Moreover, students' concept of reading is largely influenced by the types
of questions asked by teachers. For these reasons questions play a crucial
role in affecting the level of the teaching and reading process. Yet there
is little evidence to suggest that teachers are well prepared in the
formulation and analysis of fruitful questions as a diagnostic and
instructional tool.

For example, in examining seventeen newly published or recently revised
professional reading textbooks, only four of them identified the topic of

questions in either the table of contents or the index. Even here, however, the treatment of questions was rather brief and superficial, with a four- or five-paragraph descriptive and prescriptive discussion rather than an analysis with appropriate application. Perhaps in our textbooks too much attention is paid to the content of reading instruction to the neglect of how teachers teach reading.

If teachers are not competently trained in the formulation and use of questions, it is not surprising to find that investigators of teachers' use of questions report that they were found to ask regularly 150 questions per class hour (Burton 1962). Findings of this kind clearly suggest that the quality of teaching in these situations is at the level of memory of facts and details. Such an emphasis encourages students to read with a mind set to memorize as many isolated details as possible. Unfortunately, even our most able readers reflect a detail-oriented concept of reading which largely results from the types of questions they have encountered in the classroom. In a study of 1500 Harvard and Radcliffe first year students, Perry made the following observations:

1   The typical approach of 90 percent of these students was to start at the beginning of the chapter and read straight ahead. No attempt was made to survey the chapter, note marginal headings, or first read the recapitulation paragraph in which the whole structure and summary of the chapter was given. Thus, none of the clues and signals provided as a basis for raising questions were used to identify specific purposes for reading.

2   Their performance on a multiple-choice test on details as far as they were able to read in this manner was impressive. But only one in 100 – fifteen in all – were able to write a short statement on what the chapter was about. Perry describes the reading performance of 99 percent of these students 'as a demonstration of obedient purposelessness in reading'. (Perry 1959)

Obviously, setting a purpose is a potent influence on reading comprehension. But a purpose for reading can only be defined and established if the reader knows what kinds of questions to ask the author. According to both the Harvard study and the analysis of teachers' questions, it seems evident that students and teachers need to improve the quality of their questions. Perhaps in our teaching we need to shift our emphasis from giving the right answers to raising relevant and significant questions.

The purposes and formulation of questions
As a tool in the teaching of reading, questions have two main functions, diagnostic and instructional:

1   As a diagnostic tool they are unstructured, allowing the student to respond in his own fashion, thus giving the teacher opportunity to observe the variety of individual responses in a natural reading situation.

2   As an instructional tool questions are more precisely formulated and logically organized to uncover the author's pattern of thought, develop discussion, and clarify meaning.

Questions also serve to evaluate learning, but in these situations questions are primarily concerned with the content rather than the process of reading, and for that reason will not be considered here.

It is the teacher's responsibility to understand these two separate functions of questions so that she may use them independently and concurrently in appropriate situations to stimulate thinking and help the student increase his awareness of the reading process. To do this, it is essential that the teacher should first decide for which of these functions she will be using her questions. Her purpose will determine what types of questions to ask and how to formulate them. In each situation, students should also be made aware of the purpose of the questions. Otherwise, they perceive questioning as testing and the classroom atmosphere is charged with tension as the teacher conducts a threatening inquisition instead of a natural discussion.

As a diagnostic tool, questions are formulated to elicit the maximum response from an individual. In analyzing the student's response, the teacher gets insight into his process of reading, which provides a basis for planning appropriate individual instruction. In obtaining evidence of the student's ability to select, organize and relate ideas gained from reading, Strang has long advocated the use of the free response (Strang 1942). In her study of reading interests and patterns, she used as a stimulus the question, 'What did the author say?' This question is purposely somewhat vague in order to leave the subject free to express his habitual response to printed material. From analyzing the responses to this question, she concluded that all aspects of reading are involved in answering it, thus giving the most revealing single picture of the individual's reading ability.

More recently, this unstructured question has been used to diagnose reading proficiency by Gray and Rogers in their study of mature readers (Gray and Rogers 1956). Adapting Strang's stimulus question, 'What did the author say?', and a scale for rating the responses, their diagnostic procedure also emphasized more encouragement of the free response and less dependency on formally structured questions.

While the formulation of the unstructured question poses no difficulty, the analysis of the response does require the teacher to be skilful in identifying which reading skills appropriate to the material should be noted in the response. Among the insights revealing reading proficiency, the teacher may note the following:

1   the student's approach to a reading passage
2   his tendency to relate ideas rather than merely seize on isolated details
3   his ability to uncover the author's pattern of thought
4   his ability to organize and show the relation among details
5   his tendency to let his emotions or prejudices and personal experiences influence his comprehension
6   his tendency to relate what he reads to other knowledge he has gained
7   his ability to communicate in writing what he has gained from reading.

Diagnostic questions, then, reveal rather than conceal individual differences.

Instructional questions

As instructional tools, questions serve the purpose of guiding the reader to select, organize and relate the author's pattern of thought during or following the reading experience. In these situations, questions are primarily concerned with identifying the types of thought relationships developed to unify the content. In other words, the central purpose of questions at this time is to focus on the process rather than the content of reading.

How is this accomplished? First of all the teacher must be able to analyze the author's structure of thought to identify the type of relationships around which he has organized his ideas. For example, ideas that are related through comparison will be identified through signals such as: *some – others; either – or; as – so; one – both: all – none; few – many*. In this instance a question may ask for a comparison in which details are related according to likenesses and differences. If a contrast is stressed, then the question asks for a response in which just the differences are related. Frequently, details are related in a time sequence, as indicated by signals such as *long ago, later, now*. In this case, the question is formulated so that the response relates details to indicate development and/or change. In other thought patterns, sequence according to process rather than time is significant. Here the student reports details logically organized in a specific series of steps. Other types of relationship are *cause – effect; problem – solution; main idea – detail*. In each case the type of relationship suggests the formulation of a single question which requires the student to select and relate relevant details in his response rather than a series of specific questions which elicits a simple yes/no answer or an isolated factual detail.

57

Profitable instructional questions then guide and clarify various types of relationship which result in comprehension. Discussion begins with a global question which focuses on the essence of the selection and serves as a point of departure for evolving further related questions which serve to clarify, modify, or illustrate meaning. Challenging questions stimulate students to report relationships among ideas and lead to fruitful discussion. Here more time is spent in listening and supporting answers to questions than in asking them.

If the effective reader is a questioning reader, more and more opportunity should be given to students to formulate and analyze questions themselves. Perhaps in this changing world of expanding knowledge, it is more important to learn how to formulate significant questions than it is to know all the answers.

Appendix: What effect does training in the formulation and use of questions have on teaching performance?

Here are some insights student teachers at the University of Arizona have reported:

1 One of the most important things this experience has taught me is not to expect a particular answer. I feel very strongly that the diagnostic question should allow a *free* response. When I first started, I would keep on asking different people if they knew *the* answer when I didn't receive the answer I had decided was logical. I often found myself, having run through the whole group, giving the answers myself with loaded questions. Now I accept all ideas and then have students refer to the text in search of evidence for the best answer. The students read with much more comprehension and enter into discussion more enthusiastically now, for there is a real controversy to solve. They understand that any of the reasons could be possible but the question is which ones can be justified.

2 In becoming aware of the importance of questions during my semester of student teaching, I have noted several changes in approach. Before presenting the story I try to begin with at least one free response question and other supplementary questions. I've noticed that the pupils have more to say lately, and with more expression. I have also found that one effective question seems to lead to another as if it were a natural sequence so there's more continuity in our discussion. I feel I have also applied this knowledge in answering pupils' questions. When they ask questions about their work, I try to answer them with instructional questions in return, instead of answering their questions without stimulating thought.

3   From actual instruction, I found that the children were 'detail' oriented. I mean that most of the questions were asked primarily to find out if the children knew the specific facts in a particular selection. I found in my own instruction that not enough questions were thought-provoking, and that they did not promote inductive reasoning or divergent thinking. The questions did not cover many of the comprehension skills, especially inference, conclusion and generalization. After observing and asking general questions over a period of time, I did initiate some action in formulating questions in the instructional situation. I have seen results in increased interest and enthusiasm. In teaching, the proper motivation and keeping the pupils' interest is essential. The most useful technique I have found to develop motivation is thought-provoking questions.

4   I have used the information from this class almost every day in my student teaching. I used to be the type who would try to diagnose and prescribe on the basis of impressions, suspicions, feelings. I wasn't always wrong or right; that is beside the point. However, I was inaccurate, non-specific, and possibly unjust in some of my decisions. I now feel more professional. I now have a specific process to follow no matter what the reading material may be. For that matter, the process applies to many instructional areas other than reading. Making my decisions about diagnosis and prescriptions on the basis I now use, gives me a sense of security. I feel I could explain and justify what I am doing to a parent or a principal now, much better than I could before.

5   I now try to give my students a guide to their reading by having them ask questions before they read. After they have read, we spend more time listening to the answers to questions than we do asking them. I attempt to ask them questions which will guide their future reading, and I think I notice an improvement in attitude and in reading. This approach takes reading beyond interest and makes it challenging no matter what the material is.

References

Burton, W. H. (1962) *The Guidance of Learning Activities* New York: Appleton-Century-Crofts

Gray, W. S. and Rogers, B. (1956) *Maturity in Reading* Chicago: University of Chicago Press

Perry, W. G. Jnr (1959) 'Students' use and misuse of reading skills:

A report to the faculty' *Harvard Educational Review* volume 29 no. 3
  193-200
Strang, Ruth (1942) *Explorations in Reading Patterns* Chicago:
  University of Chicago Press
Taba, Helen (1964) *Thinking in Elementary School Children* Cooperative
  Research Project no. 1574 San Francisco State College, 53

*In an informal presentation, Dr Melnik synthesized the applications
and implications of this article 'The formulation of questions as an
instructional-diagnostic tool' which was published in *The Journal of
Reading* volume II, no.7, April 1968, 509-512, 578-581

Part two
The printed medium

i t a – A review of ten years research

John Downing

Professor of Education
University of Victoria, British Columbia

'The best way is . . . the Initial Teaching Alphabet'

The late Professor Frank Warburton in his review of i t a research for the Schools Council noted that the published results point unanimously in the same direction. Not one of them supports the popular belief that because our adult literature is printed in the traditional orthography (t o) of English, obviously it must be best to teach that same t o from the very beginning of learning to read. Warburton concluded with quiet certainty that not one shred of evidence could be found to support this common assumption of the self-evident superiority of t o. His rigorous examination of all the research led him to the opposite finding:

> There is no evidence whatsoever for the belief that the best way to learn to read in traditional orthography is to learn to read in traditional orthography. It would appear rather that the best way to learn to read in traditional orthography is to learn to read in the initial teaching alphabet. (pp. 234-5)

Warburton's conclusion represents a very strong claim for the effectiveness of i t a. Indeed, it is the most powerfully positive assertion of i t a's superiority which has been published during these first ten years of i t a's existence. The fact that Warburton was acknowledged as a leading authority on the design of educational research, and that the Schools Council *invited* him as an independent uninvolved expert to make this scientific critique of the i t a research, lends even greater power to his finding that 'the best way . . . is to learn to read in the initial teaching alphabet'.

In this paper I shall trace the events and summarize the evidence which led to Warburton's conclusion and to the similarly positive findings arrived at by Vera Southgate, who was Professor Warburton's partner in the Schools Council's report. What exactly have we learned from these ten years of i t a? What do we know about i t a? And about what important aspects of i t a do we still remain ignorant?

How we know about i t a: The validity of i t a research

Before I list the facts we have gleaned from i t a research over the past ten years, it seems appropriate to consider the basis for these conclusions – the level of certainty with which we can state them now.

In 1960, when I was appointed to plan and conduct the original experiments with i t a, we had no direct evidence about i t a, and the indirect evidence was not generally known. The first task therefore was to collect together this indirect evidence to see if it gave any pointers to the likely outcome of the proposed i t a experiment. During the past one hundred years or so there had been a number of attempts to introduce simplified and regularized writing systems similar to i t a. They had not been tested in scientific educational research, but there existed observational reports in various archives. My first article on this subject (Downing 1962) summarized these reports. Their general consensus was favourable with one particular finding constantly recurring in all of them: all agreed that children learned to read much more rapidly and easily when they were first introduced to written language through a simplified and regularized writing system instead of t o. Later, during the course of my work on i t a, I came across more of these older studies, and I have made a more comprehensive review of these historical developments in my book, *Evaluating the Initial Teaching Alphabet* (Downing 1967a).

At the same time that I was doing this desk research, I was planning and preparing for the first stage of the first i t a experiment. The details of these preparations are given in my book mentioned above, and in another special article on 'How i t a began' (Downing 1967b). Two major practical tasks, undertaken the year before i t a was introduced to the experimental classes, were the involvement of all British publishers who were willing to participate, and the canvassing of local education authorities and teachers for their cooperation in the proposed research.

In that year of preparation, the very important foundations were laid which have determined the status of i t a research today, ten years later. The i t a experiment was sponsored from the beginning by the two leading educational research bodies in England, the National Foundation for Educational Research in England and Wales and the University of London Institute of Education. I was appointed as director of the i t a project by a very distinguished committee of experts in relevant disciplines, and this committee gave me valuable advice during that first year of planning. We should acknowledge this committee's important contribution now that the research has eventually been accorded so much approval. Its members were Sir Cyril Burt, Emeritus Professor of Psychology at University College, London; H. L. Elvin, Director of the University of London Institute of Education; D. B. Fry, Head of the Phonetics Department at University College, London; Joyce M. Morris, past President of this United Kingdom Reading Association; W. N. Niblett, Professor of Higher Education at the University of London Institute of Education; Sir James Pitman, inventor of i t a and Chairman of the Initial Teaching Alphabet Foundation; P. E. Vernon, Professor of Educational Psychology at the University of Calgary, Alberta; W. D. Wall, Dean of the University of London Institute of Education. In addition I submitted my research plan to Professor M. D. Vernon, Emeritus Professor of Psychology at the University of Reading, and she kindly made a number of helpful suggestions which improved our plans. A number of other experts gave helpful advice. Dr Jessie Reid of the Education Department at the University of Edinburgh gave particularly valuable assistance in pinpointing some of the danger points to guard against. Percy Wilson and John Blackie at the Ministry of Education provided important practical guidance in planning the initial approaches to the local education authorities who were to be invited to join in the experiment.

Thus, during this year of preparation for the i t a experiment, a great deal of talent and expertise was brought to bear on the problem of devising and launching an experiment which would give us valid evidence on the relative effectiveness of i t a and t o. A detailed description of the design of that first experiment, planned in the way I have described, may be found in any of the following publications; Downing 1963, 1964a, 1964b, 1967a, 1969b.

Briefly, an experimental group of classes learned to read and write with i t a and their progress was compared with that of a control group of classes which used only t o from the beginning. The classes and the children in them were matched on all major variables. The methods and language content of the basic reading programme was matched also by providing the experimental group with the *Janet and John* series in i t a, and the control group with the same *Janet and John* materials in t o.

In 1963, a grant from the Ford Foundation enabled us to expand the first experiment and begin a second. This second experiment was designed by my colleague, Barbara Jones. It was intended as a check on the first investigation which it replicated except for one important change. In an attempt to match the factor of teacher competence, two teachers shared their time between a pair of classes, one class using i t a and the other t o. This constituted a valuable improvement in the scientific elegance of the

63

research design but it caused some sacrifice of reality since normally a class in the infants school has one teacher throughout the day, which was not the case in this second experiment. Details of the design of this second investigation may be found in the article by Downing and Jones (1966) which explains some of the reasons why it was conducted.

As soon as the first interim reports of the research began to come out, the experiment had to run the gauntlet of criticism. Vera Southgate's (1965) article, 'Approaching i t a results with caution' was the most searching and thoughtful of these critical commentaries. Our reply to her points of criticism is included in the article by Downing and Jones referred to above. Readers of Southgate's article and our reply must judge for themselves our defence of the validity of our research. But it is important to remember that Southgate's call to view our i t a research results 'with caution' was not a destructive attack on i t a or on the research. Indeed, one may hazard a guess that it was her constructive, unbiased and fair-minded approach in that article which caused the Schools Council to *invite* her to be Warburton's partner in the overall review of i t a which they commissioned later. Undoubtedly, the other major reason for Southgate's appointment was her acknowledged position as the leading expert on alternative methods of teaching reading to young children.

The validity of the i t a experiments was the question examined also by many of the contributors to *The i t a Symposium (*(Downing *et al* 1967). The National Foundation for Educational Research in England and Wales submitted a brief account of the results of the first three and a half years of my research to a number of experts on reading and educational research. Each one wrote his own independent judgment, and all these reviews were published together with my brief report of the results in *The i t a Symposium.* Some of these reviewers made some negative criticisms of the research methods but none was substantial. The general consensus seems to have been rather favourable, as the following quotations indicate:

No one can read the preceding report without recognizing that we now know far more about the processes of reading and of learning to read than we did before the experiments were undertaken, and that valuable experience has been gained in regard to the practicable methods of research in the bewildering field of education. *Sir Cyril Burt, Emeritus Professor of Psychology, University College, London*

This British experiment represents an important milestone attained by educational research. *Dr Marie Neale, Senior Lecturer in Education, University of Sydney*

The Downing report presents the results of a definitive and completely objective study of the value of the Initial Teaching Alphabet in early reading. *Dr Sterl Artley, Professor of Education. University of Missouri*

This reviewer is impressed with the tenacity with which Downing strove for objectivity throughout all phases of his study. His step by step analysis is thorough and cautious, and his concluding remarks are conservative. *Dr Jack Holmes, Professor of Educational Psychology, University of California, Berkeley*

The report referred to by the above writers is the one published at greater length in my book *Evaluating the Initial Teaching Alphabet.*

In 1966, when my report was nearing completion, the Schools Council decided to make their own appraisal of i t a and the i t a research. The proposal was the Schools Council's own idea and they asked Professor Warburton and Vera Southgate if they would undertake the task. The result is the very interesting book by Warburton and Southgate (1969), recently summarized in an inexpensive pamphlet by Southgate (1970).

The title of the full version of the Schools Council's report is *i t a: An Independent Evaluation,* which effectively and concisely emphasizes the neutral position of this official body in regard to curriculum in the schools of England and Wales. It also appropriately indicates the scientifically detached manner in which Warburton and Southgate approached their commission. They each worked independently, coming together only at the end when they had each arrived at their own individual conclusions which are published as separate parts in the Schools Council's report on i t a.

Warburton's part was to determine the scientific validity of the published i t a researches which were available to him at that time and to draw conclusions as to the consensus of their findings. There were seventeen such studies, six British and eleven American. Warburton found that only one of the eleven American i t a experiments had a valid design for determining whether i t a was or was not more effective than t o for teaching beginners to read. This was Robinson's study (1966) which has not yet come to fruition with any research results.

The other ten American i t a studies were all invalid for the essential purpose of comparing the i t a and t o writing systems because of serious flaws in their research designs. The common error found in these studies was what Warburton terms 'the confounding of materials and media'. Warburton comments at greater length on two examples of this serious fault in research design:

1 No proper comparison can be made between children learning to read in different media if the books and materials are different, i.e.

if the word experience, difficulty level, frequency of repetition etc of
two sets of readers are different. For example, Tanyzer and Alpert
(1965) report that in their own experiment the vocabulary count was
considerably higher in the i t a and Lippincott series than in the
Scott-Foresman series. (p. 257)

2   Mazurkiewicz (1966a) entitles his report 'Comparison of i t a and
t o achievement when methodology is controlled'. Yet the children
in the two groups used different books. His methodology is not
controlled at all. (p. 257)

Warburton sums up:

It is clearly illogical for i t a invariably to be used with one set of
reading materials and t o invariably to be used with another set, if
we wish to isolate the separate effects of the two media. The size of
the sample is irrelevant and offers no solution to the problem . . . .
To adopt an adequate experimental design is to apply logical
principles to a problem. To use different materials for different
media is as absurd as comparing tomato soup with mulligatawny
and always drowning one with ginger and the other with garlic.
(pp. 257-8)

It is little wonder that Goodacre (1968) commented as follows in her
overall review of the US Office of Education First Grade Reading studies,
of which those of Mazurkiewicz, and Tanyzer and Alpert were a part. The
title of her article is 'Lessons in reading'. Noting that these American studies
cost almost one million dollars, she remarks that they 'certainly
demonstrated the difficulty of translating educational questions into
testable hypotheses. By British research standards, this was surely an
expensive lesson!'
Yet the findings of these poorly designed American studies were not
generally in conflict with the results of the research which Warburton
judged to be more valid. They pointed to similar conclusions, and
Warburton did not reject them entirely from his total judgment of the
evidence. On its own such 'an experimental design in which the i t a pupils
always use one set of materials and the t o pupils always use another set
ensures bias, and it is logically impossible to come to any firm conclusion
about the relative effectiveness of the two alphabets' Warburton
commented. But fortunately most of the British i t a experiments avoided
this serious source of bias, and so Warburton was content to give some
consideration to the less rigorous research alongside what he judged to be
the more valid investigations.

66

Thus researches in which i t a is tied to one set of materials and t o to another cannot be taken as seriously as those of Downing (1967), Downing and Jones (1966), Harrison (1964), in which the materials were the same. (p. 258)

My own view is that the bias in the research designs criticized by Warburton is so serious as to make such studies completely worthless for determining the relative effectiveness of i t a and t o, and I have argued this in two previous articles (Downing 1967c, 1968a).

But to return to our theme how we know about i t a and the validity of i t a research, Warburton's final conclusion is one which I must quote with some embarrassment because of its personal reference to my own work. But I must do so because it is essential for your evaluation of the status of the evidence from i t a research. He writes: 'We are mainly indebted to the work of Downing'. I would hasten to add 'and his colleagues at the Reading Research Unit and those many advisors who helped to plan that work'.

For the purposes of this present paper, the essential conclusion from Warburton's review of i t a research is that the Downing reports are accounted valid scientific evidence. Therefore we shall include that evidence in listing what we know about i t a.

Before presenting that list, I must indicate two other sources of evidence for it. Firstly, Vera Southgate's part of the Schools Council's report should be taken into account. Her task was to obtain the professional opinions of teachers and other qualified educational observers in the schools with regard to i t a. Too often the scientific educational research worker is so concerned with the rigorous control of variables that he completely loses sight of the reality of the classroom. We shall compare the teachers' views gathered by Vera Southgate with the conclusions derived from the scientific experiments and their objective tests to see if they agree.

Secondly, we need to add some new results from my i t a experiments which were published too late to be included in Warburton's review. Since these came from a continuation of the research which he accepted as most valid, we may assume that they also constitute further valid evidence.

What we know about i t a
On the above basis, we may list the following seven facts which we know with maximum certainty. Below each item in the list, I will quote the relevant evidence from the Schools Council's report (which appears first) and from my own publications (which appears second).

1 *Reading in i t a is superior to reading in t o*
   Among infant teachers who had used i t a there was almost total agreement concerning its favourable effect on children's reading

progress . . . . The comments most frequently made by teachers were that i t a enables children to make a good beginning with reading; the task is simpler and consequently children can begin earlier, learn more quickly and achieve greater pleasure and satisfaction in so doing. (Schools Council p.65)

The evidence from these experiments is quite conclusive that, in comparison with the simplified and regularized system of i t a:
(a) t o slowed down children's progress in their series of readers;
(b) t o caused significantly lower scores on all tests of reading, but especially in word recognition and accuracy. The reduction in the learning efficiency of the most able pupils in the t o classes was especially remarkable. . . (Downing 1967a p. 295)

2   *Creative writing is superior in i t a*
The common features which most teachers noted in children's free writing when i t a was used were as follows: it begins at a much earlier age; it is greater in quantity; and the quality has improved in content, in the flow of ideas and in the breadth of vocabulary used. (Schools Council p.68)

(c) t o also produced markedly inferior results in written composition;
(d) t o had a seriously limiting effect on the size of the children's written vocabulary. (Downing 1967a p 295)

3   *i t a benefits children of all levels of ability*
The conclusions of the observer support those of the majority of teachers: in general, the reading and writing of children of all levels of ability was in advance of what would be found in equivalent schools using t o. Perhaps the most impressive feature of all was to watch the slowest group of children in a class, happily reading and writing at a simple level, while being certain that most of them would not have been doing so with t o. (Schools Council p.85)

Judged in terms of improvement in reading test scores, the high achieving child gains most from i t a. The slow learner gains the smallest increment of improvement in test scores from i t a. The teacher observing this result may form the opinion that i t a is best used with children who achieve well anyway with t o. But, if the teacher focuses attention on the difference between slow learners in i t a and slow learners in t o she may draw a separate and different conclusion about i t a's effectiveness with these children. In another recent article (Downing 1969a), I have made a special analysis of poor and very poor readers in i t a classes as compared with t o classes. *The results show a substantial reduction in the incidence of reading disability through the use of i t a.* (Downing 1970a)

4   *i t a produces a better attitude to reading*
Teachers' comments on children's attitudes can be summarized in this way. Children enjoy learning because of the simplicity and regularity of the alphabet; this gives them confidence so that they are eager to try; the regularity of the sound/symbol relationship means that their attempts are generally successful; and this in turn cuts out frustrations and gives them a sense of achievement. (Schools Council p.44)
(Also) The interviewer's observations in schools, which included talking to many children, confirmed what teachers had to say. Adverse attitudes to reading were not noticeable. Children's enjoyment, confidence, sense of achievement and eagerness to try to read were patently obvious. (Schools Council p.45)

Most heads feel that enthusiasm for reading is much greater and that the children show a greater love of and interest in books in the library corner. (Downing 1964a p. 36)
In summary, the headteachers report that children become independent in their reading at an earlier stage than is usual in their schools, and this seems to be supported by the objective data from the Vernon Graded Word Reading Test. (Downing 1964a p. 40)
The children learning to read with i t a are thought to be more mature than usual, and have a greater liking for school work. (Downing 1964a p.42)

5   *The transition from i t a to t o is not difficult*
Of all the verbal evidence collected in this enquiry, the fact most frequently and most emphatically stated was that children did not experience difficulty in making the transition in reading from i t a to t o. Teachers and those experienced visitors to schools who had observed the transition taking place had no doubts whatsoever on this score. (Schools Council p.168)

Most observers of i t a classes, including their teachers, seem to believe that there is no apparent difficulty in making the change from i t a to t o. It is frequently asserted that the children pass from one to the other quite effortlessly and often do not know that they are reading in a different writing system. (Downing 1967a p.238)
(But note my reservations in the next section **What we don't know about i t a.**)

6 *Children who begin with i t a, learn to spell in t o at least as well as children who have used t o from the start*

Not one infant teacher with experience of children transferring to t o spelling expressed the view that i t a had had a deleterious effect on children's spelling in t o. Hence, the verbal evidence given by infant teachers, as well as observations in schools, led to the conclusion that teachers' original fears that the use of i t a would be likely to have a harmful effect on children's spelling have not been justified. No evidence of a decline in spelling ability was noted in infant classes and there were certain indications of improvements. (Schools Council p.74)

t o spelling, perhaps surprisingly, is superior at all levels of achievement among pupils who began with i t a, and this seems to be a more generalized transfer effect of the i t a pupils' early experience of regularity of grapheme/phoneme relations in i t a. (Downing 1967a p.293) (Also, more recently) The evidence is especially strong that i t a produced fewer poor spellers. Three consecutive t o spelling tests in the third, fourth and fifth years showed the same trend. (Downing 1969a p. 554)

7 *i t a facilitates informal discovery methods of learning*

There was a growing awareness in teachers that the easier acquisition of reading skill merges with and focuses children's interest on additional activities, while at the same time further reading grows from these activities. It was being realized that discovery methods of learning in infant schools were greatly enriched when children were able to read. (Schools Council p.77)

(Also) The changes teachers reported in children's attitudes — for instance, independence, fearlessness,and confidence — had resulted in certain changes in teaching procedures. The majority of teachers commented that the greater regularity and simplicity of i t a enabled children to help themselves far more than was possible with t o. Children did not now find it necessary to ask the teacher to tell them every new word they met. They soon discovered that they could 'puzzle it out for themselves'. The resultant change in procedure represented a swing away from instruction towards individual, independent learning. (Schools Council p.54)

(And) Certain inspectors reported that in some of the more formal schools the use of i t a had led to greater informality in the grouping of children and in classroom procedures, as a result of children quickly becoming independent of the teacher when they found they could make good attempts at reading and spelling on their own. (And) A number of advisers reported that in some schools which had previously followed a reading scheme rather rigidly, i t a had had a liberalizing effect. Children who had used i t a wanted more books earlier and were interested in dipping into a variety of books, including some in t o. (Schools Council p.107)

i t a's most important educational value is the way in which it facilitates the discovery approach. (Downing 1968b p. 124)
i t a greatly facilitates this *discovery* through the clarification of structure in the three ways described above. There is no excuse whatsoever for beginning with formal synthetic phonics when English is printed in i t a. Meaningful and motivating material in natural English vocabulary and sentence structures when presented in i t a builds readiness for and leads more quickly to the *discovery* of the phonemic structure of English. (Downing 1968c p. 945)
In our original i t a experiments in Britain we deliberately avoided associating it with any particular methodology of teaching. We simply added the i t a writing system to the good approaches that were already in general use in our schools . . . . The truth is that the i t a experiment in Britain vindicates the progressive movement in reading instruction. It shows that teachers have been right to emphasize guided self-discovery in activities related to reading. It shows that they have been right to move towards a language – experience approach in which the child's need for self-expression and our need to preserve his creativity are recognized. It shows that we have been right to give priority to the development of methods which will involve children in reading from the beginning through their own interests and activities and through developing a love of books for what they contain. This is how i t a has been conceived in Britain. (Downing 1967d p. 7)

What we don't know about i t a
There are a number of important questions about i t a which still remain unanswered.

1 *Do t o pupils catch up with the i t a pupils in later years?*
Firstly, there is one problem on which the Schools Council's report and my own statistical findings are not in complete agreement. Southgate and Warburton, each independently, concluded that t o pupils do seem to catch up with i t a pupils after about the third year of school.

Warburton based his conclusion chiefly on my test results obtained from pupils who were at the end of the third school year. One test showed that i t a pupils had a statistically significant advantage over the t o group. But other tests showed no difference between the groups *at that time.* Hence, Warburton's conclusion is:

The results obtained when the children are pursued into the third year suggest that the t o groups catch up. We must await the findings of other researches, particularly Downing and Jones (1966), to obtain more conclusive evidence. (p. 235)

Southgate's finding on this point is as follows:

Comments made by teachers in junior classes, by knowledgeable visitors to schools, as well as reports of research findings, all indicate that by the age of approximately eight, the early advantages in reading and writing gained by children who have used i t a are diminishing or have almost disappeared. The observer's visits to junior classes generally confirmed this view, although certain junior teachers spoke of other advantages in the form of personal attributes which they had observed in the i t a children. (p. 164)

Southgate believes that the t o children catch up with the i t a pupils simply because of the general lack of organized educational procedures for improving reading beyond the age of eight years in English schools.

All that is happening at present is that the i t a children reach this plateau earlier than the t o children who, within two or three years, catch up with them. They are then all prevented, through lack of guidance and instruction, from making a continued surge of progress. (p. 164)

I agree with Southgate that reading instruction beyond the infant school stage is generally neglected in England. In several previous articles (Downing 1968d, 1969c, 1969d, 1970b) I have argued that this neglect of reading at the later stages is the worst feature of education in England and that the root of this problem lies in the failure of university institutes of education and colleges of education to provide adequate training in the psychology, linguistics and pedagogy of reading. The blame must lie chiefly with the institutes of education for their miserable failure in this respect. It is only one aspect of the lofty disdain for mundane practical classroom problems which has emanated from most of these ivory towers of 'higher education'.

But do the t o pupils catch up with the i t a pupils? Further tests have been administered to the children in my original experiment and these indicate that the i t a pupils are further ahead of the t o pupils at the end of five years than they were after only three years. These results were not available to Warburton and Southgate when they wrote their reports for the Schools Council. They were published by Downing and Latham (1969) only recently. Their report of tests conducted in the fifth year of school show that the i t a pupils were significantly superior to the children who had begun with t o . However the sample was rather small, and this is the only experiment which has provided fifth year test results. It may be safer, therefore, while we await data from other research, to accept the more cautious view that the t o reading and spelling attainments of i t a pupils after the transition stage are at least as good as those of pupils who have not begun with i t a.

Does this mean that i t a may not be, after all, as Warburton puts it 'the best way to learn to read'? Not at all, because whether the t o pupils catch up or not is irrelevant to the evaluation of either i t a or t o. The issue is an educational red herring. On this I am again in complete agreement with both Warburton and Southgate, for they state:

> The evidence suggests that for most children in most schools the use of i t a as an *initial* teaching alphabet would considerably raise the children's standard of reading and their rate of scholastic progress, although it seems likely that this advantage will be lost after the transition . . . . The general findings do not necessarily imply that i t a has failed. The educational and intellectual advantages of a child learning to read fluently at a very early age are very considerable and may affect his whole confidence and future progress. (Warburton in Schools Council's report pp.276-277)

> It should also be emphasized that an acceptance of the view that the reading and writing of i t a and t o children are approximately the same at the age of eight, does not discredit the use of i t a for the initial stages of reading and writing. No claim was originally made to the effect that i t a would produce better readers in the long run. The aim was to simplify the initial task of learning. Thus, even if i t a children are only at the same level of attainment as t o children after three or four years, if learning to read has been easier and more pleasant for them, if fewer children have experienced frustrations and failures and if many have known the enjoyment and value of reading a year or so earlier than they would have done, it can fairly be claimed that its use has been justified. (Southgate in Schools Council's report p.165)

In summary, we cannot be certain that i t a pupils stay ahead of t o pupils, although the new data from the tests reported by Downing and Latham allow a more optimistic conclusion about this than was possible when the Schools Council's report was written. But in any case, this is not the real issue. i t a is worthwhile because of the greater ease of learning that comes with its use in the initial stage.

There are many other things which we don't know about i t a. But, like the first problem discussed above, they do not affect the practical decision of whether to use i t a in your classroom now. I will list briefly some of the more interesting examples of aspects of i t a about which we remain ignorant.

2 Is i t a 'better' or 'best'?

Warburton concludes that i t a is 'best', but I would prefer the word 'better'. This is because none of the research evidence he reviewed was designed to test if i t a was the best writing system for learning to read and write in English. All the studies were concerned to compare t o with i t a, and no other writing systems were compared. For example, we do not know if i t a is better than UNIFON (Ratz 1966), Regularized English (Wijk 1958), or DMS (Fry 1967), to take just three examples of other available simplified and regularized writing systems. A scientific comparison between i t a and these other systems has not been made.

The certainty that i t a is better than t o is however very much greater than in the comparison of t o with each of these other systems. There is a wealth of scientific research data on the use of i t a, but none or very little on these other alternatives to t o.

The same is true of the colour systems, *Words in Colour* (Gattegno 1962) and *Phonetic Colour* (Jones 1967), except that there is a little more evidence on the effectiveness of the former in comparison with ordinary black t o, and much better evidence comparing Phonetic Colour with black t o. However, there has been no research published as yet comparing these colour systems with i t a. Jones has attempted to prove in a number of recent publications that his colour system is superior to i t a, but there is no scientific basis for Jones's claims. One cannot make a comparison between his experiment with colour and the other experiments with i t a. Any conclusions must be invalid because the samples in the different experiments are not comparable.

We can only speculate about the relative effectiveness of i t a and the colour systems. Both approaches have been shown to be superior to unmodified t o. Of this there is no doubt. My own hypothesis would be that i t a would be superior to the colour systems. This is based on the psychology of orientation in perception. i t a trains children to look carefully at the shapes of black characters on white paper, which is the essential perceptual task of reading. The colour systems seem more likely to focus attention on an aspect of print which is quite irrelevant in normal reading, except for providing an emotional cue, e.g. red for a danger sign.

The comparisons should be made between i t a and these other systems in future research. But this is no excuse for inaction now. The condemnation of t o is absolutely conclusive. The i t a claim has the greatest strength because of sheer weight of evidence, and hence for practical purposes as far as the presently available evidence is concerned, Warburton may be justified in concluding that i t a is 'best' in the quotation with which I began this paper.

3 Can i t a itself be improved?

Earlier in this paper I warned that although my research agrees with Southgate's that there is no noticeable problem at the stage when children make the transition from i t a to t o, I nevertheless have reservations on this conclusion. I have stated these in detail in my research reports (Downing 1967a, 1967e, 1968e).

Briefly, although i t a pupils transfer to t o with all the outward appearance of an easy facility and no anxiety whatsoever, nonetheless the data from objective reading tests show quite conclusively that a real setback in the learning curve does occur at this stage. The simple inescapable truth is that at the end of the second year or beginning of the third year of school, when the majority of i t a pupils are making the transition to t o, they score significantly lower on t o tests than they do on parallel i t a tests. This fact is obscured probably because although the i t a pupils read t o less well than they read i t a, yet they read t o at least as well as t o pupils can.

I believe that the good results of transfer from i t a to t o could be even better if we could modify i t a on the basis of further research on the details of the i t a alphabet and spelling system. I think we may be able to improve i t a in some other respects too, especially with regard to its use for creative writing by young children.

My view has been challenged by some of the i t a enthusiasts who seem to regard i t a as so perfect that it should be inscribed on holy tablets which must never be violated. I have discussed these objections elsewhere (Downing 1967d, 1967f, 1967g, 1967h). But the outcome is that the research has just begun in Canada. The first experiments were started just four weeks ago. We hope that these may determine which aspects of i t a are important for possible future improvement, should those who use i t a in education, publishing or printing desire to make any such improvements which may be indicated by our research.

But again this issue does not have any relevance for the essential decision of the present moment, i.e. whether to adopt i t a for classroom use *now*. We don't know if i t a can be improved, but we do know with real certainty that i t a as it is currently constituted is a great improvement on t o.

4 Can t o be improved?

The i t a experiments were quite clear about this. The fact that i t a pupils do not read t o as well as they read i t a at the stage of transition shows that it would be better to have no transition at all. Then i t a pupils would continue to read just as well as ever. Almost certainly i t a would not be acceptable as a 'spelling reform', and the way ahead would be through changes in t o. This would probably take the form of 'phonematizing' spelling in the way that Britain is now decimalizing its currency. The research just begun in Canada may provide data which could help to carry out this proposal if it should ever become acceptable to the public.

But yet again, and even more so here where the prospect of reform is so remote, we cannot wait for answers to future research. We know with certainty that at this present time the i t a we have is better than the t o we have. Therefore i t a ought to be generally adopted for use in the beginning stage of learning to read.

5   What is the best reading series in i t a?

My personal bias would be satisfied if I could prove that my own i t a *Downing Readers* (1963) were the best i t a series. Pride of workmanship leads me to believe that it is!

But seriously and frankly, we have no scientific evidence on this question as yet. Possibly we never will have. I believe that the best methods of teaching and the best materials for teaching reading vary with both the child and the teacher. The great strength of the British way of teaching beginning reading is that each school is free to select its own methods and materials. In this way a teacher can (as she should) select the methods and materials with which she works best and which best fit the individual needs of her pupils. However to accomplish this ideal the teacher must know the alternatives which are available. For this reason I have written an article describing, without any evaluation of their relative worth, the various alternative methods and materials which are available in i t a (Downing 1968c). The article does not attempt to demonstrate that any one i t a approach is better than another. This is left for the teacher to judge.

But some other sources have claimed that they have the best i t a reading series. Unfortunately their claims are based on grave errors in their quotations of i t a research reports. I will just mention these briefly here so that if you are contemplating the adoption of i t a in your school you can be on your guard against these distortions of the original i t a research reports from the Schools Council and some other sources. The following two cases will serve as examples which point to the lesson we must learn from them. Other cases of similar errors are given in two special articles on this problem (Downing 1967d and 1970c).

The first example is from an advertisement in the March 1970 issue of *The Reading Teacher* (p. 593) which runs as follows:

Tina understands thousands of words . . . . Extensive research has shown that 'the best way to learn to read and write with the regular alphabet is to begin by reading with i t a* as Tina is doing. And the best way to learn to read in i t a is with the *Early to Read i/t/a Program* by Mazurkiewicz and Tanyzer.

* *i t a: An Independent Evaluation* Warburton and Southgate.'

Quotation marks signify *quotation* by common custom, but the above advertisement does not follow the general rule. The sentence within its quotation marks is not an accurate extract from Warburton and Southgate. However this is not too seriously misleading, perhaps because it is not an unreasonable paraphrase of Warburton's actual words, which we have quoted verbatim at the beginning of this paper.

But what is more seriously misleading is the way in which the sentence claiming superiority for the *Early to Read* i t a books by Mazurkiewicz and Tanyzer is introduced. Starting that sentence with the word 'And' is suggestive that it follows on from the previous extract from the Schools Council's report. Adding below '*i t a: An Independent Evaluation* Warburton and Southgate' also is liable to cause the teacher who reads this advertisement to jump to the false conclusion that Warburton and Southgate have proved that 'the best way to learn to read in i t a is with the *Early to Read i/t/a Program* by Mazurkiewicz and Tanyzer'.

The truth is quite different. Neither Southgate nor Warburton made any comparison of the effectiveness of the various alternative i t a reading schemes. The only references in the Schools Council's report to experiments using the *Early to Read* i t a series tend to be negative. For example, Warburton found that those studies which used the *Early to Read* i t a books in America were 'illogical' and 'absurd' (p. 257) because they failed to control fundamental variables. He was not referring to the books of course, but his comments would certainly not lend support to any suggestion that he found them to be 'the best way to learn to read in i t a'.

Southgate's description of the i t a teaching she observed in the British schools would also tend, if anything, to lead to the opposite conclusion from that proposed by the advertisers of the *Early to Read* i t a reading scheme. For example, she states in the Schools Council's report:

> It would be a grave error to assume that the use of i t a had brought about an increase in formal phonic training. (p. 53)

Numerous other parts of her report lead to a picture of a way of teaching i t a which is very different from the methods laid down in the teachers' manual for the *Early to Read* i t a series. Mazurkiewicz (1966b), one of its authors, has stated that it might be termed a 'phonics' method, and Ohanian's (1966) detailed review of the *Early to Read* series confirms that in it 'the emphasis is clearly on the individual sounds and the individual forms which represent these sounds'. Therefore, she concludes that it constitutes a 'type of phonics program'.

Since the British i t a programme described by Southgate is so very different from the one found in the American *Early to Read* i t a programme, there is absolutely no justification either for any suggestion that she has proved that 'the best way to learn to read in i t a is with the *Early to Read i/t/a Program* by Mazurkiewicz and Tanyzer', as the reader of the advertisement might think.

The real truth is that neither the Schools Council's report of Warburton and Southgate nor any other published research has investigated this issue. It is one of the things we don't know about i t a.

The above example should not be dismissed as an isolated freak accident arising from the difficulty of compressing research information into an advertisement. My second example refers to serious errors in research reports. In my latest article on this problem (Downing 1970c), I have noted several errors which have been made in Mazurkiewicz's reviews of the British i t a studies. But the most extraordinary mistakes of all were discovered in an article by a different author.

The first American teacher to use i t a was Mrs Anita Metzger at her school in Ventnor, New Jersey in January 1963. She used the only i t a books available at that time – the British *Janet and John* i t a series. Mrs Metzger wrote a report of her i t a experiment, referring to the books simply as 'i t a books', not wanting to be involved with any particular commercial product. Her original manuscript actually pointed out that when she conducted the experiment there were 'at that time no [i t a] publications available in the United States'. As well as sending us a copy of her manuscript, Mrs Metzger submitted it to *The i/t/a Bulletin*, a magazine produced by the publishers of Mazurkiewicz's and Tanyzer's *Early to Read* i t a books.

Several errors were made when Mrs Metzger's report was put into print. For example, the published version states that her pupils were 'reading through Book 4 in Pitman's *Early to Read* series by Mazurkiewicz and Tanyzer before the Christmas holidays', whereas Mrs Metzger's original manuscript named no particular i t a series, and she was, in actual fact, using *Janet and John* in i t a. The error is even more curious when we remember that the *Early to Read* series had not even been written when Mrs Metzger began her experiment, and she had never used these books in her school!

Thus, the truth remains that there is no evidence to support the claim that the *Early to Read* series is the best i t a reading scheme as the advertisement claimed.

I believe that teachers should decide which i t a series to use on the basis of their own professional judgment after they have examined the various alternatives for themselves. One thing only is certain; at this present time we don't know which i t a series is best, and we should be highly suspicious of any author or publisher who claims that research has proved that his i t a books are best.

I will go even further and say something which my publisher may not like from the sales angle. I don't think the books matter all that much. The difference between one i t a series and another is not what matters most for the children. Much more important are the attitudes and methods of the teacher. This is what we will learn from our next speaker, Olive Gayford, and from reading her new book (Gayford 1970) or seeing the film about her school. This has not been proved by research. I am expressing only my personal conviction based on my experience of i t a in the past ten years.

I would add a further heresy. Despite all the research evidence, I have a hunch that the teacher's attitudes and methods are still a more important variable than the alphabet *if we are concerned with the total education of the child.* But given that a teacher's attitudes and methods are superb, and that the books she uses in her classroom are excellent, all the research evidence points clearly to the firm conclusion that t o will hinder and hamper her good efforts, while i t a will support and strengthen her in her resolve to infect her pupils with the lifelong love of reading.

References

Downing, J. (1962) 'The relationship between reading attainment and the inconsistency of English spelling at the infants school stage' *British Journal of Educational Psychology* 32, 166-177

Downing, J. (1963) 'Experiments with an augmented alphabet for beginning readers in British schools' in Traxler, A. E. (ed.) *Frontiers of Education* Washington, DC: American Council on Education

Downing, J. (1964a) *The Initial Teaching Alphabet Reading Experiment* London:Evans, Chicago:Scott-Foresman (1965)

Downing, J. (1964b) 'Experiments with Pitman's Initial Teaching Alphabet in British Schools' in Figurel, J. A. (ed.) *Reading as an Intellectual Activity* New York: Scholastic Magazines

Downing, J. (1967a) *Evaluating the Initial Teaching Alphabet* London: Cassell

Downing, J. (1967b) 'How i t a began' *Elementary English* 44, 40-46

Downing, J. (1967c) 'Methodological problems in research on simplified alphabets and regularized writing-systems' *Journal of Typographic Research* 1, 191-197

Downing, J. (1967d) 'i t a – what next?' in Schick, G. B. and May, M. M.

(eds.) *Junior College and Adult Reading Programs – Expanding Fields*
Milwaukee: National Reading Conference

Downing, J. (1967e) 'Pro-active interference in transfer from i t a to
traditional orthography' *British Psychological Society Bulletin* 20,
18A-19A

Downing, J. (1967f) 'Can i t a be improved?' *Elementary English* 44,
849-855

Downing, J. (1967g) 'What's wrong with i t a?' *Phi Delta Kappan* 48,
262-266

Downing, J. (1967h) 'Will i t a copyright prevent improvements?' *Phi
Delta Kappan* 48, 524

Downing, J. (1968a) 'A closer scrutiny of the research data on i t a'
Education (Boston) 88, 308-312

Downing, J. (1968b) 'Self-discovery, self-expression, and the self-image
in the i t a classroom' in Douglass, M. (ed.) *Claremont Reading
Conference 32nd Yearbook* Claremont California: Claremont Graduate
School. And, in 1969, in Bintner, A. R., Dlabal, J. J. and Kise, L. K. (eds.)
Readings on Reading Scranton, Pennsylvania: International Textbook
Company

Downing, J. (1968c) 'Alternative teaching methods in i t a' *Elementary
English* 45, 942-951

Downing, J. (1968d) 'Reading in America as compared with Great
Britain' in Clark, Margaret and Maxwell, Sheena (eds.) *Reading:
Influences on Progress* United Kingdom Reading Association

Downing, J. (1968e) 'Some difficulties in transfer of learning from i t a
to t o' in Figurel, J. A. (ed.) *Forging Ahead in Reading* Newark, Delaware:
International Reading Association

Downing, J. (1969a) 'New experimental evidence of the effectiveness of
i t a in preventing disabilities of reading and spelling' *Developmental
Medicine and Child Neurology* 11, 547-555

Downing, J. (1969b) 'Initial Teaching Alphabet: Results after six years'
Elementary School Journal 69, 242-249

Downing, J. (1969c) 'Neglect of reading most serious defect in training'
Times Educational Supplement, March 28th

Downing, J. (1969d) 'Are current provisions for teacher training adequate
for the effective teaching of reading and related skills?' *Proceedings of
Annual Conference of the British Psychological Society, March 1969*, 8-9

Downing, J. (1970a) *The Effectiveness of i t a in the Prevention and
Treatment of Disabilities of Reading and Writing* Paper presented at the
World Mental Health Assembly, Washington DC, November 1969.
Reprinted as pamphlet London: Initial Teaching Alphabet Foundation

Downing, J. (1970b) 'Functional literacy: future needs and current
progress' *Symposium*, 9-15

Downing, J. (1970c) 'Cautionary comments on some American i t a reports' *Educational Research* November, 70-72

Downing, J. *et al* (1967) *The i t a Symposium* Slough: NFER

Downing, J. and Jones, B. (1966) 'Some problems of evaluating i t a: A second experiment' *Educational Research* 8, 100-114

Downing, J. and Latham, W. D. (1969) 'A followup of children in the first i t a experiment' *British Journal of Educational Psychology 39*, 303-305

Downing Readers (1963) London: Initial Teaching Publishing Company

Early to Read (1963) New York: Initial Teaching Alphabet Publications

Fry, E. (1967) 'The Diacritical Marking System and a preliminary comparison with i t a' in Downing, J. and Brown, A. L. (eds.) *The Second International Reading Symposium* London: Cassell

Gattegno, C. (1962) *Words in Colour: Background and Principles* Reading: Educational Explorers

Gayford, O. (1970) *i t a in Primary Education* London: Initial Teaching Publishing Company

Goodacre, E. (1968) 'Lessons in reading' *Times Educational Supplement* March 22nd, 985

Harrison, M. (1964) *Instant Reading* London: Pitman

Jones, J. K. (1967) *Research Report on Colour Story Reading* London: Nelson

Mazurkiewicz, A. J. (1966a) 'A comparison of i t a and t o reading achievement when methodology is controlled' in Mazurkiewicz, A. J. (ed.) *i t a and the World of English* Hempstead, New York: i t a Foundation

Mazurkiewicz, A. J. (1966b) 'Materials of instruction for beginners' in Mazurkiewicz, A. J. (ed.) *i t a and the World of English* Hempstead, New York: i t a Foundation

Ohanian, V. (1966) 'Control populations in i t a experiments' *Elementary English* 43, 373-380

Ratz, M. S. (1966) *UNIFON: A Design for Teaching Reading* Racine, Wisconsin: Western Publishing Educational Services

Robinson, H. M. (1966) 'Effectiveness of i t a as a medium for reading instruction' in Mazurkiewicz, A. J. (ed.) *i t a and the World of English* Hempstead, New York: i t a Foundation

Southgate, V. (1965) 'Approaching i t a results with caution' *Educational Research* 7, 83-96

Southgate, V. (1970) *i t a: What is the Evidence?* London: Murray and Edinburgh: Chambers

Tanyzer, H. J. and Alpert, H. (1965) *Effectiveness of three different basal reading systems on first grade reading achievement* Hempstead, New York: Hofstra University

Warburton, F. W. and Southgate, V. (1969) *i t a: An Independent Evaluation* London: Murray and Edinburgh: Chambers

Wijk, A. (1958) *Regularized English* Stockholm: Wiksell

i t a – A teacher's viewpoint

Olive Gayford

Headmistress
West St Leonard's County Primary School

Introduction

We have heard from Dr Downing a review of ten years of research which has been carried out into the teaching of reading through the medium of the Initial Teaching Alphabet. I would like to consider i t a from a teacher's point of view.

With i t a now so well established I am only one among hundreds of headteachers using this medium which has countless advantages over the traditional alphabet as a means of introducing young children to reading and writing.

When we first became involved in an experiment in the use of i t a, now more than seven years ago, ours was a comparatively small unit, comprising six teachers and approximately two hundred children between the ages of five and seven plus. Children who reached the age of seven by the first day of September in any year were transferred to the adjoining junior school. In April 1967 the two schools were amalgamated under my headship, making one primary school unit.

For many years we were faced with the very real problem which faces countless teachers in infant schools today – the lamentably short time which some children spend in an infants school. Children born in the summer month have, in the main, less than two years in which to complete their entire infant school course and, irrespective of the medium by which they are being taught to read and write, this time is grossly inadequate.

Teachers in infant schools are the first to recognize that learning cannot be hurried, yet it is surely understandable that they should at times feel a sense of urgency, especially if they are required to send their children to a junior school where a child still reading in i t a would be regarded as backward in reading.

It is then as the headteacher of a primary school, who over the past seven years has seen the tremendous impact that i t a can have on children's reading performance and creative written work, that I offer this paper. I do so in the hope that teachers will feel that, despite the problem of the all too early transfer to the junior school, it is well worthwhile giving children the flying start that i t a can offer.

The need for i t a

I should like first to consider the need for i t a in our schools today. The

82

society in which our children are living must of necessity influence life in our schools. Contemporary society is marked by frequent and far reaching social and economic changes. The present primary school children will grow into adults in this changing society. They will have the choice of a wide range of occupations unheard of by their parents let alone their grandparents, but the pressures on them will be great. Children growing up in this society will need to be self-reliant and independent. They will need to be resourceful and discriminating. Throughout their lives they will need to be capable of learning and of discovering knowledge.

It is apparent then that the primary school of today must do more than equip children with skills in the three Rs. It must be a community and the way of life within that community must transmit values and attitudes. It is the responsibility of the school deliberately to encourage the development of positive attitudes towards learning, attitudes which can only develop in an environment in which creativity and initiative and making discoveries are encouraged and in which children are allowed to develop as individuals. If we believe in the discovery approach to all learning, learning to read can be no exception. The way in which i t a facilitates this discovery approach is one of its greatest educational assets.

It is evident that it is easier for a child to discover the relationship between printed characters and spoken sounds if the characters always represent the same sounds and if they occur in the same order in which they are heard in the spoken word. This is where i t a has its undoubted advantage over traditional orthography. Because of the consistency of i t a, when a child makes a discovery of a sound/symbol relationship, it works in all circumstances.

First steps in learning to read

Before teachers can help children towards an understanding of what reading will mean to them in terms of enjoyment and discovery, they must be clear in their own minds what reading involves. Reading is, in the first instance, a means of communication, a recorded form of speech. It is obvious therefore that unless a child possesses the ability to make himself clearly understood and to understand others by means of the spoken word, it is pointless to attempt any sort of instruction in the printed word. The majority of children, on coming to school, have learned to communicate their thoughts and feelings to others, first by gesture and then by speech. But as children vary considerably in their rate of development, they will not all have reached the same degree of fluency. Some children come to school from homes where they have had little encouragement to develop their powers of speech. They are often shy and uncommunicative and are reluctant to make contact either with adults or with other children. It is only the friendly encouragement and approval of an understanding teacher in a happy and relaxed environment that will help them to overcome their speech difficulties . As these shy and inarticulate children begin to talk, the teacher must help them to express their thoughts and feelings. With the extension of their vocabulary will come an extension of confidence which will bring about emotional stability. Even children who make contacts easily, who have acquired a fairly high degree of fluency in speech, need the opportunity for conversation provided by participation in a wide variety of practical experiences. One of the main functions of an infant school, therefore, must be to provide a stable, stimulating environment in which a child can explore and investigate the world around him; an environment in which he will not only increase his vocabulary and the power to use it, but in which he will gain a reservoir of experience that will bring understanding to what he reads and a purpose for learning to express himself in writing.

Many children are made aware of the printed word long before they come to school. Letters, newspapers, catalogues and a variety of printed material arrive through the letterbox, and these become an accepted part of daily life. Picture and story books play an important part in a child's early life. When a child becomes aware that familiar objects can be represented on the page of a book, and he is able to distinguish and isolate one particular object from a mass of colour on an illustrated page, he has in fact taken a step in learning to read. Many children will have experienced the pleasure of being read to by a parent while they themselves follow the story through the pictures and words of the book. These early associations with the printed word lay the surest foundations for learning to read.

How important it is that this kind of association with reading should continue when a child comes to school. Instead of launching little children on a formal course of instruction in letters and words – an experience foreign to that which they have come to know as reading – an understanding teacher will realize that the best contribution she can make is to create for them a lively environment in which books and reading become a necessary and integral part of living.

Creating the need for reading and writing
Experience has shown that it is through his own activity and personal involvement that a child finds the need and desire to learn a new skill. John Dewey (1906) discovered this over fifty years ago and wrote:

> An end which is the child's own carries him on to possess
> the means of its accomplishment.

When a child is actively engaged in painting, modelling, pretending, investigating and discovering, the need for reading and writing frequently arises. The emphasis is more on the child's learning than on the teacher's teaching, but the teacher's part is far from a passive one, as one example of this type of learning may show.

A group of five year olds had constructed a ship using large wooden boxes. Their interest had been sustained for several days while the ship was painted, equipped and finally 'launched'. Colin, the self-appointed captain, announced that his ship was going to sail round the world. 'How do you write "Captain"?' he said to his teacher, 'I want to write it on my hat.' This was the first of many reading and writing experiences which sprang from this activity. A discussion followed on the proposed voyage, involving the names of the countries which were to be visited. Books were consulted and it was discovered that some countries were hot and some were cold. 'Will you read what it says?' was the frequent request. As Christmas was approaching and making a Christmas cake had already been discussed, the ship's crew arranged to call at the appropriate countries to collect the ingredients. Meanwhile, in school and at home, the children searched through magazines for colourful pictures of sultanas, eggs, flour, oranges etc and each picture was mounted on coloured card on a wall board. Cards bearing the names of each commodity were prepared in large clear print and slotted beneath each picture. A duplicate set of cards was left on a nearby shelf and the children used them in devising a number of games. They matched them to those on the wall, used them as 'flash' cards in their self-chosen groups, removed the cards from the wall and played 'Snap' with the two sets, and then tried to replace the cards under the right pictures. Later, when it was time to make the cake, the children were each allowed to choose a card and they went with their teacher to a grocer's shop near the school to buy the necessary ingredients. More games followed. They mixed up all the cards and, setting out all the ingredients on a table, tried to attach the right card to each one and so on. A great deal of writing drawing and painting ensued and a book entitled 'ѻur Cristmas cæk' was compiled and was eventually added to the many other large homemade books in the book corner where it was read over and over again as the children relived their experiences.

So far the children's attention had not been drawn to individual words or characters, but an awareness of the significance of the printed word was undoubtedly developing and later when the soundsymbol relationship had been discovered, this and other homemade books were reread and discussed. With i t a the similarity of, for example, the symbol for ɛɛ in words like 'pɛɛl' and 'trɛɛcl' could be found in captions such as 'ѻur swɛɛt ʃhop' 'dꙍ not fɛɛd ɹhe birds' and 'cum and rɛɛd' which could be seen around the room.

No learning can prosper in isolation, and often activities devised to promote an understanding of mathematical concepts serve equally well to give experience in reading and writing. This is true of the classroom shop. If the shop is a cake or sweet shop, the children enjoy helping to make the cakes and sweets. Recipes are read and ingredients measured and each morning the 'shopkeepers' sort, arrange and count the stock in their shop. Beside the transparent plastic boxes that hold the various types of wrapped and homemade sweets will be a box containing printed cards bearing the name and price of each variety together with notices such as 'œpen', 'clœsd', 'sæl'. The names of the shopkeepers for the day are displayed in the shop and those who are to help with the cooking have their names laid around the cooking table. The printed word becomes an accepted and necessary part of living.

Individual approaches to reading

Because children are individuals and their rate of development varies considerably, it is easy to see that they do not all respond to the same stimuli. The incentive for learning to read may come through a love of books and stories or because some piece of construction or planning requires the ability to read, or perhaps because it is necessary to be able to read in order to participate fully in the daily life at school. Some children are attracted to reading through drawing and writing about their personal experiences.

᾿ Reading and writing in the infant school cannot be separated. When there is access to paper, pencils, crayons and paint, children will express themselves through their drawings and paintings. At first their efforts are purely pictorial, but they soon find that drawing alone is not sufficiently satisfying. They wish to offer verbal interpretations of their pictures which prompt such requests as 'Will you please write "My new house" or "My dad's new car"?' As the child explains his drawing to his teacher, so he establishes a personal contact with her. As she writes what he dictates so the idea of reading and writing as connected means of communication takes root in his mind. His desire for written explanation soon extends to include aspects of expression other than drawing and he requests captions to accompany his paintings and models.

Children enjoy possessing a book in which to draw and write, especially if it is large and has gaily coloured covers. As confidence increases, these drawings will depcit episodes in a child's home life and original stories in which the interest is often sustained for several days. At first the child may or may not attempt to copy what he has dictated to his teacher, but later he writes each word beneath her writing, reading it as he writes. After a time, having come to terms with the printed word in a variety of situations, he will begin to write unaided. Teachers working with i t a have noticed that a child reaches this stage far more quickly and asks how to spell fewer words than if he were learning with t o. This because he can begin to rationalize the recording of speech using a regular alphabet.

Children's writing — discovering characters and sounds

The most significant contribution i t a has made to children's learning
is in the field of creative writing. Through the use of pre-reading material
and through the daily experiences related to a child's own needs, a teacher
can help him to discover an individualized approach to reading and writing ,
although the order of procedure cannot be set out in any universally ideal
sequence. Several significant facts emerge. First, the most purposeful early
reading material for young children is material they write themselves. Second,
any printed material, whether made by the teacher or obtained from a
publisher, should arouse immediate interest and meaning and be of such a
design as to ensure a child's personal involvement.

Yet as soon as a child becomes actively involved in writing his attention
is focused not on a sentence as a whole, but on the order in which symbols
occur within a single word. Undoubtedly the ability to memorize a word
as a whole is a great help when a child needs to write that word, nevertheless
the order of the letters is important, because the very act of writing necessitates
following one letter with another. As soon as a child writes a word and says to
himself 'This one, then this one, then this one' he is aware of the individual
symbols in order from left to right, although it takes some time before he
becomes aware of the fact that the symbols represent sounds which are made
in that order.

Claims have been made that children can be taught to read without ever
learning individual symbols and the sounds which they represent. For some
children learning to *read,* this may well be true, but when they need to
write they must of necessity recognize character order. Many teachers have
found that although there is no place for word analysis in the early stages,
at some time children need to know the sound values of the printed
symbols. The fact that children need to learn these sound values does not
mean that a teacher has deliberately to set about teaching them through
formal phonic drills. A good teacher will never lose sight of the fact that it
is the children who do the learning; her skill lies in contriving situations in
which this learning can take place.

If two sets of character cards are provided children will sort them,
match them and play 'Snap' with them long before they are aware of
their significance as symbols representing sounds. When i t a is used
only lower case letters have to be reckoned with and this considerably
reduces the number of shapes. As these cards are handled, sorted and
matched, the shapes are gradually absorbed. Children will soon become
aware that similar shapes are used when the teacher is writing underneath
their drawings and that they occur again in the captions on the wall and
in their books in the book corner. Because of the consistency of i t a
a child is offered greater opportunity for practice in identifying the
characters.

When a child recognizes a character shape and says 'I have got this one in my name' or 'I can see one like that up there' he is on the way to the discovery that words are made from a number of symbols put together. Once this discovery has been made, he will go on to appreciate that the symbols represent sounds. For example many a child noticing the recurrence of the word 'mıe' in a 'ſhaŋk yꭴ' book they have made, will read 'ſhaŋk yꭴ for mıe muſher, mıe faſher, mıe hœm' and will say 'That one says 'mıe' and so does that, and that'. A child who has noticed this will inevitably go on to notice 'ıe' in the caption 'ıe lıek mıe ıescreem'. The frequent recurrence of this character in another book, although made primarily as an aid to mathematical discovery, cannot fail to attract a child's attention. After making sugar mice the children put in small pink balls for their eyes and a page from the book reads: '1 mꭴs has 2 ıes; 2 mıes hav 4 ıes; 3 mıes hav 6 ıes' The nature of i t a makes such discoveries possible.

Naturally the capacity for reaching these conclusions unaided differs from child to child, depending on the mental and visual maturity level reached, and the age at which this level is reached will vary considerably. Once a child has become aware of the repeated occurrence of certain characters in different words, he will go on to discover others in similar situations and his reading and writing achievements will make dramatic progress.

Nothing contributes more to ultimate success than a child's confidence that he can succeed. Yet in t o he is more likely to meet with failure and frustation which could completely undermine his confidence, for often the recurrence of a sound in the spoken word is represented by a different printed symbol each time it occurs. The unnecessary complexities in traditional print have been responsible for the frustration and deeprooted sense of failure in learning to read experienced by countless children.

Learning to read and learning to write should be complementary but with the traditional code for written English making rationalization difficult for so many young children, the beginning of free writing can be delayed unnecessarily. The Initial Teaching Alphabet has changed all this and made it possible for the first time for reading and writing to be truly complementary.

It might be appropriate at this point to stress the vital importance of the way in which i t a is presented in schools. We have seen that i t a's greatest assets are the way in which it facilitates the discovery approach to learning and promotes creativity in writing. Yet it is quite possible to use i t a and achieve neither of these great benefits. There are several reading schemes on the market which were produced originally in the traditional alphabet and have now been transliterated into i t a. The vocabulary of these schemes is often unnaturally restricted and contains

constant repetition. i t a frees children from vocabulary restriction
and yet many children continue to be hamstrung by this limited
vocabulary. Work books which require children to supply a missing
word to complete a sentence can also have a restricting influence and
detract from sponteneous creative writing and the great bonus which
i t a gives can well be lost.

As soon as children realize that a knowledge of the characters is the
key to decoding and constructing any word, they express themselves
as easily and spontaneously in writing as they do through their
drawings and paintings. One timid, withdrawn little boy who was
not quite six was unable and unwilling to face the reality that his
mother had left home. One morning he covered a paper with
writing which, when it was sorted out, went something like this:

> My mummy and me went to the wood. We went for a
> walk in the wood. I walked next to my mummy. We
> came out of the woods and went in another wood.
> My mummy couldn't get up so I helped her up. We
> went in another wood. I walked next to my mummy.

There were no spaces and the spelling was far from perfect but
the turmoil in the child's mind was clearly etched in his writing.

Through the medium of i t a, children's confidence that they
can write whatever they want to say grows with dramatic rapidity
as this extract from a story of one child who was just six will
show.

> . . . and the lædy druŋk brandy until ſhee wos druŋk
> and ſhee colapst and wos pœt in hospital bie amblens and
> ſhee wos very very ill and had tœ hav an operæſhen
> becos ſhee wos sœ ill and ſhee wos unconſhus for a loŋ
> tiem. the clock went fast and ſhee didn't nœ whot wos
> gœiŋ on and the nurs cæm in the waud. the nurs wos
> hœldiŋ a træ ov cups ov tee and biscits, wun eech for
> evry wun in the waud and thæ wer aull asleep. ſhee wœk
> them up wun bie wun and gæv them aull thær fœd and
> then sent for the dokter. the dokter cæm in the rœm
> and sed hœs first. mee sed a littl vois. œ gaud sed
> the dokter. . . .

There were twelve pages of this, all in the same conversational
tone in which she would have told her story orally. With the mastery
of calligraphy skills many aspects of school life provide stimuli for

creative writing. Children will write about anything which touches them personally and which rouses their feelings. For some it may be a vivid personal experience, for others a piece of creative work into which they have projected themselves and for others it may be the impact of a piece of music, a picture or a poem. A child who is slow at reading or mathematics may react quite differently to music. The confidence and pleasure he may gain from such experiences could well help him to develop his powers of communication, including of course writing. Even in this somewhat specialized field the advantages of i t a are to be seen. The child's desire to express himself, which has been latent until a particular subject has made its impact on his emotions, can now be satisfied by using a simplified alphabet.

Learning which comes about through a child's own needs covers a much wider field than that which is teacher-directed. For the teacher there would at first appear to be fewer lessons to prepare and less specific teaching to be done, but the quality and extent of a child's learning is dependent upon the skill of the teacher in contriving learning situations. Some teachers have found that although a completely free approach has much to commend it, with large numbers of children in a class it is difficult to ensure that each individual child is in fact taking full advantage of the opportunities provided and above all that progress is being made. The development of a system of individual assignments, related wherever possible to the task chosen by the child, enables every child to have the maximum opportunity for learning through his own self-chosen activities but at the same time ensures a balance of reading, writing and mathematical experiences.

The ease with which children use i t a in their written replies to their teacher's messages reveals the true purpose of reading and writing as a means of communication.

The transition period in reading

The community at large, and teachers in particular, who have had no first hand experience of teaching reading through the medium of i t a are quite understandably concerned lest there should be difficulties at the transition stage. Many will concede that learning to read with i t a is far easier and far more pleasurable for the majority of children in the initial stages, but to the uninitiated it is the ultimate transition to traditional print that gives rise to apprehension.

If absolute fluency in reading in i t a is observed as a pre-requisite for the transition, many children do not appear to notice the difference when they pick up a book of equal difficulty printed in traditional orthography. One of i t a's special features is that it has been designed for the transfer through its preservation of the 'upper coast line' of printed words and sentences of conventional print. When a child has developed the skill of allowing his eye to skim along a line of print picking up the outstanding features in the upper coast line of words, he should be able to do the same by picking up the same or very similar minimal cues in t o.

The use of context to detect the meaning of new words is an essential skill in reading which should be developed during the i t a learning period. A child will then use this skill during the transition to t o.

It has been said that the environment in which a child learns to read can make as much as 10 percent difference to his ability to learn. His ability to make a smooth transition from i t a to conventional print is similarly dependent on the environment and the attitude of the teacher within that environment. In a relaxed and happy atmosphere where the teacher does not accentuate the difference between i t a and the traditional print, the children will not be self-conscious or anxious and the transition will begin gradually, almost imperceptibly. From the earliest stages it is wise for the occasional book in conventional print to be introduced. The teacher will often read a story or bring in a reference book in traditional print, which is afterwards left in the book corner. Conventional print will be found on packets of sweets, bags of flour and sugar and pots of jam as they come from the shop into the classroom and many children will have books at home printed in traditional orthography. It is a mistake for parents and teachers to think that a child who is learning to read with i t a should be kept away from conventional spelling. In an environment where both i t a and t o are accepted as printed forms of the same spoken word, the opportunity for both being unconsciously assimilated is much greater.

At first sight, it would appear that a teacher might find problems where one or two children have begun reading t o and the rest are still reading i t a. Where a system of individual assignments is used, the problem is at once minimized. Assignment cards in t o replace those in i t a in the books of the children who have made the transition. Suggestions for classroom organization during the transition period are given in my book *i t a in Primary Education*. (Gayford 1970) Any teacher who has had teaching experience with this medium will be able to recall instances of children whom she has come upon unexpectedly and found reading avidly in conventional print. This can happen at any age according to the level of maturity reached by individual children.

It is now recognized that the use of i t a requires a longer course than was at first contemplated. Certainly for the slow learners at least, it needs to extend into the junior school.

Mr Maurice Harrison, until recently the Chief Education Officer for Oldham, wrote:

In Oldham, where every child is now being taught to read by

i t a, the junior schools expect some twenty-five percent of
the children who come to them to be still reading in i t a.
There is no effort to impose t o − not even in the first junior
year and all junior teachers have had instruction in i t a.

This attitude towards transition is clearly in the best interests of the
slower learning quarter of the population.

While it is clear that no hard and fast rule can be made about the exact
point of time at which every child must be ready to make the transition
to t o, there are two general principles which teachers should always bear
in mind. In the first place, the transition should not be forced too early
and in the second, careful account should be taken of the children's
individual differences in learning rates and attitudes. Many children are
ready to transfer during their second and some during their first year
in school. It is important to remember that part of the transfer design
of i t a is based on the similarity between configurational cues in i t a
and those in conventional print. For this reason teaching in a step by
step manner is not advocated. If attention is drawn to individual letters
and their place within words, a child's progress can be slowed down
considerably, for his attention is directed away from reading for meaning.
Only when a child is reading confidently in traditional orthography
should his attention be drawn to structural analysis and this is usually
better done in relation to writing.

Transition in writing
Long before the invention of i t a, teachers in Britain encouraged young
children to express themselves in writing and were prepared to accept
that the emphasis should be more on creativity than on the way in which
words were spelt. There can be few teachers of young children (and
indeed of some not so young children) who have not at some time
encountered 'sed' for 'said' and 'nite' for 'night' and indeed many
other purely phonetic versions of the irregularly spelt words in the
decidedly inconsistent spelling of our English language. Yet there was
never any question about the advisability of allowing children to write
nor was there any anxiety lest these early spellings should persist
indefinitely. Why then should there be anxiety about a child's ability
to leave behind his i t a spellings? i t a has given the child a regularized,
logical, phonemic spelling system which will be no more difficult to
leave behind than the phonetic spellings of his own invention. But
just as there would be no dramatic and sudden change to correct spelling
before the invention of i t a, so there can be no specific moment at
which a child gives up his i t a spelling for traditional spelling. At first,
reading traditional print will serve as a preparation for transfer in writing.

The more a child reads in t o the more he will absorb the different ways of spelling many words and be encouraged to use them in his creative writing. It must be remembered, however, that the transfer in writing takes longer than the transfer in reading. Consequently, a teacher must expect a mixture of i t a and t o spelling for some considerable time after the reading transition has begun.

When a child has mastered reading in conventional print, his attention needs to be drawn to the position of letters in words as this will aid his writing in t o. Correct spelling can be aided by games and specially prepared apparatus, and word books or dictionaries can be used with advantage at this stage. However at no time should a teacher lose sight of the fact that the main aim of children's writing must always be to encourage creativity and freedom of expression.

Beyond the transition

When the transition is complete and children are reading fluently in t o, this is by no means the end of a teacher's responsibility for their reading. The classrooms at the top of an infant school and all through a junior school must continue to emphasize the part played by books in an environment designed to stimulate observation and investigation. The mastery of reading skills will be an incentive for children to practise those skills, consequently enticing books must be awaiting them on the shelves. There must be a graded range of stories, some imaginative and adventurous, others from other lands and cultures, books of poetry as well as informative reference series.

All through the infant school, in addition to the classroom book corners, a central collection of books plays an important part in developing literacy. After the transition and all through the junior school this collection will have even greater significance.

It is a mistake for a teacher to think that when children have mastered the skills and are reading widely for themselves there is no longer any need for her to read to them. All through the infant and junior school a teacher should read to her children.

When a child is reading fluently it is important that the choice of what he reads should be largely his own. It will not be necessary for *every* child to progress through graded readers which are often bought in sets of three or four dozen. Half a dozen books from any one grade from several different series are a better investment. The children will then have a choice and will be able to discuss them and recommend them to each other. Money saved by buying fewer readers can be better spent on library books.

The conception of English as a living language is often clouded by the fear that unless children are given countless tedious exercise they will be unable to spell and punctuate correctly. To inhibit communication by restricting thought processes to a straight-jacket of neat, markable exercises will create an imbalance which could waste much of the creativity released by i t a.

Reading and writing are development processes and must be carried on throughout the primary school. A child who has attended an infant school in which there is a lively interest in books will have come to include in the term 'books' not only those which are printed and bound by a publisher, but those which can be built up by the children themselves around any subject which has excited their interest. The skills demanded when using reference material should be developed throughout the junior school, leading naturally into the study of subjects which will involve the use not only of books, but of film strips, tape recorders and other audio-visual aids.

Where i t a has been used from the start, children are far more conscious of the phonemic structure of the English language and are more likely to develop a keen awareness of spelling sounds which later lead to a more uninhibited writing of good readable English.

References

Dewey, John (1906) *The School and the Child* Chicago: University of Chicago Press

Gayford, O. M. (1970) *i t a in Primary Education* London: Initial Teaching Publishing Company

Harrison, M. (1967) in *The Times Educational Supplement* 17th February

Colour codes compared with i t a

Vera Southgate Booth

Lecturer in Curriculum Development
School of Education, University of Manchester

Written English

If the written or printed form of the English language had one symbol,
and only one symbol, to represent each of the sounds of the
spoken language, it could be regarded as a completely regular code,
having a one-to-one relationship between spoken sound and written
symbol. With a written form of the language based on an alphabet
of twenty-six letters and a spoken language consisting of forty-odd
sounds, we are clearly a long way from this goal.

The relationship between a spoken language and its written form
is exercised in two distinct processes: decoding and encoding. Decoding
is reading; the process whereby the child or adult looks at the written
symbols and recognizes them as sounds, words, phrases and so on of
spoken language which he understands. He may utter these sounds
aloud or abstract their meaning silently. Encoding is writing; the
process whereby symbols are recorded as visual representation of
the spoken or non-verbalized language, in the form of sounds, words,
sentences, information or ideas. With a regular code, mastery of the
skills of both decoding and encoding would be simpler than is the case
with an irregular code.

But written English is not a regular language, either in the decoding
or the encoding sense. The different pronunciations of the letter
'c' in 'cat' and 'cinema', or the different sounds attached to the letter
'o' in 'on', 'rose', 'one' and 'women' are two examples of
irregularities encountered in decoding.

With regard to the encoding process, consider the young child who
wants to write a word containing the sound 'ee'. He could find himself
floundering over the choice of double 'ee' as in 'see', 'ea' as in 'clean' or
a single 'e' as in 'he'. Additional variations of spelling for this sound
are also available in English; for example 'ei' in 'ceiling' or 'ie' in 'belief'
and 'e' combined with a silent 'e' at the end of a word as in 'these'.
Fortunately for the child, he may at that time be unaware of the complete
range of alternatives. It is unnecessary to give further illustrations of
how an irregular spelling system (or writing system as linguists often
prefer to term it) necessarily increases the difficulties of learning to
read and write.

95

Two main methods of beginning reading

As far as reading is concerned, our written language consists of two broad categories of words. First, there are those words which are regular and may be decoded fairly easily by the child who knows the code and can utter the sounds which the letters represent. (In order to simplify the main theme, the undoubted difficulty experienced initially by some children in mastering the technique of blending sounds together is being disregarded.) The famous or infamous words 'cat' and 'mat', as well as longer words such as 'fantastic', are examples of words which follow simple regular rules.

This first category of words, usually described as 'phonic' words, can be considerably extended to include many more words which are considered to conform to more difficult rules. The British rule that a 'silent' or 'magic' 'e' at the end of the word like 'cake' makes the 'a' say 'a', or the American rule for words such as 'boat' and 'seat', that 'When two vowels go walking the first one does the talking', are examples of such rules.

In passing it is worth noting that some of these rules do not have such general applicability as teachers often imagine. Clymer (1963) for example, shows that of forty-five phonic generalizations most commonly taught in elementary schools in the USA, only eighteen are of general utility in that they are applicable to all or a majority of the words the child is likely to meet. For example the rule 'When a word begins with "wr" the "w" is silent' has a '100 percent utility' as there are no exceptions whatsoever. In contrast, the rule 'When words end with silent "e", the preceding "a" is long' has only 60 percent utility; 60 percent of words, such as the word 'cake' for example, conform to the rule, while 40 percent, such as 'have' represent exceptions to the rule.

In contrast to the phonically regular words are others which are quite irregular such as 'said' and 'would' — words which a child cannot be expected to decode. These are words which the teacher must first tell the child, and which will then require extensive practice until they are recognized instantly on sight. Moreover , many of the most commonly used words in our language fall into this category of irregular words, as can be seen from McNally and Murray's (1962) *Key Words to Literacy*. Here are found, among the 'thirty basic words accounting for more than one third of running words met with in ordinary reading, junior or adult, irregular words like 'the', 'was', 'all', 'he', 'are', 'have', 'one' and 'said'.

It is the difference between the most appropriate modes of learning and teaching regular and irregular words which has been partially responsible for teachers' preferences for beginning reading tuition with either a phonic or a look-and-say method. Whichever is chosen as the initial method, it is clear that neither can serve as the sole method and that a fluent reader needs to have mastered both techniques.

Herein lies one of the main difficulties of an irregular code for the beginning reader. The pupil quickly appreciates, even if this is not put into words by his teacher, that there are unknown words which he can tackle with reasonable success on his own, and that there are others which do not respond to 'sounding out' and which he must either guess or ask his teacher or a fellow pupil to tell him. Even more seriously, the child has no means of knowing which of these two methods is applicable to the unknown word confronting him. Of course the bright child in time devises a workable form of attack. It might include first trying phonic analysis and, if this fails, discarding it as inappropriate or supplementing if by recourse to contextual clues. The slower child frequently merely gives up.

The movement to simplify the code

Attempts to regularize the written code of English have a long history. Pitman and St John (1969) for instance discuss 'Four Centuries of Spelling and Alphabet Reform'. It is only more recently that such reforms were viewed in the light of transitional codes aimed at easing the task of beginning reading and intended to be discarded in favour of t o (traditional orthography) when the pupil had reached an appropriate stage of reading fluency.

In *Formulae For Beginning Reading Tuition* (Southgate 1968) the writer has defined media currently being used or considered for the initial stages of learning to read. Such attempts to regularize the code are polarized in two main directions. First, there are codes which accept the twenty-six letter alphabet and the current rules of English spelling, and superimpose signals in the form of colours or diacritical marks as aids to pronunciations. These are termed 'signalling systems'. Secondly there are 'simplified spelling systems' which are likely either to employ an alphabet of forty odd characters or to regularize the spelling rules governing the use of the present twenty-six letter alphabet.

In this paper, three signalling systems in the form of colour codes — *Words in Colour* (Gattegno 1968), *Colour Story Reading* (Jones 1967) and *Reading by Rainbow* (Bleasdale 1966), and one simplified spelling system, the Initial Teaching Alphabet, usually referred to as i t a (Pitman 1959) are compared. It is not possible here either to fully describe or examine in detail all four media. They will be appraised in general terms only, in the light of their effectiveness as media for beginning reading, i.e. as decoding devices, although their effectiveness as encoding devices will also be mentioned.

Possible advantages and disadvantages of regularized media

A summary of the possible advantages and disadvantages of using some form of regularized medium for beginning reading tuition in preference to t o is likely to form a useful background against which to examine these media. (The following list of advantages and disadvantages is similar to the one given in *Reading – Which Approach*? (Southgate and Roberts 1970).)

Advantages

1 A regularized medium, whether it takes the form of a signalling system or a simplified spelling system, usually makes the earliest stages of learning to read easier for the child.

2 If the medium represents a complete code to pronunciation, the child can learn to adopt one invariable techinque for attempting to decipher new words, and the employment of this technique is almost certain to guarantee success.

3 The use of simplified regularized media in place of t o is thus likely to lead to a number of beneficial effects for the child, including the following:

   i   there is less likelihood of failure

   ii   he soon experiences success, pleasure and satisfaction

   iii   his desire to read and his interest in reading increases

   iv   he more quickly becomes independent of the teacher.

4 The task of helping children to learn to read becomes less arduous for the teacher, with the result that she has more time to devote to other aspects of the curriculum and the special needs of individual children.

5 If the medium provides a regular encoding device, children's ability to express themselves freely in writing will be facilitated. Simplified spelling systems which provide a one-to-one relationship between sound and symbol, or approach closely to this ideal, are likely to gain in this respect over signalling systems which are usually concerned with decoding.

6 The more regular the medium the more likely is it to result in an improvement in children's spelling. Again, simplified spelling systems are likely to show the greatest advantage in this respect. Signalling systems, while not aimed specifically at improving spelling, may nevertheless do so by drawing attention to both the regularities and irregularities of t o.

Disadvantages

1 Certain difficulties may be encountered by both the children and their parents when the medium of instruction differs greatly from the traditional spelling system in use outside school. The closer the appearance of the new medium to t o, the less important is this

difficulty likely to be. On this count, signalling systems may have the advantage over simplified spelling systems which employ numerous new characters.

2 The quantity and variety of reading materials published in new media may be limited.

3 The published reading materials may be restricted to one scheme of books or apparatus, applicable only to a definite method and with certain procedures which the teacher does not support. This disadvantage applies particularly to signalling systems.

4 Children who have to move to another school before they have transferred from the alternative medium to t o may experience difficulties.

Colour codes and i t a

New media currently in use in British schools consist mainly of i t a and the three colour codes already mentioned. The number of schools using these new media is certainly only a small proportion of those using t o, but definite figures are not available. Warburton and Southgate (1969) found that in 1966 9·2 percent of all schools containing infant pupils were using i t a to some extent with infants. This percentage has probably increased since then but the extent of the increase is a matter for conjecture. No accurate information has been published regarding the number of schools using the various colour codes, although one would estimate their combined total to be less than that of schools using i t a.

Some of the principal similarities and differences between the three colour codes and i t a are summarized in the table overleaf.

The medium

The colour codes are all examples of signalling systems. They retain the twenty-six letter alphabet and the accepted spelling patterns of English, and all use colours to varying extents as signals to pronunciation. In *Words in Colour* Gattegno identifies forty-seven sounds in the English language and, by employing different shades and tints of the basic colour as well as two-coloured letters, has produced a colour code of forty-seven colours, one for each sound. On his charts all the letters are coloured; none are black.

In *Colour Story Reading* Jones identifies forty-two sounds. The colour code consists of black, together with red, blue and green. The majority of the letters are printed in the latter three colours, while a few are in black against the normal background of white paper. In addition, certain of the single letters or groups of letters are printed in black on red, blue and green backgrounds in the shape of a square, a circle and a triangle.

In *Reading by Rainbow* Bleasdale does not mention the number of sounds identified in English, as this colour code is clearly not aimed at

99

A comparison of colour codes with i t a

Approach Author	*Words in Colour* Gattegno, C. (1962)	*Colour Story Reading* Jones, J. K. (1967)
Medium	A signalling system — using 47 different colours for letters.	A signalling system using a few black letters, but most letters in 3 colours or on coloured background shapes.
No. of sounds identified	47	42
Regularity of code		
(1) decoding	1 Absolute regularity, one-to-one relationship.	1 Not an entirely complete code: 2 signals — shape and colour needed for many letters; also some danger signals.
(2) encoding	2 As with t o — including its irregularities.	2 As with t o including its irregularities.
Beginning method	Phonic (synthetic)	Phonic (analytic) — but Jones says look-and-say and phonic.
Materials	Limited range — coloured wallcharts, 3 children's basic books and 1 story book in black type, worksheets, etc in black.	Limited range — 3 children's basic books and activity kit of illustrations and games, all in colour.
	Only these materials to be used.	Other reading materials in black t o can be used alongside.
Procedures	Very formal throughout. Class and group instruction at first. Directed exercises, including dictation.	Less formal than other 2 colour codes. Begins with stories read to children. Children's books require teacher direction and the symbols need to be taught.
Approximate estimates of range of reading attainments	Scheme covers *all* the 274 sound/symbol relationships of English. The child is learning to spell as well as read. Estimated R. A. of 9-10 at end of course — possibly higher.	Total vocabulary of 3 children's books is only 121 words — although supplementary work may have extended this total. Thus — only an introduction or aid to beginning reading.

Reading by Rainbow	*i t a*
Bleasdale, E. and W. (1966)	Pitman, J. (1959)
A signalling system — 1/3 of letters in 3 colours, and the rest in black.	A simplified spelling system — in the form of an augmented alphabet.
(number not identified)	44
1 A partial code — not always consistent.	1 Almost a completely regular decoding device.
2 As with t o — including its irregularities.	2 An almost completely regular encoding system.
Phonic (synthetic)	Can be used with any method or any combination of methods.
Limited range — 4 children's basic books and 2 supplementary readers, all in colour.	Wide range — 10 or more reading schemes. Almost 1,000 titles including maths, information story books, etc.
Materials in black t o could probably be used towards end of scheme.	Only i t a materials to be used until the transition stage.
Formal teaching required for the early books. Teaching activities suggested for mastering the sounds of the letters.	The teaching and learning procedures can be as formal or as informal as the teacher chooses. Teacher has absolute freedom of choice.
Estimated level of Book 4 — R. A. of 7 or 7½.	Average R. A. of approximately 8 on t o tests just after transfer from i t a to t o.

providing signals for each sound. Approximately two-thirds of the letters are black; the remainder are blue, red or yellow.

i t a is an example of a simplified spelling system in the form of an augmented alphabet. Twenty-four of the twenty-six letters of the alphabet are retained, the letters 'x' and 'q' being discarded. Twenty additional characters make up the complete total of forty-four characters which comprise the alphabet. Many of the 'new' characters consist of two t o letters which have been ligatured, for example 'i' and 'e' or 'c' and 'h' joined together. Pitman (1959) states that i t a leaves 50 percent of t o words virtually unchanged while a further 10 percent have only minor modifications such as the omission of an 'e' from the word 'have'.

The regularity of the code
1 Reading (i.e. decoding)
Words in Colour is a complete colour code in which the colour of every letter or group of letters indicates the pronunciation. It is also an absolutely consistent code with no deviation from the invariable rule that a letter or group of letters printed in a certain colour represents a particular sound. This code thus fulfils one of the main criteria suggested by the writer, as it presents the pupil with an invariable rule for decoding unknown words.

Colour Story Reading, while providing signals to the sounds of the majority of letters and words, is not a complete code in the sense of *Words in Colour,* nor does it achieve absolute regularity. With forty-four of its fifty-three colour symbols the child must look at both the shape and colour of the letter in order to know how to pronounce it; with the nine black letters on coloured background shapes, recognition of the background shape is sufficient to establish the relevant sound. The fifty-three symbols of this code thus provide the child with accurate and, in two distinct ways, consistent clues for decoding. However, the inclusion of black letters on the ordinary background of white paper – for example the 'ai' in 'said' and the 'a' in 'was' causes the code to diverge from the role of providing a clue to pronunciation. Such letters act only as danger signals, alerting the child to the fact that these letters are not to be pronounced as might be expected. Thus *Colour Story Reading* may be considered as a partial code which is fairly but not entirely complete. It gives the child clues to the pronunciation of the new words he may encounter but only supplies him with danger signals for a number of our common irregular words.

Reading by Rainbow needs also to be classified as a partial code but one much less complete than the code of *Colour Story Reading.* The use of coloured letters is confined to a few of the more common rules which cause children difficulty; for example, letters printed in yellow to indicate they are silent letters, and the use of a blue 'd' to distinguish it from a black 'b'. While there is no doubt that such devices do help beginning readers to master cerrain irregularities of written English, a code incorporating only a few simple rules does not constitute a complete colour code. It cannot and does not overcome the child's dilemma about which words he can 'sound out' and which are look-and-say words. Neither is *Reading by Rainbow* entirely consistent within its own limited code; for example, although two blue 'o's are used for the sound found in the middle of the word 'took', the words 'good' and 'foot' are printed in black and termed 'look-and-say' words.

When i t a is examined, it will be found that as far as decoding is concerned, the general rule applicable is that each written symbol represents one sound. This rule is not absolutely consistent as it is in *Words in Colour* where the same colour invariably denotes the same sound, but deviations from complete regularity are of a minor nature. For example, double consonants are retained in such words as 'little' and 'sitting' and the letter 'y' is pronounced in two different ways at the beginning and end of words like 'yes' or 'silly'. Neither is a special character employed for the indeterminate vowel sound, as found for example in the word 'the', which can only be learned as a look-and-say word.

In summing up on how these four approaches provide pupils with an infallible and completely regular decoding device, the writer would rank them as follows:

1st   *Words in Colour* is an absolutely complete and regular code
2nd   i t a is an almost complete and regular code
3rd   *Colour Story Reading* provides two different kinds of colour clues relating to a majority of English words but does not supply direct clues to the pronunciation of a number of irregular words
4th   *Reading by Rainbow* does not attempt to supply a complete decoding device, but employs a minimum of colour clues to help overcome certain common difficulties.

2 Encoding (i.e. writing)

These four new media were primarily designed to help children to learn to read more easily, yet a brief word ought to be said about their effect, if any, on children's free written work.

A simplified spelling system by its very nature must make it simpler for children to put down in writing the ideas they wish to express. By eliminating all or most of the irregularities found in t o, a barrier to spontaneity of free expression in writing is removed. The result is that the child's confidence about expressing himself in writing is not undermined. Thus, one of the main advantages of i t a as reported by teachers, observers and researchers – for example Downing (1964 and 1967), Harrison (1964), Sceats (1967), Warburton and Southgate (1969) and Southgate (1970) – is a marked increase in the quantity and quality of children's free written work, with greater accuracy in i t a spelling than was formerly experienced with t o spelling.

In contrast, none of the signalling systems mentioned can be considered specifically as encoding devices. For example, when *Words in Colour* is used as the medium for beginning reading, Gattegno does not suggest that children's free writing should be encouraged. The children are expected to carry out written exercises concerned with the sound combinations they are currently being taught. In this way, as they learn to read they are also learning to spell in t o, including the many variations of spelling for identical sounds. By the end of the course, if Gattegno's methods have been followed closely, a child would be able to read and spell the entire 274 sound/symbol relationships which he identifies in the English language. How this affects children's written expression in the long run would depend on the influence and inspiration of the teacher in that part of the school day not devoted to reading tuition.

The preceding sentence is equally applicable to *Colour Story Reading* and *Reading by Rainbow*. Neither is intended as an encoding device. A child's free written work would still be in t o and the standards reached would depend largely on the teacher's expectations, help and encouragement. Nevertheless a child whose attention has been drawn to the regularities and irregularities of English spelling, either by the use of a colour code or by phonic training, will be likely to be more interested in the spelling of words, and consequently a better speller, than the child who has learned to read largely by a look-and-say method. In this respect children who have used a colour code for beginning reading should find spelling less of a deterrent to free writing than children whose reading and writing experiences have been confined solely to ordinary t o accompanied only by limited phonic training.

Method
Words in Colour employs a synthetic phonic method; that is individual letter sounds are taught first and are later combined to form regular words. *Reading by Rainbow* also begins in this way and should therefore be similarly classified. *Colour Story Reading* must also be counted as a method which begins with phonics. However, although the first book begins with the sounds made by various objects – for example, Sam the snake says 's' – the writer is inclined to regard it as basically employing an analytic method in which the word is the basic unit which the child analyzes into its component parts.

With i t a, in contrast, the teacher can use any method he prefers.

104

Most teachers in Britain have tended to begin reading in i t a with a look-and-say method.   For instance, Warburton and Southgate (1969) found only one teacher in England who began by teaching children the sounds of the characters. In the USA the reverse has been the case. The majority of schools began to use i t a with a phonic method, although some found it a valuable medium for use with a look-and-say method, including the Language Experience Approach.

Reading materials
When colour codes are employed for beginning reading, the range of available reading materials is generally limited. This is true of the three colour codes being examined.

In *Words in Colour*, materials printed in the colour codes are confined to twenty-nine large wallcharts showing single letters, groups of letters and discrete words. The material to be used by the children, namely three basic books consisting of words similar to those on the wallcharts, with the addition of unconnected sentences and one story book, are all in black and white. The children's worksheets and word-building books are also in black and white. While learning to read by means of *Words in Colour*, children are expected to be restricted to these reading materials.

In *Colour Story Reading* three children's books and an activity kit of illustrations and games are printed in the colour code. The children's books consist of prose in the form of simple stories related to characters named after the vowels. In contrast to *Words in Colour*, the author suggests that other t o materials could be used alongside the colour code materials.

Reading by Rainbow also has a limited range of children's reading materials – four children's books and two supplementary readers – printed in the colour code. In contrast to the two preceding colour codes, the continuous prose fairly soon reaches the level of interesting stories embodying a variety of characters. A simple version of the story of Red Riding Hood forms the final part of Book 2, while Books 3 and 4 include stories about pirates, penguins and various animals. While no directions are given about whether or not t o books should be used alongside the scheme, one would imagine that towards the end of the scheme this practice would be acceptable and possibly even desirable.

i t a contrasts with the colour code approaches in the large amount of children's reading materials now obtainable in this medium. There are now about 1,000 titles of children's books printed in i t a available in Britain. These include ten or more beginning reading schemes, of which a few are designed primarily as remedial schemes, as well as supplementary story books, reference books, mathematics books and various games and activities. Other books in i t a are published in the USA. Whilst this breadth and variety of children's reading materials is the direct opposite of the limitations imposed in this respect by *Words in Colour*, the two approaches have one common feature; children's initial reading experiences are expected to be limited to materials printed in the appropriate code.

Procedures

When the kinds of classroom regime which could be adopted with these four approaches are examined, *Words in Colour* stands out as the most structured. Very formal teaching procedures are laid down throughout the scheme, with the teacher as the focal point, giving class and group instructions. *Reading by Rainbow* also requires the teacher to instruct at first, although teaching activities are suggested for mastering the sounds of the letters and later in the scheme children would be likely to require less and less teacher guidance. *Colour Story Reading* possibly requires the least formal teaching procedures of the three colour codes. The stories which the teacher reads to the children before they are given their own reading books introduces an informal note. Nevertheless, any scheme which requires children to master sound/symbol relationships in the early stages, as do all three colour codes, cannot avoid placing the teacher initially in the role of instructor.

The use of i t a allows the teacher to adopt formal or informal procedure as she chooses. The children can be taught or they can discover for themselves.

Range of reading attainment

Just as with t o reading schemes, so also do schemes using new media attempt to cover vastly different amounts of ground in terms of vocabulary content, complexity of skills and range of content of the reading materials. Accordingly the average reading attainments of pupils who have completed various schemes using new media can show wide divergences.

If learning to read is regarded as a continuous developmental process extending from infancy to adulthood, and necessitating mastery of different subskills, *Words in Colour* makes by far the greatest progress along this path in terms of mastery of decoding skills. A child who has completed this course will have learned, or at least met, the 274 sound/symbol relationships of English. He should then be in a position to decode literally any word he wishes to read. On the other hand, if no other reading materials have been allowed, the child's practice in reading and enjoying continuous prose will have been seriously limited. A child who managed to complete the scheme would have achieved a reading age of at least nine to ten years on a test consisting of decoding skills. His ceiling may even be considerably higher. The level of his reading

106

comprehension would depend largely on the skill with which his teacher had encouraged him to utilize his increasing decoding skills.

If *Words in Colour* takes children the furthest along the road of learning to read, *Colour Story Reading* takes them the least distance. The *total* vocabulary of the first three books is only 121 different words, although the child's vocabulary may well have been extended by some of the work which it is suggested should be undertaken alongside the scheme. Thus *Colour Story Reading* is best considered as an introduction or aid to beginning reading.

On the basis of coverage, *Reading by Rainbow* comes somewhere between the preceding two colour codes. It introduces some of the phonic rules and helps children to tackle certain of the irregularities of t o, as does *Colour Story Reading*. On the other hand, more continuous children's reading material is available than with *Colour Story Reading*. Children who have completed the *Reading by Rainbow* scheme would certainly be able to read the simple supplementary story books which accompany or follow the final basic books of many of our well known t o reading schemes; a stage which is often equivalent to a reading age of about seven and a half on both mechanical and comprehension reading tests. The better readers would no doubt score higher than this on standardized reading tests.

On completion of an initial course of reading using i t a, the appropriate figures to consider are scores on t o tests shortly after children have transferred from i t a to t o books. An abundance of research evidence is available on this point. An examination of the results of Downing's and other people's researches indicates that on tests of both decoding and comprehension skills an approximate reading age of eight soon after transfer is about the norm.

Summarizing this comparison of colour codes and i t a

The authors and inventors of the four new media which have been examined share one common attribute. They all believe that the irregularities of t o increase children's difficulties in beginning reading. This common belief led each author to devise a code which would abolish or diminish the inconsistencies of t o in the initial stages of learning to read. In each case the new code required the printing of special reading materials, which in turn resulted in laying down methods and procedures to be adopted and, in varying amounts, limitations on the use of other reading materials. These points have been examined in detail in the preceding section.

The use of ordinary t o, whether a phonic or a look-and-say method is employed initially, causes the child the same difficulty; he is bound to encounter two kinds of words, regular and irregular, which require different modes of attack. Accordingly, one of the most important questions to ask regarding each new medium relates to the extent to which it succeeds in providing the child with a uniform method of decoding unknown words. Secondly, one should probe for evidence of complications or disadvantages, and equally of possible additional bonuses, which might accompany the solution to this problem.

Words in Colour employs a complete and absolutely consistent colour code, so that any child who masters it develops a uniform method of reading unknown words printed in this code. The exercises which form an integral part of the approach will help the child to recognize letters in black print and reinforce his knowledge of the sounds they represent; they will also give flexibility in analyzing and recombining both phonemes and graphemes in a manner that will lead to an appreciation of t o spelling rules. To achieve this effect, the teacher's own flexibility of approach must be largely sacrificed. The teacher must be willing to follow the rules laid down for his guidance, to confine children's reading materials to a limited set of books and apparatus, and to divorce reading tuition in the early stages from many of the other activities of the class.

Colour Story Reading, although it does not provide either a complete code or an absolutely consistent method of attempting to decode unknown words, does supply a partial colour code which will help the child by overcoming some of the anomalies of ordinary t o and by drawing attention to certain of the phonic regularities and conventions of t o. In contrast to *Words in Colour*, it provides only a brief introductory course to beginning reading; it allows the teacher freedom to utilize it either as supplementary or basic materials and to choose other reading materials for use alongside it, and it presents the child with colourful books.

Reading by Rainbow also provides only a partial code, much less complete than *Colour Story Reading* and not as consistent. Again it draws attention to certain phonic rules but fails to remove entirely the child's dilemma of irregular sight words alongside regular words which can be 'sounded'.

Neither does i t a provide an absolutely complete and regular code for decoding new words, as does *Words in Colour*, but it approaches much more closely to this level than does *Colour Story Reading* or *Reading by Rainbow*. It has certain advantages over *Words in Colour*, as a teacher can choose to use any method and any procedures, and can also select whatever reading schemes and supporting materials he considers most appropriate. i t a also has one other advantage over all three colour codes, as it comprises a fairly regular encoding system which teachers have found to be a definite incentive to children's free writing. This in turn makes it easier for reading and writing to arise from, and be integrated with, the total activities of the primary school.

On the other hand i t a has two drawbacks which certain teachers may think important and which do not apply to the three colour codes. First, with i t a the alphabet used in school is different from the one used outside. However, the writer does not consider this to be a drawback which need cause teachers concern. (See Warburton and Southgate 1969 and Southgate 1970.) Secondly children have eventually to transfer from i t a to t o both in reading and spelling, a problem which does not exist with the colour codes, as children use black print in t o alongside the colour code. While in normal circumstances the stage of transfer from i t a to t o does not appear to cause children difficulty, (see Southgate 1970), it may do so if the transition is unduly hastened or if the child has to be transferred suddenly to a school which uses only t o.

This brief appraisal of four new media, three colour codes and i t a, shows that each has certain advantages over the use of ordinary t o, although the advantages vary between the media. Any teacher who is convinced that the irregularities of the traditional spelling system of English are a hindrance to children who are learning to read and write would be failing in his professional capacity if he omitted to examine these approaches carefully. If the teacher also considers it important to find a simplified encoding system for children, if he wishes to encourage children's free writing from the beginning and to provide opportunities for an individualized, discovery method of learning, he cannot fail to note that i t a fulfils these criteria while the colour codes do not set out to do this.

In this appraisal, it has also been noted that as well as advantages, each new medium has certain features which different teachers will consider to be drawbacks. Whether to use a new medium in preference to t o, and if so which one to select, is a personal choice to be made by the staff of a school. They cannot make it until they have listed their own criteria of assessments based on their own priorities regarding children's acquisition of the skills of reading and writing, against the framework of their total beliefs, aims and plans regarding the whole sphere of primary education.

References

Bleasdale, E. and W. (1966) *Reading by Rainbow* Bolton: Moor Platt Press

Clymer, T. (1963) 'The utility of phonic generalizations'
The Reading Teacher volume 16, no. 4, 252-258

Downing, J. A. (1964) *Examples of children's creative writing
from schools using i t a* Reading Research Document no. 4
London: University of London Institute of Education

Downing, J. A. (1967) *The i t a Symposium* Slough: NFER

Gattegno, C. (1962) *Words in Colour* Reading: Cuisenaire

Harrison, M. (1964) *Instant Reading:The Story of the Initial
Teaching Alphabet* London: Pitman

Jones, J. K. (1967) *Colour Story Reading* London: Nelson

McNally, J. and Murray, W. (1968) *Key Words to Literacy and the Teaching*
London: The Schoolmaster Publishing Company

Pitman, J. (1959) *The Ehrhardt Augmented (40-sound 42-character)
Lower-case Roman Alphabet* London: Pitman

Pitman, J. and St John, J. (1969) *Alphabets and Reading* London:
Pitman

Sceats, J. (1967) *i t a and the Teaching of Literacy* London: Bodley
Head

Southgate, V. (1968) 'Formulae for beginning reading tuition'
Educational Research volume 11, no. 1, 23-30

Southgate, V. (1970) *i t a: What is the Evidence ?* Edinburgh:
Chambers and London: Murray

Southgate, V and Roberts, G. R. (1970) *Reading - Which Approach ?*
London: University of London Press

Warburton, F. W. and Southgate, V. (1969) *i t a: An Independent
Evaluation* Edinburgh: Chambers and London: Murray

Readiness for reading with i t a and t o – A research report

D. V. Thackray

Head of Education Department
St Paul's College of Education, Rugby

A comparison between the reading readiness and early reading progress of children learning to read with the initial teaching alphabet (i t a) and of children learning to read with traditional orthography (t o).

My report falls fairly naturally into three parts. First I would like to give you the background to the research, then go on to describe the investigation and finally to present the results.

Background to the research

I have been interested in the field of reading readiness in England for a number of years. In my first research I tried to determine the relative importance of the generally accepted reading readiness skills, such as visual and auditory discrimination, mental ability and vocabulary development, in learning to read and making progress in reading. Research of this kind has been carried out by American research workers over a period of almost forty years, from the time reading readiness tests were first published. In England however, to the best of my knowledge, mine was the first experiment of this kind. The reasons for this are firstly, English children begin school when they are five, which is considered rather too young an age for widespread testing, and secondly, there are no published British reading readiness tests.

In my first experiment I followed the approach commonly used by American research workers. A representative sample of 183 children was tested in a number of reading readiness skills using an Anglicized version of the Harrison-Stroud Reading Readiness Profiles (1969), when beginning their second term in school (average age 5 years 4 months). The children were also assessed in terms of three other important factors in reading readiness – general ability, home environment, and emotional and personal attitudes. Later when beginning their fourth and fifth terms (average age 6 years and 6 years 4 months respectively) the children were given the Southgate Group Reading Test (1950) to measure reading achievement.

The earlier reading readiness results were correlated with the later reading achievement results. The individual reading readiness skills which correlated the most highly with reading achievement were those of visual and auditory discrimination. These correlations were higher than that for mental age, showing that in this experiment the readiness skills of visual and auditory discrimination were as important – perhaps more important – than mental age in learning to read in the early stages.

The main i t a experiment began in England in 1961 under the direction of Professor Downing. When describing the differences between i t a and traditional orthography (t o) both Pitman (1961) and Downing (1964) have stressed that i t a is simpler both in its visual and auditory characteristics. It is simpler visually because in i t a there is a consistent visual pattern for each whole word or sentence; it is simpler from the auditory standpoint because each symbol in i t a stands effectively for its own sound.

Because of its simplicity, protagonists of i t a have suggested that children using i t a should be ready to read at an earlier age than if learning to read with the more complex t o. Knowing from my first experiment the importance of visual and auditory discrimination, I felt that this hypothesis was a reasonable one and in my second experiment – the one with which this paper is concerned – I decided to test it experimentally.

Purpose of the research
The main purpose of my research was to test the hypothesis that children learning to read with i t a are ready to read at an earlier age than children learning to read with t o.

The investigation
The method of approach was to enlist the cooperation of sixteen schools – eight schools where the children were learning to read with i t a and eight schools, matched as well as possible with the i t a schools, where the children were learning to read with t o. The original total sample was 300 children with 150 in each group, but family removals and the matching of the two groups reduced these numbers to 119 in each group during the first two years of the experiment and to 102 children in each group during the third year.

The children in the experiment were studied over a three year period, during which time the children learning to read with i t a had transferred to t o and had been given the opportunity to make good any setback in reading achievement experienced after transfer. Reading readiness was the main consideration in the investigation, but it was realized that true reading standards, needed for comparison with standards on reading readiness measures, are not established until the children who started to read with i t a have been reading for a reasonable length of time in t o after the transfer. This meant testing and observing the children who were taking part in this experiment over a period of three years.

112

After being in school for approximately six weeks, all the children in the sample were given the Harrison-Stroud reading readiness tests of visual and auditory discrimination, and also tests of visual and auditory discrimination that I constructed. They were also given the WISC (1949), and my own vocabulary test. At the same time class teachers of the children were asked, firstly, to rate each child on a five point scale for a number of reading readiness evaluations including mental abilities, physical attributes, social and emotional traits and language development; and secondly, to give the fathers' occupations and details of any homes which were other than normal. This information gained from tests, evaluations and teachers' reports facilitated the later matching of the i t a and t o groups and subgroups.

At the beginning of the children's third term in school, two reading readiness tests of visual and auditory discrimination were given again to the whole sample. These two tests were given again firstly, to measure progress made in these two skills and secondly, to see if the children learning to read with i t a had in any way developed these skills differently from the children learning to read with t o. This comparison was made because the results of a small experiment carried out by Sister John (1966) suggested that i t a might develop perceptual skills to a greater extent than t o, and it was decided to test this hypothesis. At the same time a first reading achievement test, the Schonell Graded Word Reading Test (1950) was given to all the children. The usual form of test was given to the t o group, but a transliterated version of the same test was given to the i t a group. In this way initial progress in learning to read was assessed.

After a further term, that is at the beginning of the children's fourth term in school, the same reading achievement test was repeated together with a second more comprehensive reading test, the Neale Analysis of Reading Ability (1963). Transliterated versions of the tests were used with the i t a children.

Reading achievement and progress was again measured at the beginning of the children's sixth term in school. At this stage it was found that many children had transferred to t o and where this had occurred the children concerned were tested in t o. Those children still reading with i t a were tested both in i t a and t o. In these cases the t o test was given to the children first; since it was more difficult the taking of the t o test would not affect the i t a scores to any great extent. A comparison of i t a and t o scores made by the same children, at the same time, on the same test, provided interesting evidence about the ease of transfer from i t a to t o.

The final reading achievement tests of the investigation were given at the beginning of the children's ninth term in school, when some of the children had moved on to junior schools or junior departments, and all but four had transferred to t o reading. The same two reading achievement tests were given, but this time only the t o versions were used.

Analysis of the data

In order to compare the reading readiness requirements of children learning to read with i t a and with t o, two groups of children were matched for age, sex, reading readiness skills of visual and auditory discrimination, intelligence, vocabulary and social class. The two matched groups of i t a and t o children were then compared in three main ways. Firstly, the mean reading achievement scores of the i t a and t o groups were compared throughout this experiment. Table 1 illustrates this approach.

Table 1
Showing a comparison between the mean scores of the i t a and t o groups on the Schonell Graded Word Reading Test given for the first time (given in i t a to the i t a children; given in t o to the t o children).

Group	No.	Mean Score	S.D.	Diff. in means	S.E. of diff.	C.R.	P
i t a	119	6·8	9·55				
				3·25	·94	3·46	·01
t o	119	3·55	3·6				

This table is just to illustrate my first approach which was to compare the mean scores of the i t a and t o groups on the reading achievement tests given from time to time throughout the three years. Column 1 indicates the two groups; column 2 the number in each group (119); column 3 — the important column — shows the mean reading achievement score of each group on the Schonell Test given at the end of the first year in school. Column 5 shows the difference in the mean score of 3·25 in favour of i t a. The other figures need not delay us, as I am only trying to illustrate my approaches.

Secondly, five levels of performance achieved by subgroups of i t a and t o children on the various reading readiness measures were taken, and for each level the mean scores attained by the subgroups of i t a and t o children were calculated and compared. Table 2 illustrates this approach.

Table 2
Showing a comparison of the mean scores attained on the Schonell Graded Word Reading Test by subgroups of i t a and t o children who attained similar levels of performance on the writer's Visual Discrimination Test.

114

Range of scores	Group	N.	Mean score	S.D.	Diff. in means	S.E. of diff.	C.R.	P
28–34	i t a	8	24·00	15·81	19·75	3·61	5·47	·001
	t o	24	4·25	3·74				
21–27	i t a	53	7·92	9·27	4·04	1·58	2·56	·05
	t o	33	3·88	5·39				
14–20	i t a	26	4·96	6·40	2·66	1·37	1·94	NS
	t o	27	2·30	2·83				
7–13	i t a	23	1·87	2·50	·58	·63	·92	NS
	t o	28	1·29	1·90				
0–6	i t a	9	1·33	·95	1·04	·41	2·54	·05
	t o	7	·29	·46				

This table illustrates my second approach which was to compare the mean scores attained on the reading achievement tests by subgroups of i t a and t o children who attained similar levels of performance on the measures of reading readiness skills given soon after the children entered school.

In this particular table, column 1 shows the range of scores possible on my Visual Discrimination Test divided into five levels of performance: 0–6; 7–13; 14–20; 21–27 and 28–34. Column 4 shows the mean reading achievement scores of the i t a and t o children who attained similar levels of performance on visual discrimination. Column 6 shows the difference in the mean scores of the i t a and t o subgroups.

A clear pattern can be seen — the mean scores of the i t a groups are consistently higher than the mean scores of the t o groups although they had the same level of performance on the Visual Discrimination Test given initially. From such an approach it is possible to see that i t a children with a lower level of performance in visual discrimination than t o children, could reach the same reading achievement level. For example within the range of scores 28–34 the t o reading score was 4·25 (column 4). If we enter the range of scores 14–20 we see the i t a children's mean reading score was similar (4·96) but with a lower level of performance in visual discrimination.

Thirdly, a comparison was made between the mean scores attained on the reading achievement measures by subgroups of i t a and t o children with similar mental ages. Table 3 illustrates this approach.

Table 3

Showing a comparison between the mean scores attained on the
Schonell Graded Word Reading Test, given the first time, by subgroups of
i t a and t o children with similar mental ages.

Mental ages (years months)	below 3–6	3–6 3–11	4–0 4–5	4–6 4–11	5–0 5–5	5–6 5–11	6–0 6–6	6–6 6–11
No. of i t a children in each mental age group	2	5	15	23	36	30	7	1
No. of t o children in each mental age group	4	7	14	20	25	27	20	12
Mean score of t o children on Schonell	·5	2·0	3·13	3·69	6·69	10·93	11·71	20
Mean score of t o children	0	1·71	1·8	1·65	2·24	3·0	5·22	12

This table illustrates my third approach which was to compare
the mean scores attained on the reading achievement tests by
subgroups of i t a and t o children with similar mental ages.

Across the top of the tables you see eight mental age
ranges from below 3 years 6 months to 6 years 6 months
to 6 years 11 months. If you look at the column
headed 4 years 6 months to 4 years 11 months, you see
23 i t a children and 20 t o children fell into this mental
age range. The mean scores of the i t a children in the group
was 3·69 and the mean scores of the t o group 1·65. This is
a common pattern indicating that with similar mental age
levels i t a children score consistently higher than t o children.

Main findings

1   In my sample i t a had no more favourable effects on the growth
of perceptual discrimination skills than had t o, so Sister John's
earlier findings were not borne out. (Tables 4, 5, 6 and 7 give
the relevant figures.)

Table 4

Showing a comparison between the mean scores of the
i t a and t o groups on the writer's Visual Discrimination Test
given for the first time.

Group	No.	Mean score	S.D.	Diff. in means	S.E. of diff.	C.R.	P.
i t a	119	18·16	7·47				
				1·17	1·02	1·15	NS
t o	119	19·33	8·25				

Table 5

Showing a comparison between the mean scores of the i t a and t o groups on the writer's Visual Discrimination Test given for the second time.

Group	No.	Mean score	S.D.	Diff. in means	S.E. of diff.	C.R.	P.
i t a	119	24·01	6·51				
				1·41	·86	1·64	NS
t o	119	25·42	6·69				

Table 6

Showing a comparison between the mean scores of the i t a and t o groups on the writer's Auditory Discrimination Test given for the first time.

Group	No.	Mean score	S.D.	Diff. in means	S.E. of diff.	C.R.	P.
i t a	119	11·47	6·66				
				·15	·83	·18	NS
t o	119	11·32	6·15				

Table 7

Showing a comparison between the mean scores of the i t a and t o groups on the writer's Auditory Discrimination Test given for the second time.

Group	No.	Mean score	S.D.	Diff. in means	S.E. of diff.	C.R.	P.
i t a	119	17·5	7·65				
				·57	·97	·59	NS
t o	119	18·07	7·14				

2 Regarding the first statistical approach in which mean reading scores of the matched groups were compared throughout the experiment the following results were established. In this short report only sample evidence can be provided.

i When the i t a group was tested in i t a, there were significant differences between the mean scores of the i t a and t o groups in favour of i t a. As the two groups were well matched it is clear that the children in my sample learned to read more easily and made better progress with i t a than with t o. Conversely, the traditional alphabet and spelling of English used with an eclectic approach was a more difficult medium for the teaching of reading than i t a. (See table 8)

Table 8
Showing a comparison between the mean scores of the i t a and t o groups on reading accuracy as measured by the Neale Analysis of Reading Ability (Form A), given for the first time. (Given in i t a to the i t a children; given in t o to the t o children.)

Group	No.	Mean score	S.D.	Diff. in means	S.E. of diff.	C.R.	P.
i t a	119	9·55	10·30				
				3·6	1·16	3·13	·01
t o	119	5·95	7·35				

ii When the two groups were tested in t o at the end of their second and third years in school, there were no significant differences between the mean scores of the i t a and t o groups. When i t a children read in the relatively more difficult medium of t o, the average score was lowered and the i t a group lost its early lead. (See Table 9)

Table 9
Showing a comparison between the mean scores of the i t a and t o groups on reading accuracy as measured by the Neale Analysis of Reading Ability (Form A), given for the third time. (Given in t o to both i t a and t o groups.)

118

Group	No.	Mean score	S.D.	Diff. in means	S.E. of diff.	C.R.	P.
i t a	102	32·04	17·8				
				·11	2·49	·04	NS
t o	102	32·15	17·8				

iii　At the end of the second year a comparison was
made between the mean scores attained on the
i t a and t o versions of the two reading achievement
tests by 50 i t a children who had not transferred
to t o. There was a highly significant difference
between the mean scores on the i t a and t o versions
of both tests indicating that for these 50 children
at this stage the t o version of the test was much
more difficult for them to read than the i t a version,
which again shows that in my experiment there was
a setback in reading progress during the transfer stage.
(Sample evidence is given in Table 10)

Table 10
Showing a comparison between the mean score attained on
the i t a and t o versions of the Neale Analysis of Reading Ability,
Form B (Accuracy) by 50 i t a children who had not transferred
to t o.

Neale Accuracy	No.	Mean score	S.D.	Diff. in means	S.E. of diff.	C.R.	P.
i t a version	50	13·5	10·05				
				5·8	1·61	3·6	·001
t o version	50	7·7	5·5				

3　Regarding the second statistical approach which compared the
mean reading achievement scores of subgroups of i t a and t o
children who attained similar levels of performance on the reading
readiness measures given initially, the following results were
established:

i　When the i t a group was tested in i t a
the results show that for nearly all levels
of performance on the reading readiness
tests, the mean reading achievement scores

attained by the i t a subgroups are greater
than the mean reading achievement scores
attained by the t o subgroups and in many
cases significantly greater. This pattern of
results indicates that i t a subgroups with
lower levels of reading readiness than t o
subgroups can reach reading achievement
levels similar to those t o subgroups , whilst
reading in i t a. If i t a children can learn to
read with lower levels of reading readiness
than t o children, then i t a children, on
average, will be ready to read earlier than
t o children. (Sample evidence is given
in Table 11)

Table 11
Showing a comparison of the mean scores attained on
reading accuracy as measured by the Neale Analysis of Reading
Ability, by subgroups of i t a and t o children, who attained
similar levels of performance on the writer's Auditory Discrimination
Test.

Auditory Discrimination Thackray			Neale Analysis of Reading Ability Form A Accuracy — first time					
Range of scores	Group	No.	Mean score	S.D.	Diff. in means	S.E. of diff.	C.R.	P.
27–33	i t a	1	27·0	0				
	t o	1	10·0	0				
20–26	i t a	15	21·47	13·15				
					13·39	5·17	2·59	·05
	t o	12	8·08	12·25				
14–19	i t a	26	10·5	11·92				
					1·91	2·83	·68	NS
	t o	29	8·59	8·67				
7–13	i t a	43	7·77	7·68				
					4·79	1·44	3·33	·001
	t o	52	2·98	6·08				
0–6	i t a	34	2·82	6·0				
					·98	1·29	·76	NS
	t o	25	1·84	3·87				

ii   When the two groups were tested in
t o at the end of their second and third
years in school, and a comparison again made
of the mean reading scores of i t a and t o
subgroups who attained similar levels of
performance on the reading readiness measures
given initially, a new pattern of results emerged.
The mean reading scores of the subgroups were
similar, again providing evidence of the setback
in the progress of i t a children at the transition
stage. (Sample evidence is given in Table 12)

Table 12

Showing a comparison of the mean scores attained on
reading accuracy as measured by the Neale Analysis of Reading
Ability, by subgroups of i t a and t o children who attained
similar levels of performance on the writer's Auditory Discrimination
Test.

Auditory Discrimination Thackray			Neale Analysis of Reading Ability Form A Accuracy — third time					
Range of scores	Group	No.	Mean score	S.D.	Diff. in means	S.E. of diff.	C.R.	P.
27–33	i t a	1	46·0	0				
	t o	1	65·0	0				
20–26	i t a	13	45·76	18·06				
					7·21	7·94	·91	NS
	t o	11	38·55	19·11				
14–19	i t a	23	33·26	14·32				
					9·16	4·6	1·99	NS
	t o	24	42·42	16·7				
7–13	i t a	35	34·57	16·6				
					7·32	3·64	2·01	·05
	t o	44	22·25	15·3				
0 – 6	i t a	30	22·1	14·39				
					1·85	3·84	·48	NS
	t o	22	23·95	14·63				

4   Regarding the third statistical approach which compared
the mean reading achievement scores of subgroups of i t a and
t o children with similar mental ages initially, the following
results were established:

i   When the ita group was tested on i t a the
figures indicated that i t a children were able
to learn to read as well as t o children with
an average mental age of six months to a year
less than the average mental age of the t o children.
(Sample evidence is given in Table 13)

Table 13
Showing a comparison between the mean scores attained on
reading accuracy by subgroups of i t a and t o children with similar
mental ages initially as measured by the Neale Analysis of Reading
Ability given for the first time.

Mental ages (years, months)	below 3–5	3–6 3–11	4–0 4–5	4–6 4–11	5–0 5–5	5–6 5–11	6–0 6–5	6–6 6–11
No. of i t a children in each mental age group	2	5	15	23	36	30	7	1
No. of t o children in each mental age group	4	7	14	20	25	27	20	2
Mean score of i t a children on Neale	0	3·2	3·4	5·3	9·3	14·4	12·6	10
Mean score of t o children on Neale	0	·7	1·8	1·2	3·93	6·6	9·0	20·5

ii   When both groups were tested in t o the
results indicated that the i t a and t o subgroups
with similar levels of mental ability initially
had similar levels of reading ability, again
providing evidence of the setback in the
reading progress of the i t a children in the
transition stage. (Sample evidence is
given in Table 14)

T able 14
Showing a comparison between the mean scores
attained on reading accuracy by subgroups of i t a and t o
children with similar mental ages initially as measured by the
Neale Analysis of Reading Ability given for the third time.

122

Mental ages (years, months)	below 3–6	3–6 3–11	4–0 4–5	4–6 4–11	5–0 5–5	5–6 5–11	6–0 6–5	6–6 6–11
No. of i t a children in each mental age group	1	4	13	22	33	23	5	1
No. of t o children in each mental age group	3	5	12	8	21	22	19	2
Mean score of i t a children on Neale	5·0	20·2	24·9	28·5	29·6	41·4	46·0	17·0
Mean score of t o children on Neale	12·7	10·6	30·1	27·6	28·3	34·5	44·3	53·0

5 In order to see the comparative importance in my experiment of the factors making for reading readiness and early reading progress, comparisons were made throughout the experiment of the correlation coefficients (calculated for the i t a and t o groups separately) between the initial tests of reading readiness abilities, and the two measures of reading achievement. The averaged results obtained towards the end of the children's second and third years in school when the tests were given in t o are as follows:

	End of 2nd term	End of 3rd term
visual discrimination	·48	·58
auditory discrimination	·46	·41
intelligence	·38	·38
vocabulary development	·38	·44

The above correlation coefficients show that visual and auditory discrimination have a substantial relationship with later reading achievement and are more important than mental ability and language development in learning to read by t o through the medium of i t a, or in learning to read by t o from the start. These results are in keeping with those I found in my first experiment. It is therefore important for the reception class teacher to gain some estimate of her children's abilities in visual and auditory discrimination so that if weaknesses are detected, exercises to develop these skills may be used during the pre-reading activities where necessary.

I feel my research showed experimentally that:

1 i t a is simpler than t o in its visual and auditory structure

2 i t a children are ready to read earlier and make quicker
progress than t o children taught with an eclectic approach
3 there is a setback for the i t a children during the transfer
stage which resulted in similar mean reading scores for the
i t a and t o groups at the end of three years in school.

Conclusion

If firstly, children learning to read with i t a were taught with
confidence at a rather earlier age than is normal for the teaching
of reading with t o and secondly, the transfer to t o could be made
easier in some way, then i t a children could keep their lead and
reading standards could be raised.

Perhaps I should finish by making my position clear regarding
the use of i t a. Although my research shows that after three years
children learning to read with i t a had similar mean reading scores
to children who have learned to read with t o, I believe i t a is still
worth trying because of the other benefits it brings in its train, the
main ones being an improvement in creative writing and increase
in confidence on the part of the young learner. i t a is worth trying
only if the teacher prefers this medium and believes it will bring
results. i t a should not be imposed from above on unwilling schools
and unwilling teachers; if it is it will surely fail.

References

Downing, J. A. (1964) *The i t a Reading Experiment* London: Evans
Harrison, M. L. and Stroud, J. B. (1965) *The Harrison-Stroud Reading
Readiness Profiles* Boston: Houghton, Mifflin
Neale, M. D. (1963) *Neale Analysis of Reading Ability* London:
Macmillan
Pitman, I. J. (1961) 'Learning to read: An experiment' *Journal of Royal
Society of Arts* 109, 149-180
Schonell, F. J. and Schonell, F. E. (1950) *Graded Word Reading Test*
Edinburgh: Oliver and Boyd
Sister John (1966) 'The effect of the i t a medium on the development
of visual and auditory awareness of symbol differences' in Downing, J. A.
(ed.) *The First International Reading Symposium* London: Cassell, 112-
123
Southgate, V. (1959) *Southgate Group Reading Test 1* London:
University of London Press
Wechsler, D. (1949) *Manual for the Wechsler Intelligence Scale for
Children* New York: Psychological Corporation

Part three
The TV medium

Television and reading

Joyce M. Morris

Language Arts Consultant

In recent years, whenever and wherever the subject of this morning's session is discussed, the works of Marshall McLuhan are almost certain to be cited. This is mainly because he argues that literacy has now outlived its usefulness, and should be regarded simply as an aid to technology. He also suggests that, of all modern media, only television is appropriate to our age.

Needless to say, I do not share these views. On the contrary, I believe literacy will long remain of vital importance for individual and communal development. Moreover, I am convinced that instead of continually debating whether, how far, and in what manner television replaces print, it is more worthwhile to explore ways in which television could make a greater contribution to the achievement of literacy through programmes specifically devised for this purpose.

Whilst it is reasonable to assume that all conference members agree about the continuing importance of literacy, to my knowledge, a few are somewhat sceptical about the value of televised reading programmes. There are also others who will not have formed a judgment on this issue because, until today, they have had no opportunity to view and subsequently discuss such programmes. Accordingly, Miss Sharpe, Miss Chovil and I realize the necessity of putting forward a strong case for television as an aid to reading acquisition.

As my role in the proceedings in primarily to provide a background for the contributions of my colleagues, I shall begin with a historical outline of the 'union' between television and reading in the United Kingdom.

BBC as 'Pioneer'

In the summer term 1964, Miss Chovil came to see me at the National Foundation for Educational Research where for eleven years I had been the officer responsible for reading investigations. She had studied my publications and those of other British research workers in the reading field, and felt that perhaps BBC School Television might help to solve some of the problems they disclosed. She especially asked for my opinion on the possible contribution a series for backward readers aged seven to nine might make in assisting them and their teachers in their respective tasks.

At that time, Miss Chovil and other television producers had made programmes which helped to develop children's oral language skills and generally contribute to their progress in various aspects of the school curriculum. But the proposed reading series had no precedent in the UK and hence, if transmitted, would be a pioneer undertaking on the part of the BBC involving considerable risk in terms of money, time and effort as well as reputation.

Naturally, I could not forecast how effective such a series might be, especially as important details such as its length, content and format had not been decided. Nevertheless, there were a number of reasons why I encouraged Miss Chovil to try very hard to get her skeletal proposal accepted. Since these reasons helped to bring about the 'trial marriage' between television and reading it might be of interest to summarize them here.

Research findings

By 1964, the reading research department of the NFER had accumulated a great deal of evidence to suggest the need for a national campaign to raise reading standards generally and to solve the problem of 'functional' illiteracy among the 'educable' population. Some of this evidence had been published, but far more of it consisted either of research findings awaiting publication or of information which could never be publicly disclosed because it had been given in the strictest confidence. Consequently, I was in the privileged position of having much inside knowledge whilst at the same time being unable to use it fully to support measures I knew to be urgently needed.

However, without divulging details, I was able to assure Miss Chovil that certain research findings awaiting publication amply justified a series of televised programmes for backward readers in lower junior classes. For example, they provided fresh evidence to warrant the following conclusions:

1 On transfer to the junior school or department, about 50 percent

126

of seven year olds still require expert help with the basic mechanics of reading.

2 The prognosis for backward readers aged eight is very poor in that only one in eight is likely to achieve normal competence, and over half will have serious reading difficulties to the end of their school days.

3 One of the main reasons for this prognosis is that teachers responsible for the progress of backward readers tend to be ill-equipped to teach reading.

The above conclusions drawn from research eventually published in Morris (1966) and Goodacre (1967), plus other accessible data, constituted only part of the rationale behind my desire to see television harnessed in the service of reading. The rest came from an appraisal of prospects for improvement in the national reading situation and the kind of contribution I might make to it.

Prospects for improvement

During the five years prior to Miss Chovil's visit, I had urged the establishment of a national institute for the development of reading and related language arts. This was because I believed (and still believe) that progress in the reading field would be far greater if there was a central body responsible for coordinating various important activities in addition to taking a leading role in the execution of their aims. These activities would include research, the dissemination of information, and the provision of courses for experienced teachers designed to equip them with the 'specialist' knowledge of language arts necessary to give 'expert' pre-service and in-service training as well as advice in the school situation.

However, in 1964, there was no immediate prospect of a national institute being established. There was also little hope of expanding the resources of the NFER's reading department, despite increasing demands on it for information, advice and more research focused on questions with implications for classroom practice. Furthermore, research findings were so slow to be implemented that one wondered whether the effort required to conduct professional research on a shoe string might be better spent helping to solve the problems it had already disclosed.

In the circumstances, the idea of television as an aid to reading acquisition was particularly attractive to me because it implies what McLuhan calls 'the involvement in nowness'. Television has the potential for making an instant and widespread contribution to the necessary speeding-up of improvements in the national reading situation. For instance, it could improve the quality of teacher training by vividly portraying how different theoretical approaches to the development of reading skills actually work in practice. It can also, as we hope to convince you today, favourably influence children's attitudes to the learning task as well as making it easier for them.

Accordingly, when the BBC gave the go ahead for an experimental unit of four reading programmes, I welcomed the challenge presented by my role as consultant in that here was a unique opportunity to help solve problems my own research had highlighted.

In 1965 I went on a three month lecture/study tour of the USA with several objectives in mind. One of them was to collect data for the Department of Education and Science relevant to my proposal for a reading development institute. Another was to bring back ideas for the pioneer television series on which Miss Chovil and I had already started work.

Television and reading in the USA
Thanks to the generous cooperation of many Americans, I accomplished all my objectives except that of bringing back ideas for the television series. This was because educational producers working in every television network I was recommended to visit told me they had very restricted budgets which prevented them making the best use of television for reading development. They regretted that their programmes had to be based on a master teacher taking a reading lesson, and longed for the day when animations and other expensive but more appropriate techniques could be employed.

Thus I returned with the unexpected news for Miss Chovil that what we were proposing to do was in advance of anything on American television in 1965. In other words the BBC series would be a pioneer project in a wider context than we had imagined.

The experimental series
We decided to devise a series whose content was different from but related to classroom reading activities. The presenter was to be a primary school headmaster whose personality seemed likely to appeal to the target audience. But even if this proved to be the case, an important ingredient for success in the teaching/learning situation would be lacking, namely close teacher/pupil relationships. However, we felt we could add 'spice' to the classroom and motivate backward readers afresh in ways not open to teachers e.g. by animations, filmed stories and so on.

Although we were by no means satisfied with *Fishing for Fivers* as the pioneer series was called, teachers generally welcomed it and some sent helpful suggestions for a second series in the hope that it would be decided to continue the project. Since, on the whole, the reaction of the committees advising the BBC's School Broadcasting Council was also favourable, this decision was taken and a series called *Tom, Pat and Friday* was broadcast the following year.

'Look and Read'

Response to the experimental series suggested that the time had come to meet teachers' requests for a longer series lasting at least a school term. Accordingly, we devised a ten-week series called *Bob and Carol Look for Treasure* which was first transmitted in 1967 under what has now become an established umbrella title *Look and Read*.

This series is based on a film adventure story containing an element of fantasy and split into weekly episodes with cliff hangers to promote continuing interest. Its approach to the problems of retarded readers is eclectic, but there is an emphasis on word-attack skills. Words are drawn mainly from lists compiled from research into the speaking (Burroughs 1957) and writing (Edwards and Gibbon 1964) vocabulary of young children and from those most frequently encountered in their reading matter (McNally and Murray 1962). Various television techniques are used and the series is supported by printed material for pupils and a pamphlet for teachers outlining suggestions for preparatory and follow up activities.

As we shall be showing you an episode from the latest *Look and Read* series and Miss Sharpe will be talking about it, I need only point out the main ways in which it differs from our earlier efforts. First, the filmed story *Len and the River Mob* is set in the context of what might be described as 'social realism' and, though produced with lower juniors in mind, is considered by secondary school teachers to be suitable for older retarded readers. Second, the presenter is not a teacher but the actor who plays the leading part of Len, thereby facilitating the switch in each programme from dramatic episode to studio presentation of reading content.

'Words and Pictures'

Reports on *Len and the River Mob* from the BBC's feedback sample of schools and its education officers were generally encouraging as were a number of unsolicited letters. Consequently, Miss Chovil and I might have worked on another *Look and Read* in 1969 had it not been for our belief that 'prevention is better than cure' and therefore, it would perhaps be better to use available resources for top infants making slow progress with reading.

We were reasonably certain that the target audience for such a series would be large enough to make it a viable proposition. This was because a recent national survey (Kellmer Pringle, Butler, Davie 1966) had shown once again that approximately 50 percent of children do not reach a primer 4 level of reading ability by the end of their infant schooling.

129

However, it was not doubts about potential audience size which caused the official proposal to have a difficult passage. It was a feeling amongst those considering it that it would be unwise to try and accelerate the reading progress of infants by means of a television series since this was best left to the discretion of their teachers. Whereas it was appropriate for the BBC to continue *Look and Read*, especially as it was apparently successful in helping to meet a widespread need.

Eventually, after considerable further debate based on additional research evidence and teachers' requests, the advising committee agreed to the proposal for a new series *Words and Pictures* which was broadcast this summer. Miss Chovil will be discussing the series later and a part of it will be shown. Therefore all I need say is we welcome your comments and criticisms especially because we hope to have the chance of devising further reading programmes for infants.

Problems
At this point, it might be useful if I discussed some of the problems involved in the kind of union so far achieved between television and reading.

Competing with 'orthodox' television
As the series are concerned with helping children learn to read they must include didactic material. In other words, they cannot be wholly devoted to motivational aspects important though these are. In contrast, at home children grow accustomed to viewing attractive television programmes which do not require them to learn anything specifically. Hence, our first major problem is to devise programmes as capable of sustaining children's interest as more 'orthodox' programmes whilst simultaneously getting across to them some of the things they must learn to make headway with reading.

We try to solve this problem by making the filmed story as imaginative, exciting and fast-moving as possible. Each episode is then followed with practice in particular reading skills using ingenious devices such as teleprinters and, of course, animations. The presenter asks the viewers to answer questions or respond in other ways, pretends to trick them or appears not to be as quick off the mark as they are, and puts over all material with vivacity and friendly good humour.

Since our programmes are aimed at retarded readers, it is particularly important to ensure that the impetus of one programme is carried over to the next and into classroom activities which consolidate what has been learnt. For this purpose, we recommend pupils and teachers to use the inexpensive material which accompanies each series and is available from the BBC * before the first programme is transmitted.

Defining the target audience

Advance publicity about a new series must obviously give a clear definition of the target audience as well as some indication of aims and content. Otherwise teachers cannot decide whether it is worthwhile, in the interests of their pupils, to make the organizational arrangements for taking it and to order the supporting publications.

So far, defining the target audience for each series has been one of our biggest headaches. This is because there is no generally agreed definition of such terms as 'backward readers' and, in the limited publicity space available, a choice has to be made from many possibilities.

Clearly it is not much good using space to say that a series is suitable for children whose reading ages on a stated test fall within a stated range since many potential viewers will not have taken that particular test or any standardized test for that matter. (Administering standardized reading tests to young children is not a generally accepted procedure in UK schools.) Therefore we have to resort to less 'scientific' definitions which we hope will be reasonably helpful to teachers in all circumstances.

Of course, we cannot prevent some teachers interpreting our definitions too precisely and hence deciding that a series is unlikely to be suitable for their pupils when in fact it would be. We are pleased that others do not take them too literally insofar as this has allowed retarded readers of secondary school age to benefit from series not advertised as appropriate to their needs. But we are concerned about the misunderstandings which are evident in the reports of teachers who have found a particular series less satisfactory for their purposes than they had hoped.

Deciding content and pace

Every series involves difficult decisions regarding content and pace. The filmed story must appeal to a target audience of both sexes with widely different home backgrounds and school conditions. Of necessity the didactic material has to be highly selective. Yet, despite gaps in the coverage of specific skills, it has to be arranged in a manner which helps to promote satisfactory reading progress. It must also take account of the varied methods of teaching reading in the UK. As for the pace of presentation, in general this should be just right for the middle ability range of the target audience with variations here and there to allow quicker and slower children to proceed at their own rate and maintain their interest.

On the whole, teachers appear to be satisfied with the content and pace of the series broadcast to date. Understandably however, there are wide divergencies of opinion especially among those whose reports suggest that their pupils were not the kind we had in mind when planning a particular series. For example, at one extreme there are teachers who seem to hold the mistaken view that television can do a 'comprehensive' job in promoting reading progress, and when a series fails to do so think it is through an insufficiency of didactic content. At the other extreme, teachers would appreciate either less of this sort of content or a smaller range of it devoted to the mastery of a few subskills. Some, of course, would like a generally faster or slower pace according to the degree and type of reading problem with which they are coping in the classroom.

Though it is impossible to devise a series which suits everyone, divergent opinion about content and pace is carefully considered as pointers to future series. Requests for changes are also useful as evidence in support of a plea for more resources to make additional series.

Considering differences in English pronunciation

In the UK, English is spoken in a wide variety of ways and there is no generally accepted 'correct' form of speech. This makes it necessary to effect a number of compromises when planning each reading series. For example, the speech of the presenter and leading characters in the filmed story has to conform fairly closely to what is called 'Received Pronunciation' for want of a better term. In other words, they have to speak the kind of English which can be most easily understood by the target audience, though it is the speech actually used by only a small proportion of the population. At the same time, for obvious reasons, provision must be made for other forms of speech to be represented.

Of necessity Received Pronunciation is also used as a baseline for didactic content designed to help children understand relationships between speech and print. But here it is not so satisfactory because it involves limiting the choice of example words and constituent word elements to those which will not confuse children whose speech is not Received Pronunciation or an approximation to it. For instance, the italicized letters in f*er*n, f*ir*, w*or*m and f*ur* represent only one phoneme for Received Pronunciation speakers whereas they represent different phonemes for most Scottish speakers. Therefore, a demonstration of such phoneme/grapheme relationships would not be generally helpful.

Whilst on this subject, it might be useful to explain why presenters of each series have sometimes 'sounded' single consonant letters with an intrusive vowel and thereby caused concern to some teachers. This is mainly for the technical reason that by themselves some consonant phonemes cannot be heard by children sitting more than a few feet from the television screen.

132

Financial stringencies

The budget for each series has been sufficient to permit the use of appropriate television techniques instead of relying on a teacher taking a lesson. But it has not been enough to carry out all good ideas in the best possible manner. For example, though the puppet characters in *Words and Pictures* have been much appreciated by viewers, they could have been more effective for the purposes of the series if they were of the more expensive kind which create the illusion they are actually speaking by mouth movements synchronized with their dubbed voices. It is also disappointing that animations for every series have had to be limited in number and type because of financial stringencies.

Here it is appropriate to recall that in 1965, when the BBC forged the union between television and reading, American television producers could not follow suit because of restricted budgets. Now it looks as if some of them will be able to take the lead in this sphere of activity since comparatively immense funds have been allocated for a reading series next year. This project, incidentally, is one of the conseqences of the overwhelming success of *Sesame Street* which can be attributed not only to the talents of the personnel involved but to the fact that it was launched with a budget of eight million dollars.

A greater contribution?

Subjective evidence suggests that television has already proved to be a valuable aid to reading acquisition. Many teachers, for example, have reported that the BBC series have motivated backward readers to make progress and enabled them to do so. They have also found the series useful as nuclei for numerous classroom activities. Furthermore, the requests for more and/or longer series each year indicates a belief that television could make a greater contribution to the achievement of literacy in the future.

Unfortunately money for school broadcasting is limited and reading is far from being the only priority. Hence there is no immediate prospect of BBC School Television producing more than one new reading series each year and this is unlikely to be as long as many teachers have requested. However, it is planned to broadcast repeats of the steadily accumulating series so that every term a reading series will be available for schools.

We urge all teachers who have found a series beneficial for their pupils to write to the BBC** instead of only expressing their appreciation orally after lectures etc. We also hope they will persuade teachers in other schools with television, but who have not yet taken a series, that it would be worthwhile to try one out. Perhaps I should add that, to my knowledge, a number have already done this to good effect and some have been so enthusiastic about *Words and Pictures* that several schools are having television installed especially to give their pupils a chance of seeing the repeat.

Len and the River Mob has been taken by over 6,500 schools and will be broadcast for the third time in the spring term 1972. Miss Chovil and I will soon be starting work on another *Look and Read* to be transmitted in the autumn term 1971. It would therefore help us to ensure that it is a worthy successor to *Len and the River Mob* if you critically appraise the episode you are about to see and suggest improvements to be incorporated in the new series. Of course, as Miss Sharpe's contribution will demonstrate, the success of any televised reading series is determined largely by teachers being prepared to spend time, effort and professional skill in getting the maximum benefit from it. Indeed, it is this variable which will mainly decide the future of television as an aid to reading acquisition.

References

Burroughs, G. E. R. (1957) *A Study of the Vocabulary of Young Children* Edinburgh: Oliver and Boyd
Edwards, R. P. A. and Gibbon, V. (1964) *Words your Children Use* London: Burke
Goodacre, E. J. (1967) *Reading in Infant Classes* Slough: NFER
Pringle, M. L. , K. Butler, N. R. and Davie, R. (1966) *11,000 Seven Year Olds* London: Longmans

* British Broadcasting Corporation, 35 Marylebone High Street, London W1M 4AA
** British Broadcasting Corporation, Villiers House, Haven Green London W5

Words and Pictures

Claire Chovil

Producer
BBC Schools Television

Watching television is usually a passive activity; it is enough to put yourself where you can see the picture adequately, and then no further activity is required — except perhaps to change channels or switch off. In a television reading series, where children are expected to make a response to the programme and to read from the screen, positioning becomes much more significant. No television *picture* (let alone *words* shown on the screen) can be seen clearly at a distance greater than twelve screen widths from the set; children handicapped in reading will have an additional difficulty if they are seated further away than that. Also, beginnings and ends of words may be lost if the set is not correctly adjusted, so it is worthwhile looking at the tuning signal before the programme, and making sure that it is circular, rather than egg-shaped. But over and above these technical details, it is worthwhile considering your usual method of dealing with a question and answer situation in the classroom. Maybe you normally ask the children to put up their hands to answer a question, and you reserve the right to choose the child who will speak. If so, where do you sit while a television programme is going on which might contain a sequence where children are asked questions? If you sit at the back of the group the children will have to turn right away from the screen to offer their answers. Time will pass; the programme will move on at its own momentum; the children will 'lose the thread'. It is probably better if you sit at the side, near the front, and encourage the children to make their answers directly to the presenter of the television programme. The teacher's presence near the front of the class does also seem to act as an encouragement for children reluctant to join in.

After two complete terms of *Look and Read* had been made and transmitted, the BBC had received a considerable amount of feedback from schools as teachers reported on how the series had succeeded with their classes. Many reports were favourable, but there was a fair amount of comment that teachers would find a slightly easier series, which concentrated on fewer difficulties at a time, useful for younger children and those with greater reading problems. It was not possible to think only of the really poor readers in first and second year junior classes as the new potential audience. Educational television has to make its money go as far as possible and series for children in top infant classes, who were not making good progress in reading, which could also be taken by groups of first and second year juniors. We wondered if the junior part of the audience would find the stories too babyish, but there was no such problem.

It was decided to broadcast two programmes each week (lasting fifteen minutes each) with two repeats. So the first programme each week could be seen on Monday and Tuesday, the second programme could be seen on Wednesday, with a repeat on Friday. For any teacher wanting regular English and reading work from television and for a teacher valuing repetition, there was a series broadcasting four days out of five; an innovation at present in educational television, though one hopes it will not remain so. *Words and Pictures*, as the series is called, is to be broadcast again in summer term 1971, on Mondays (repeat Wednesdays), and Tuesdays (repeat Fridays).

A few points about the planning of the programme; first of all it must be stated that *this is not a series for children who cannot read at all.* If the BBC were to make one it would probably need to be suitable for five year olds, as well as for older children. At the time of planning, it did not appear that infant teachers, who have many ways of preparing their children for reading, would welcome television at a stage where the approach to reading is often personal and depends on the teacher's assessment of each child's reading readiness. (Maybe the new Independent Television series will change that viewpoint.)

Two of the possible solutions to backwardness in reading were in the forefront of our minds when planning the programmes. Firstly, recent research (see bibliography) indicates that whole-word methods for beginning reading need to be backed up by phonic instruction after the initial stages if the child is going to progress to a situation where he can tackle new words on his own. Secondly, other research has established that many of the children who find learning to read difficult, also tend to have a small speech vocabulary and use a limited range of words. So we felt that programmes which would help in oral English work and in phonic work were needed. This is why the first programme in each week of this series contains a puppet story, without any reading work in it at all. It can simply be used for oral English work; it *could* be used on its own; equally, it could lead to an extension of the *oral* vocabulary as a prelude to reading. The second programme contains a small amount of general reading in look-say words and sentences, but its main part is phonic work, on a different phonic concept each week. The range of phonics covered in the eight weeks of the series is:

Week 1 — Consonants

136

2 – Short vowels
3 – Word building
4 – 'Lazy' letters
5 – Magic 'e'
6 – 'Hard' and 'soft' letter sounds
7 – Consonant blends
8 – Word endings

Obviously it would have been a pity if the two weekly programmes were not connected to each other, so the characters from the story programme always appeared in the teaching programme, and helped with the teaching.

When I spoke at Durham, I showed extracts from a pair of programmes at this point. As a substitute, I should like to tell you a little about the contents of a pair, to give some idea about how the theory worked out in practice.

In the story, the presenter of the programme is looking for a house. He goes over an old empty house, and finds an attic at the top. He says he likes an attic: 'It's a room in the roof, like a nest at the top of a tree.' On the floor of the attic is an old Aladdin's lamp. When he rubs it the empty attic is suddenly magically filled with all sorts of toys and clutter. He sees a toy Noah's Ark amidst it all, and thinks of rubbing the lamp again to see if Mr and Mrs Noah will talk to him and tell him how they managed to sort all the animals out when they first arrived in the Ark. When he rubs the lamp it starts to rain! He sees that the animals are coming into the toy Ark. At first Mr and Mrs Noah allow them to go to any cabin, but this is disastrously confusing at feeding time. So they sort the animals by the initial letters of their names; the bears go into a cabin with bison, buffaloes and bees, and this is done throughout the Ark. This story was, like all the others, produced as a puppet play using string puppets. The animals were simply wooden cut-outs.

The second programme concentrates on the recognition of a few initial consonants, following on the idea of the first story. After some look-say and sentence practice at the beginning, the children in the audience are asked to look and listen to an initial consonant in a given word and then detect its use in other words. They are also asked to suggest other words with the same initial consonants. They are, in fact, involved with Mr and Mrs Noah in the business of resorting the animals, because Mrs Noah has been springcleaning. Obviously, only a few consonants can be covered in such a short programme, but the basic idea of Noah's Ark (not a new one) can be used by the teacher for further work on consonants.

Here is a short extract from the script to give an idea of manner and pace, and to indicate how the characters and teaching are combined:

137

PRESENTER: Who's to go in the next cabin Mrs Noah?

MRS NOAH: All the animals with names beginning with this sound.

(*On 'magic' mirror the letter 'r' is written*)

PRESENTER *(out of vision)*: The sound is 'r' *(Mirror writer adds 'as in rat')* . . . as in rat. *(in vision)* Should these animals go in the cabin with the rats? Listen, and call out yes or no.

(He picks up cut-out animals and shows them to camera)

Here's a dog. *(Pause)* A lion. *(Pause)* A monkey. *(Pause)* A parrot. *(Pause)* One of the rhinos. *(Pause)* A rabbit. *(Pause)* These are the ones that go in the 'r' cabin with the rat.

(Mirror writer writes 'r cabin')

PRESENTER *(reads words as they appear superimposed at bottom of picture)*: Rhinos; rabbits; rats.

MR AND MRS NOAH: But the rabbits went into another cabin.

RHINO: Why?

PRESENTER: Yes. Why?

MR AND MRS NOAH *(to children)*: You tell him. Go on.

(Pause as caption saying 'Mrs Rabbit does not like the rhino' is shown)

MRS NOAH *(whisper)*: Mrs Rabbit does not like the rhino.

Each week the presenter rubs the magic lamp, makes a wish and brings a different toy in the attic to life. There are toy soldiers, a jigsaw puzzle, a skeleton puppet, a shadow puppet etc. In each case the story and the characters are used as a basis for the week's phonic teaching. For instance, the jigsaw puzzle story is used as a basis for a programme on word-building.

Few people think of using a reading scheme without looking into its vocabulary. The vocabulary used in the programmes occurs in the *Key Words to Literacy* list compiled by McNally and Murrary (which many teachers are using in the *Ladybird* books), or from the first list in Burroughs' *A Study of the Vocabulary of Young Children.* Thus most of the words used *should* be in the speech vocabulary of a seven year old child. From these words spoken in the programme a smaller vocabulary was selected from the brief retelling of each story which occurs in the pupils' pamphlet called *Up in the Attic: A Words and Pictures Reading Book.* This was an essential accompaniment to the series and cost 5p a copy. There was also a handbook of notes for the teacher. This included a longer version of the story for reference and reading aloud, followed by suggestions for work after the programme written by a teacher, Barbara Tyler. The work suggestions included ideas for oral English work, a list of the most important look-say words in the week's story, and ideas for practice of the week's phonic concept. These ideas were as varied as possible; they included suggestions for games and written work as well as oral phonic work. It was intended that the reading of the story in the pupils' pamphlet should be the final activity after many different kinds of preparation. Here, for example, is an extract from part of the work suggested for the programme on initial consonants:

Oral work

1. Listening for sounds at beginnings of words.
   Listen for the words beginning with b.
   e.g. Bears, donkeys, badgers, Noah, bees
   Repeat with m and c.

2. Listening for the 'odd man out':
   e.g. parrots, pigs, rabbits, porcupine, dogs, ducks, dormice, kangaroos.
   Make sure that the child explains the difference in terms of letter-sound.

Game—'Filling the Ark'

'Mrs Noah is filling the Ark with things beginning with the sound 'b', e.g. butter, beans, bicycles etc. Repeat with other letters.

Activities

(a) Sorting for initial sounds.
It is suggested that pictures of objects which represent three of the consonants can be cut from old

| b | m | t |

magazines etc. The children can be given three cards, each with an initial consonant on it, and can sort the pictures on to the cards. As children become more competent so further letters and objects might be added. At a later stage, objects beginning with k. and c. can be sorted.

(b) Matching animals and initial consonant, on cards as shown. If necessary the letter can be cut in such a way that the exercise is self-corrective.
Here also the objects on the cards could be cut from magazines, or the animal stamps could be used.

m

Many of the things that have been said so far imply time to be spent on following up the programmes, and quite a lot of time. A television series is planned in the same sort of detail as a reading scheme, and no teacher expects to get far with a reading scheme if children only spend fifteen minutes working on a story. Yet some teachers seemed to expect that this would be all that was necessary after a television series; not surprisingly their children found the time too short, and the work to be done in it too difficult. At the other end of the scale, where teachers were prepared to make the series the basis of their reading work, they found much in it that was useful to them and the children.

Television is not a means of instilling instant learning: it does not mysteriously alter the normal speed at which a child learns. But it can be an intense stimulus to learning, not only because it brings new ideas into the classroom, but also because it can combine the potent force of a moving picture with the spoken and the written word. Yet these things are of no significance at all unless the teacher makes use of them after the broadcast, and personally consolidates their value. This takes time, and it is probably not worthwhile contemplating taking such a series unless at least an hour and a half is available for consolidation work during the days that follow the programme. But if you can find such time to spend you may well be surprised at how rewarding it can be.

Bibliography

Research on reading
Central Advisory Council for Education (1967) *Children and Their Primary Schools* (Plowden Report) London: HMSO
Chall, J. (1967) *Learning to Read: The Great Debate* New York: McGraw-Hill
Lewis, M. M. (1969) *Language and the Child* Slough: NFER
Morris, J. M. (1967) *Standards and Progress in Reading* Slough: NFER
Pringle, M. L. K., Butler, N. R. and Davie, R. (1967) *11,000 Seven Year Olds* London: Longmans

Teaching reading
Moyle, D. (1968) *The Teaching of Reading* London: Ward Lock Educational
Roberts, G. R. (1969) *Reading in Primary Schools* London: Routledge and Kegan Paul
Southgate, V. and Havenhand, J. (1960) *Sounds and Words* London: University of London Press

Vocabulary sources
Burroughs, G. E. R. (ed.) (1957) *A Study of the Vocabulary of Young Children* Edinburgh: Oliver and Boyd
Gill, W. S. and K. (1952) *The Phonic Side of Reading* London: Cassell
McNally, J. and Murray, W. (1968) *Key Words to Literacy and the Teaching of Reading* London: Schoolmaster Publishing Company
Stott, D. H. (1962) *Programmed Reading Kit Teachers' Manual* Glasgow: W. and R. Holmes
Tansley, A. E. (1961) *Sound and Sense* Leeds: E. J. Arnold

Len and the River Mob in the classroom

Helen Sharpe

Remedial Reading Service
Hull

The BBC series *Len and the River Mob* provided an excellent opportunity for some varied and interesting work with a group of slow learners in an opportunity class in Hull. This culminated in a booklet, with the same title, made by the children for Dr Joyce M. Morris.

Dr Morris had visited this class the previous year and making the booklet was undertaken with obvious enjoyment. From this booklet slides were made by the BBC for use in colleges of education. The appropriate tape was made by teachers and pupils.

Details of participants

Number of children	Age range	IQ range	Reading ages	Number with some mental or physical handicap
16	8 – 11	66-87 (only 4 above 76)	5·0 – 5·1 (2) 6·1 (1) 7·3 – 7·6 (4) 7·7 – 7·8 (5) 8·0 – 8·2 (4)	9

Story content

The story *Len and the River Mob* was of particular interest to pupils living in this dockland area and gave them a sense of community identification. For example, five pupils had fathers who went to sea on trawlers or cargo boats, one was a docker and one a caretaker at the Humber Conservancy Board. All the children were familiar with cranes, derricks, wharves, sheds and the coloured funnels of ships which could be seen from the classroom windows and from the streets in which they lived. A number of pupils visited the fish dock and Corporation Pier at weekends. Loaded lorries and car transporters were part of their everyday experience. One pupil owned an Alsatian dog. A policeman on patrol was a common sight and Hammonds' Toy Fair was one of the highlights in the city at Christmas time. (A toy shop and a Dutch doll appeared later in the story.)

141

Choice of names

Len Tanner's surname was an excellent choice. A number of pupils readily accepted that he was the son of Elsie Tanner (a character from a television series entitled *Coronation Street*). Mrs Green, who had been in the cast of *Coronation Street*, was a person they had met previously and liked. An ESN pupil called Pat identified herself with Pat Green.

Moral standards

In most cases clear cut divisions were made between good and bad characters. Micky was considered a 'wide lad'. The boys, and some of the girls, had a sneaking regard for him until Len was ill-treated by Mr Moon's gang.

Programme

Each twenty-minute programme was seen twice a week. The BBC publications essential to the success of the series were provided; these included the teachers' notes and a pamphlet for each pupil.

Method

The timetable revolved round the series. The class teacher did some direct teaching and also provided learning situations where she acted as advisor rather than instructor. Her careful preparation made this practicable.

Before each broadcast the plot words were displayed on wall charts and discussed.

As the Thames was to play a major part in the series, a comparison was made between the Humber and the Thames (both rivers empty into the North Sea, both rivers are tidal) and Drypool Bridge and North Bridge were compared with Tower Bridge. The existing experiences of the pupils were therefore extended quite naturally.

Following the broadcast, only the appropriate chapter from the pamphlet was read. No pupil 'flicked the pages'. In this way interest was sustained and curiosity stimulated.

Practical work, which included a variety of models, colouring outline drawings and free illustrations, was part of the weekly pattern. Games made by the teacher from suggestions in the teachers' notes were an additional stimulus and proved most valuable in group reading lessons with the less able readers. Simple exercises in comprehension and free writing based on the text were taken at least once a week.

It was very noticeable that at the second viewing the pupils were able to participate more fully.

Some pleasurable activities combined with short periods of concentrated study produced satisfactory results, e.g. a block of flats was made from a biscuit carton covered in red brick paper and in each window a word beginning with 'fl' was written.

Some measurable achievements

There was a development of community spirit. The less able were supported by the more able pupils. All achieved some degree of success which resulted in improved social behaviour.

Improvements in attitude to school work were marked. All were prepared to find something to do in spare moments. Pupils proved their ability to work individually, in a group and as a form.

Enthusiasm and interest were maintained throughout the series. A number of pupils viewed the programme at home during halfterm. The supervisory assistant, in addition to parents, helped to provide apparatus. Pride in work was obvious in the standard produced. An interest in books developed. There was a more confident approach to all subjects and a willingness to make an attempt.

It was the considered opinion of members of staff that all pupils had increased in mental stature; they had reached the stage where some measure of success was a possibility.

Making the appropriate tape

Our first venture in this field was not without its problems. Some pupils were in awe of the microphone and became tongue-tied, while others felt they were 'on the set' and became overconfident. It was very soon apparent that if any degree of success was to be realized, the normal vocabulary of the child would have to be used. The method employed throughout was one with which the pupils were very familiar, i.e. question and answer. In this situation, the words used by pupils were allowed to stand, but when replying the teacher used words more readily acceptable, for example:

QUESTION: What is Roy doing?

ANSWER: He is *getting* a message over the radio.

QUESTION: Can you guess what message he is *receiving*?

A number of speech problems occurred. For example:

1 The 'h' aspirate was dropped constantly.
2 Lazy speech left much of the tape meaningless.
3 A sense of the unknown made some pupils develop a whisper.
4 Some of the questions phrased by the staff came through in almost unrecognizable voices.

However these results made the children feel that here was something we were in together. The teachers made much of their own mistakes, thus helping the pupils to get theirs in proportion. Through constant practice, all showed marked signs of improvement and at last on 20th December at 3.00 p.m. the tape was completed. We all breathed a sigh of relief!

Conclusion

The success of the series depended on its form, the excellence of the supporting publications and the enthusiasm and untiring efforts of the teacher in charge of the class.

143

Part four
Readability

The assessment of readability –
An overview

Jack Gilliland

Senior Lecturer in Education
Teesside College of Education

The concern for effective communication in speech and print is of long
standing. If historical precedents are relevant, then the problem was
defined by an early teacher who stated:

> Except ye utter by the tongue words easy to be understood
> how shall it be known what is spoken? (St Paul, Corinthians
> 14:9)

Introduction
All teachers are concerned, in different ways, with the problem of
matching a variety of printed materials to a variety of children with
specific reading abilities. Usually, an attempt is made to minimize
the difficulties which a given child will encounter so that the
reading undertaken will be efficient, profitable and enjoyable.
The problem is that the reading materials are extremely varied as
are the characteristics of the children for whom the material is to
be chosen.

Amongst the various kinds of reading materials, conventional
reading schemes present the least problem. In most cases teachers'
manuals, giving details of vocabulary control, levels of difficulty
and graded alternative readers, provide evidence upon which the
suitability of the scheme for given children may be judged. However,
either by choice or by direction, children will be looking at a range of
reading materials for pleasure, for projects and assignments, about
which little evidence is available upon which to pass judgment.

Publicity material may be available but all too often this is inadequate. Matching a book to a child can hardly be reliable when based upon such comments as 'suitable for eight years and above' or 'for boys and girls aged six to sixteen years'. One's personal reading offers some basis for subjective judgment, but the unreliability of subjective judgments in many spheres has been well established, and no less so in the selection of reading materials. Chall (1958) has shown that while experienced teachers were able to rank reading material in an order which corresponded closely to objective measures of difficulty, these rankings were inaccurate and inadequate when matched with children. Researchers into readability are attempting, however imperfectly, to produce objective and reliable means by which the levels of difficulty in texts can be measured, and matched to levels of reading ability in children.

Definitions of readability

Readability has been variously defined but two typical definitions, given below, indicate the essential attributes which are included in the concept of readability:

1 In the broadest sense, readability is the sum total (including interactions) of all those elements within a given piece of printed material that affects the success which a group of readers have with it. The success is the extent to which they understand it, read it at optimum speed, and find it interesting. (Dale and Chall 1948)

2 The quality of a written or printed communication that makes it easy for a given class of persons to understand its meaning or that induces them to continue reading. (English and English 1958)

Although ease of reading and speed of reading have been incorporated into the Dale Chall and other definitions, the most frequent and most heavily emphasized elements have been comprehensibility and interest. McLaughlin (1968) extends the English and English phrase 'that induces them to continue reading' and makes 'compellingness' an essential part of his definition. He argues that compellingness is a necessary component in any measure of readability, and his suggestion for the use of readability tables, incorporating this factor, rather than the use of formulae will be discussed later.

Following these definitions, the many variables which contribute towards the comprehension and interest of a passage may be conveniently grouped under four main headings:

1 factors in the reader, e.g. age, sex, motivation, state of knowledge
2 factors in the print, e.g. type size, leading, format
3 factors in the content, e.g. fact, fiction, topic
4 factors in the language, e.g. vocabulary, grammar, style.

This picture is complicated by the fact that these do not merely make an independent contribution but interact with each other to influence readability. For example, the format and style of a scientific paper may be affected by the subject matter and details given, and a reader's state of knowledge may affect his response to vocabulary factors.

Methods of assessing readability

Attempts to evaluate the factors affecting readability, singly or in combination, have involved comparing an assessment with a criterion measure. The three measures most commonly adopted in the past have been:

1 visibility of print, as measured by visual acuity tests and number of fixations
2 ease of reading, as reflected in speed of reading and
3 ease of understanding, as measured by tests of comprehension.

Each of these criterion measures incorporates only one of the alternatives involved in the definitions of readability described earlier, and clearly different assessments of readability may not be comparable if they have been matched against different criteria, since the criteria themselves are not equivalent. Reading speed, for example, cannot be equated with reading comprehension. Visibility of the print, on the other hand, measures an important but subsidiary element which is common to both. Even within one kind of measure, there are many practical problems.

For example consider the difficulties involved in producing satisfactory measures of comprehension. The question and answer technique, although frequently used, is of little use to readability research since it is impossible to establish whether difficulties in understanding are due to difficulties in understanding the passage or the questions. Answering difficult questions about an easy passage cannot be compared with asking easy questions about a difficult passage.

Again, the conditions of testing may be critical. If the text is removed, memory factors and reliance upon cues in the questions will influence the result, and this cannot be regarded as a comparable exercise to matching cues in the questions with cues in the context when the passage is retained.

The utility of 'objective' measures such as multiple choice test items is also limited. Here responses of items may be influenced by the range and type of alternatives given, as well as by guessing.

An interesting and potentially very useful variation of the sentence completion principle has been developed by Taylor (1953) and labelled the 'cloze procedure'. Bormuth (1966) argues that it has fewer limitations than other methods and its potential as an improved measure of comprehension is now being examined by several researchers. Although in readability studies it is being used mainly as a criterion measure against which other measures are compared, it will be argued later that it could be used as a readability measure itself.

In general it may be said that the concept of readability and the problems involved within it are now fairly clearly established. Recent research is less concerned with redefining the concept than with increasing the accuracy of measurement by the refinement of existing procedures or by the introduction of new bases for measurement. Many different procedures are available and like the criterion measures reflect the various components in the definitions. Attention is now directed to an evaluation of some of these methods used in the assessment of interest, language and legibility.

The assessment of interest

Attempts to define and quantify the degree to which a given text is compelling to a given reader are not numerous, perhaps because the problem is more daunting than that of dealing with textual factors or legibility. Yet, as has been seen, interest or 'compellingness' is an essential factor in the concept of readability and, as mentioned earlier, McLaughlin has argued that any measure of readability should use as a basis those materials which children have chosen to read.

One basis for the selection of types of reading material has been the frequency with which books in libraries have been used. Lists have been prepared upon this basis but few attempts seem to have been made to follow up the use of selections made or to relate the selections to other measures of readability. Although of only general application, surveys of this kind into children's interests have provided crude guides as to the likely use of books. Analysis of subject matter and themes, reported by Chall (1958) led to some easily anticipated generalizations in that interests were largely individual and showed large differences in the groups studied. Some trends in choices were related to maturity and sex.

1 Children between six and eight years were found to be interested in stories of animals, children, familiar experiences, nature, fairies and lively stories containing elements of surprise and humour.
2 Between eight and twelve years, boys showed preference for adventure, mystery, sport and realistic animal stories, while girls preferred stories of home and school life. Action and humour were the factors found to exert the greatest common influence.
3 Over twelve years boys and girls showed preferences for adventure and humour while girls also showed an increased interest in love stories.

In addition to the low predictive value of such generalizations concerning American children, cultural differences in the amount and types of reading interest reduce considerably the use to which these conclusions might be put in this country.

McLaughlin's idea of collecting lists of books actually read and enjoyed by children of different ages, rather than searching for areas of interest, may be more relevant to the precise assessment of readability. Also Abernathy *et al* (1967) report an investigation into the reading habits of Belfast school children. If extended, this type of survey could provide a series of reading materials to be used as a basis for a measure of readability reflecting interest, particularly in the choice of fiction.

Chall (1958) reports findings of a series of studies which investigated the relative importance of content, style format and organization. Leary and Strong in separate studies reported by Chall both found content and style to be stronger influences than format and organization and she also reports a study by Engelman in which conversational style was preferred to narrative expository style. As far as is known, only two studies appear to have quantified this type of factor and applied them in the assessment of readability.

Flesch (1948), using the frequency of personal pronouns and the number of personal sentences in the sample, devised a 'human interest' formula, which was claimed to be measuring the level of abstraction. This, with his reading ease formula, was very widely used but has since been superceded by more recent formulae.

In a study reported by Klare (1963), Morriss and Halverson used a method of analyzing 'content' words in context, thus attempting to measure the relationship between 'ideas' and reading difficulty. This technique, so different from others of the time, has been found cumbersome to apply and has been criticized for its lack of validity and applicability, though Klare reports a study which examined this system and found a significant correlation between the word classifications and the McCall-Crabbs Standard Test Lessons in Reading. The significance of this study lies in the attempt to produce an assessment of readability which reflected the effect of word meaning and context.

Interest and ideas reflect the meaning or significance which the words have for individuals. Many psychologists have examined the learning of verbal material and the meaning which individuals attach to words. In particular, Osgood *et al* (1957) devised a measure of meaning, the 'semantic differential'. While this tool does not yet seem to have been used in the assessment of readability, the principles involved seem applicable and its use has been advocated.

Although there is an absence of detailed and systematic research, two general factors related to interest and readability have been examined and are relevant to this section of the overview. The effect of motivation upon reading speed and comprehension has been reported by Klare. Examining the truism that motivation is necessary to achievement in the context of reading, he suggests that a specific kind of motivation, a 'set to learn', has a noticeable effect upon readability scores. He found that while the presence of a strong set to learn had little or no effect upon the number of words read per second or the words read per fixation, this strong set to learn produced significantly higher scores in a recall comprehension test.

The second general factor considered relevant is the 'principle of least effort' expounded by Zipf (1949). This 'principle' involves the notion that a human being will minimize the amount of work necessary to reach a certain goal. Preferences for reading material have been shown to be governed by the simplicity of the text, and the fact that the reader usually reads more of simpler texts than he does of harder. This does not mean to say that the reader will never tackle something difficult, it means that he will only do so when motivation is high. What the reader *chooses* to read will therefore be generally below the level which he *could* read.

It may be concluded that measures of readability based upon free choice and reading for pleasure will involve a reading level determined by the principle of least effort and which may be noticeably below the potential reading level of an individual when motivated. The assessor of readability has the problem of deciding which of these two general factors he bases his work upon, since texts read on the basis of choice and those read under a strong 'set to learn' will produce different patterns of results when assessed for readability.

The difficulties posed by these points may be reduced by the consideration of two possible approaches to measurement. Firstly, following McLaughlin's argument in favour of readability tables.

Such a table would constructed from the selection of books which children at different ages had actually read and enjoyed, and would indicate the proportion of a particular group of readers who find a specific kind of material compelling. Secondly, the extended use of 'cloze' passages to include children's ranking as well as reading performance might permit the incorporation of interest factors without involving cumbersome analyses of texts.

The measurement of language

No other basic factors involved in the assessment of readability have produced so many variables used in measurement as language. Since the characteristics of paragraphs, sentences and words are numerous and easily quantifiable, it is perhaps inevitable that the study of language should provide so many measures. More than 150 different linguistic variables have been examined and found to be be related to reading difficulty. Happily, most of these factors vary together because of underlying relationships between them, and so only main groupings will be referred to. Variables have been sought which relate to reading difficulty at passage, sentence and word levels. The largest groupings involve sentence and word factors.

An interesting attempt to classify paragraphs in a way which reflects their structure has been made by Bissex (see Strang and Bracken 1957). Developing the idea from his teaching, he has produced a system of visualizing paragraphs and grouping them under main and subheadings. Three theoretical forms of a paragraph (inductive, deductive and balanced) are proposed and broken down into subtypes. Bissex points out that variations in the structure of paragraphs, though great, are not infinite, and that examining the structure of a piece of writing can assist in the comprehension of it. Plotting the ranges and frequencies of occurrences of these types of paragraph, if they are found to be linked to understanding, might well be of use in the assessment of the readability of a text. This approach is particularly valuable, in view of its potential as a means of quantifying organization of the paragraph and thought structures involved in a text, an aspect of readability which seems to have received scant attention. Hopefully, it might even lead to the adoption of a more systematic approach to paragraph structure!

Measures of readability incorporating sentence and word factors have conventionally been expressed as a formula which has been used to produce a reading grade (since all the published work of note with one exception has been related to the American situation). The application of the formula usually involves the teacher in the selection of a sample of the text, counting some characteristic of sentences and words (for examples see below), and then a calculation which produces the level of difficulty in the form of a reading grade. The constructors of measures have frequently had to resolve the problem of choosing between a formula which was easy to calculate but low in reliability and validity or a complicated formula which is unwieldy and difficult to apply but reliable and valid.

Two typical and frequently used formulae are given below. The frequent use of both word and sentence variables in the formula is reflected in each example.

1 *Dale and Chall readability formula (1948)*
$$X_{c50} = 0.1579X_1 + 0.496X_2 + 3.6365$$
where X_{c50} is the reading grade score of a pupil who could answer one half of the series of test questions correctly.
X_1 is the Dale score (the relative number of words outside the Dale list of 3,000 words)
X_2 is the average sentence length
3.6365 is a constant

2 *Farr-Jenkins-Paterson*
New reading ease index = 1.599 nosw $- 1.015$ sl $- 31.517$
nosw = number of one syllable words per 100 words
sl = average sentence length in words
31.517 = constant

Most formulae incorporating a sentence factor have used the length of the sentence as a measure of its readability. Research has repeatedly shown that there is a sentence factor affecting readability. Since it is easy to accept that the longer a sentence becomes the more difficult it is to read and understand, sentence length has continued to be used, particularly as it is a variable which is easily measured. It is arguable, however, whether this measure can be regarded as adequate in the light of more recent linguistic analyses.

In an article concerning the structure of language, Yngve (1960) quotes two sentences which are of use in this context:

1 If what going to a clearly not very adequately staffed school really means is little appreciated, we should be very concerned. (21 words)
2 We should be very concerned if there is little appreciation of what it really means to go to a school that clearly isn't very adequately staffed. (26 words)

Using sentence length as a measure, one might be led to expect that sentence 1 would be easier to read and understand than sentence 2! These, and many other examples, indicate clearly that difficulty at the sentence level may have more to do with grammatical complexity than with simple sentence length, and that an assessment of readability should reflect the complexity variable as well as length. The former measure may reflect the linguistic capability of the reader while the latter measure reflects memory span.

In the paper referred to above, Yngve has proposed a model for language structure based upon certain assumptions concerning the production of sentences. A counting system is applied to the syntactic structure and relationships in a sentence. This quantification of sentence complexity enables one to use it in the assessment of readability.

Bormuth stated, as a result of his research, that 'word depth' as defined by Yngve seemed a useful readability measure which correlated highly with difficulty of comprehension. 'Word depth analysis' is difficult to grasp and apply and so for practical reasons may find less favour than traditional and other more modern techniques.

McLaughlin cites another recent form of linguistic analysis which he considers suitable for readability measures. He uses Harris's string analysis to produce a measure of 'separation'. He devised an experiment using original passages and rewritten passages with varying degrees of 'separation'. Using the cloze procedure as a measure, he found significant differences in comprehension related to the degree of separation and not simply to sentence length. He goes further and offers a theory to explain the psychological difficulty involved in separation, in a way which takes account of linguistic and memorizing phenomena which affect reading performance. While extremely valuable at an explanatory level and in research contexts, in terms of practicability both word depth and analysis and string analysis require simplification. Using different approaches, they appear to be reflecting the same aspect of reading difficulty, namely sentence complexity.

Bormuth also highlighted the possibility that the examination of independent clause frequency may give higher predictions of readability than other sentence measures used in his study. He reported that six of the eight highest predictors of difficulty involved independent clauses, and that the most successful traditional sentence measure (syllables per sentence) was ninth. The ease of counting and sorting independent clauses may make it preferable to word depth analysis for many readability assessments. A further conclusion from Bormuth's results was that though sentence length and complexity are correlated, they each have an independent correlation with difficulty.

Memory span and its effect upon the recall of sentences has been examined. Memory span for sentences has been found to be related to the degree of approximation to English. Approximations to

English have been described and evaluated by Miller (1951) and also by Carroll (1964). Essentially, higher approximations to English enable a reader to use his previous learning and increase the predictability of words and phrases. The more he can predict, the fewer words the reader has to read carefully in order to proceed. In this way, a proportion of words in the text become redundant. The response to contextual clues in this way may have more to do with the reader's linguistic competence than with the 'meaning' of the passage. It is nevertheless a significant variable in the assessment of readability.

Redundancy has received little attention to date. Klare argued that while redundancy is closely related to readability, its inclusion as a factor would rob readability formulae of their usefulness, since redundancy can only be estimated through a try out of written material on subjects. Bormuth, on the other hand, suggests that if some of his correlations are to be believed, then redundancy variables (letters not words) may be among the best used in his study. Results from the use of the cloze procedure, which permits redundancy to have an effect upon scores, also suggests that readability measures may reflect a reader's response to this linguistic factor without affecting the measure of comprehension.

The importance of the continued attention to measures of sentence difficulty is supported by such reports as that of Strickland (1962), which indicates relationships existing between the language of children's textbooks, the spoken language of children and reading attainment.

Word factors used in the measurement of readability have usually been based upon word frequencies, word length or grammatical classifications. Word frequency indices most commonly used have involved reference to the word lists compiled by Thorndike and Dale. It is considered that the more infrequent words there are in a passage, the more difficult comprehension will be.

However, it is unlikely that a general frequency count such as Thorndike's will reflect the word frequencies peculiar to an individual. The use of such a count will more often than not lead to an underestimation of frequencies, and thus level of comprehension, of specific individuals. Additionally, the frequency of a word is not the same as its familiarity to a given individual. Frequency and familiarity do not share a one-to-one relationship and therefore readability formulae using the former will be sampling imperfectly the familiarity of the words used. A more accurate prediction of readability would involve familiarity as a measure.

Finally, the use of word frequency has been justified in measures of readability using ease of reading as a criterion, since this factor has been found to be related to speed of word recognition. These results reflect the influence of word and letter redundancy which has already been discussed.

Readability of texts has been found to be influenced by the length of the words used. This measure of difficulty has usually involved counting the frequency of polysyllabic words or the calculation of an average word length expressed in syllables or words. Such measures have the advantage of being easy to work out and seem to retain acceptable levels of reliability and validity. In the past, as isolated measures, they have not been found very useful, though recently McLaughlin (1969) has proposed a formula using a polysyllabic count as the sole variable.

Assessments of word length and word frequency would appear to be different reflections of two characteristics of language. Firstly, much of the grammatical glue which holds sentences of English together is composed of short words of Anglo-Saxon derivation referred to as 'function' words. These 'function' words occur very very frequently. By contrast, 'content' words tend to be derived from the Romance languages in which words are very frequently polysyllabic and so tend to be long. Secondly, words are affected by a 'law of abbreviation', described by Zipf (1935). This law refers to the tendency for words to be abbreviated with frequent usage, e.g. 'tele' for 'television' and 'bus' for 'omnibus'. Measures of word length and word frequency therefore reflect a common element in language — either abbreviation through usage or origin and grammatical function.

Few assessments of readability have yet incorporated a measure based on grammatical class. Bormuth did include a number of such variables in his research. Among other things he compares the frequency of occurrence of certain classes of word and parts of speech ratios with previous word measures. His correlations, if reliable, showed that this type of predictor may be worthy of further investigation. He predicts that major advances in the assessment of readability will stem from the further study of the new linguistic variables referred to here and more fully in his article.

The measurement of legibility

An overview of readability must necessarily include a reference to studies of legibility and situational conditions which affect visibility. However, although some definitions of readability include ease of reading as a factor, and although there is much useful research available, legibility will not be dealt with to the same extent as other factors referred to. Firstly, the experiments and evaluations are thoroughly reported by Tinker (1963), (1965) and (1966). Secondly, control of many variables is outside the direct sphere of influence of teachers. Thirdly, recent developments do not have the same application to readability measures as others mentioned in this paper. Fourthly, the technical nature of the forms of measurement of such perceptual processes as visual acuity and saccadic movements involved in legibility cannot be readily utilized by a teacher. This section will therefore be confined to a description of the main conclusions considered relevant to an overview of readability measures.

Studies of legibility have involved the investigation of the following major factors:

1   the visibility and legibility of letters, digits and other symbols
2   the influence of type faces
3   the size of type, line width and leading
4   the influence of colour of print and background
5   the influence of printing surfaces
6   the influence of illumination and other situational conditions.

The findings of Vernon (1929) and Shaw (1969) support Tinker's conclusion that such factors as simplicity of outline, serifs, and the way they are used affect the readability of the text. It has long been recognized that the upper coastline of print is more informative than the lower, and more recently Kolers (1969) has shown that a fluent reader finds the right hand side of letters more informative than the left. Also the presence of single distinguishing features — areas of white space enclosed in outlines and heaviness of stroke — will be critical in children's reading, particularly under non-optimal reading conditions and also where little contextual meaning is being extracted.

There are literally dozens of studies investigating the other factors referred to above. Singly, each of these factors has been found to affect readability but interaction effects have also been found which further affect reading ease. Findings from researches have led Tinker to establish 'safety zones'. These are limits within which variables may be altered without significantly affecting the legibility of type. Tinker particularly stresses the effect of introducing non-optimal features into a reading situation. He states that a combination of non-optimal factors produces a severe disorganization of the oculomotor system which does not seem to occur when an optimal set up is used.

Spencer (1968) has vividly illustrated the effect of angles of vision, curvature of the page and vibration upon visibility. Glazing of paper and directional lighting have also been shown to seriously reduce the efficiency of capable readers. In these respects knowledge of legibility studies can have a direct effect upon the work of a reading teacher.

Second thoughts on measures of readability

After a period of stagnation the renewal of interest in readability would seem to be accounted for by the increased interest in psycholinguistics and by the improvement of measures of comprehension.

Studies of psycholinguistics and the development of theories to account for levels and processes involved in language behaviour have provided new tools with which to describe and quantify characteristics of different readers and texts. Bormuth's thorough examination of the correlations between comprehension difficulty of texts and new and traditional linguistic measures indicates that several new factors might be utilized to provide new improved formulae and refine existing ones.

Of the new measures of reading comprehension, Taylor's cloze procedure, referred to earlier, has proved most interesting to researchers in readability. This procedure involves the preparation of a sample of text by removing every 'n' th word (usually the fifth) and replacing it with a blank of standard size throughout the passage. The subject then has to attempt to replace the deleted words. The subject's score reflects the extent to which he has used the exact words of the author and thus is a measure of the subject's ability to estimate the author's intentions as well as to respond to purely linguistic factors. The methods of testing and scoring, together with the use of the actual readers for whom readability is being measured, make this procedure the measure which, to date, most adequately reflects the elements and interaction defined by Dale and Chall. It has in addition several practical advantages such as ease of preparation and simplicity in scoring which are likely to make it of interest to teachers.

Conclusions

In a society becoming increasingly aware of the necessity for efficient and pleasurable communication through print, the control of difficulty of comprehension is critical, particularly in educational situations.

The concept of readability is now clearly defined. In view of its relevance to the problem of selecting reading materials, it should be an essential part of the body of knowledge of anyone concerned with reading. Teachers and children could profit from the use of readability measures. This argument has been accepted in the USA but regrettably it has been given much less consideration in this country.

The traditional approach to readability assessment has been through the production of formulae. Alternatives such as the cloze procedure and the construction of readability tables have been suggested which may provide the accuracy and ease of application required by teachers which readability formulae do not yet have.

In addition to removing the need for a reliance upon traditional testing procedures, recent methods of linguistic analysis have produced a number of variables and measures likely to improve the assessment of readability. The explanations of the generation of language offered may also be utilized in the prediction of reading difficulty.

Bibliography

Abernethy, D., Ferguson, S., McKay, Y., Thompson, D. F. (1967) 'Children's in-school reading in Belfast — A suggestive survey' *Reading* volume 1, no.3

Bormuth, J. R. (1966) 'Readability: A new approach' *Reading Research Quarterly* 1, 79-132

Carroll, J. B. (1964) *Language and Thought* Englewood Cliffs: Prentice-Hall

Chall, J. S. (1958) *Readability: An appraisal of research and application* Bureau of Educational Research Monographs no. 34 Ohio State University

Dale, E. and Chall, J. S. (1948) 'A formula for predicting readability' *Educational Research Bulletin* 27, 11-20

English, H. B. and English A. C. (1958) *A Comprehensive Dictionary of Psychological and Psychoanalytical Terms* London: Longman

Farr, J. N. , Jenkins, J. J. and Paterson, D. G. (1951) 'Simplification of Flesch Reading Ease Formula' *Journal of Applied Psychology* 35, 333-37

Flesch, R. (1948) 'A new readability yardstick' *Journal of Applied Psychology* 32, 221 -33

Klare, G. R. (1963) *The Measurement of Readability* Iowa State of University Press

Kolers, P. A. (1969) 'Clues to a letter's recognition: Implications for the design of characters' *Journal of Typographical Research* 3, 145-167

McLaughlin, G. N. (1968) 'Proposals for British Readability Measures' in Brown, A. L. and Downing, J. (eds.) *Third International Reading Symposium* London: Cassell

McLaughlin, G. N. (1968) 'SMOG grading – A new readability formula' *Journal of Reading* 12, 639-646

Miller, G. A. (1951) *Language and Communication* New York: McGraw-Hill

Osgood, C. E., Suci, G. J. and Tannenbaum, P. H. (1957) *The Measurement of Meaning* Urbana: University of Illinois Press

Shaw, A. (1969) *Print for partial sight – a research report* London: Library Association

Spencer, H. (1968) *The Visible Word : Problems of Legibility* London: Lund Humphries

Strang, R. and Bracken, D. K. (1957) *Making better readers* Boston: D. C. Heath and Co.

Strickland, R. G. (1962) 'The language of elementary school children: Its relationship to the language of reading testbooks and the quality of reading of selected children' *Bulletin of the School of Education* Indiana University volume 38, 4

Taylor, W. L. (1953) 'Cloze procedure: A new tool for measuring readability' *Journalism Quarterly* 30, 415-433

Tinker, M. A. (1963) *Legibility of Print* Iowa State University Press

Tinker, M. A. (1965) *Bases for Effective Reading* University of Minnesota Press

Tinker, M. A. (1966) 'Experimental studies in the legibility of print: An annotated bibliography' *Reading Research Quarterly* volume 1, no. 4, 67-118

Vernon, M. D. (1929) *Studies in the Psychology of Reading: A The Errors made in Reading* London: HMSO, 5-26

Yngve, V. H. (1960) 'A model and a hypothesis for language structure' *Proceedings of the American Philosophical Society* volume 104, no. 5, 444-466

Zipf, G. K. (1935) *The Psycho-Biology of Language* Boston: Houghton-Mifflin

Zipf, G. K. (1949) *Human Behaviour and the Principle of Least Effort* Cambridge, Massachusetts: Addison-Wesley Press

Readability—The use of cloze procedure

Donald Moyle

Senior Lecturer in Education
Edge Hill College of Education, Ormskirk

Cloze procedure, as a new approach to the assessment of readability, was first used by Taylor (1953). It is an empirical measure which uses the performance of children upon the text being measured to obtain the readability level. Though it would seem obvious that an examination of the performance of children on the actual text has more face validity than the use of formulae, it has as yet been employed infrequently. In the USA, where both reading materials and subject texts are often assessed for readability before publication, formulae are normally employed no doubt due to the greater expense and trouble which would be occasioned if an empirical measure were used. In Britain there has to date been little interest in measures of readability other than the grading of books by committees of experienced teachers using subjective judgments e.g. Pascoe (1962) and Lawson (1967). Cloze procedure has to date been employed only experimentally and even here usually at high levels of reading attainment.

Cloze procedure: what is it?

Gestalt psychologists applied the term 'closure' to the tendency to complete a pattern which has a part missing. Thus we tend to see a circle even when a small gap is left in the drawing. The fluent reader will often substitute a word of similar spelling and meaning to the one in the text or read correctly a word from which a letter has been omitted. A current advertising stunt to promote pre-packed bacon is based upon this principle. Spelling errors are to be located, one being the omission of the 'h' from the word 'when'. Though this appears in large print in a four word sentence a group of intelligent adults took on average 3½ minutes to locate the error.

Cloze procedure, applied to reading, requires the subject to fill in a gap, usually a whole word, which has been left in the text. In order to do this the subject must complete the language pattern of the writer by filling the gap, e.g. by supplying 'ran' in 'The dog — after my cat'. In order to complete such blanks in an extract from a book, the child must be able to react according to a number of criteria:

159

1   select a word according to grammatical rules
2   select a word with the correct meaning
3   choose a word which fits in best with the language patterns and
    vocabulary employed by the author.

For example, in the simple sentence given above the word omitted could
equally well have been 'runs'. However if the sentence had been preceded
by 'Yesterday my cat scratched a dog' the word 'runs' would no longer be
acceptable for the omission must be a verb in the past tense. The synonym
'chased' could possibly be employed but is perhaps less likely to occur than
'ran' in the given text.

   Cloze procedure involves accuracy, in that the child cannot hope to fill in
the blanks if he cannot recognize the majority of words given. It also involves
fluency and a knowledge of grammatical structure. Further, it necessitates
understanding the text and therefore comprehension. As such it would
seem to measure total readability much more nearly than any of the
formulae or other measures so far developed.

Cloze procedure: how does it work?

There are a number of alternative approaches to the application of cloze
techniques. It is usual to sample the text by taking a short passage from
the early pages, another midway through the book and a third from near
the end. This gives some idea of the internal consistency of the book with
regard to reading level. Sampling of course has the danger that the extracts
used may not be fully representative of the level of the book as a whole.
It is necessary therefore to examine the complete text subjectively to
assess whether the extracts used are representative.

   Passages can be presented either with deletions, i.e. the use of the
original text with chosen words obliterated, or with omissions, i.e., with
the passage retyped, each word omitted being represented by a blank of
equal size. Both methods have their advantages and disadvantages. In the
former the presence of illustrations and the clue given to the size of the word
omitted may influence results. In the latter the use of a different type face
may alter the difficulty of the task, especially among very young children.

   Omissions or deletions from the text can be selected on a structural or
lexical basis. Rankin (1959) found structural deletions correlated at a
significantly higher level with vocabulary and reading comprehension scores
than did lexical deletions.

   In structural deletion a certain percentage of words are removed from
the text no matter what words these prove to be. In lexical deletion certain
parts of speech are omitted e.g. nouns or verbs.

   Structural deletions can be determined by a table of random numbers or the omission of say every tenth word. Taylor (1953) found that though both methods achieved a similar grading of the passages he employed, the deletion of every fifth word gave the best discrimination between passages. It must be added, however, that Taylor was working with adult subjects and it may be that there will be differences from one age to another in the deletion rate which gives the best discrimination. Indeed Smith and Dechant (1961) suggest that among young children a passage cannot be understood if more than one word in ten cannot be read. If this is so then to omit more words than one in ten would prevent the child using his ability to understand the text in order to fill in the blanks.

The two passages below have been treated in an identical manner, every tenth word being deleted. Actual deletions are shown in italics. Quite by chance the parts of speech selected are heavily different and it could be that the difficulty of the passages presented as cloze tests could be significantly affected by the nature of the words selected. The two passages are graded by their respective authors as having a reading level of nine years. No information is available on how this grading was achieved.

Passage 1 From *The Village That Was Drowned* by P. Flowerdew (Oliver and Boyd 1965)

'You haven't seen Foxy. Isn't he a pretty little *thing* ?'
Carol gave the animal scarcely a glance. She was *bursting* with news of her own.
'Have you heard?' she *asked*.
'Heard what ?'
She paused to give full effect to *her* coming announcement.
'This village,' she said in a dramatic *voice*, 'this village is going to be drowned. All the *houses* will be covered by water. The church will be *covered*. The school will be covered. The whole valley will *become* one great lake.'
'What do you mean?'
'What are *you* talking about?'
'It's true. People in the town of *Westhill* haven't enough water, so it's going to be stored here for them.'

Passage 2 From SRA International Reading Laboratory IIA

About forty men live on this island, each man *an* expert in one of the many jobs there are *to* do.
'Any luck yet?' Bill asks, as he and *his* team get ready to take over from another drilling *team*.

'No,' one man tells him, shaking his head. 'And *you* won't
find gas on your shift. Rock's hard now *and* there's still half
a mile to go.'
The experts *had* said that there might be gas at this point,
but it would be two miles under the sea. Bill *and* his team
take over.
To reach the place under *the* sea-bed where the gas is trapped,
great drills are used.

Cloze procedure : possible uses

1 The method would seem to commend itself to authors and publishers
  as a realistic means of assessing the reading level of books of all types
  prior to publication.
2 The teacher could employ the technique for grading the books within
  his/her own classroom.
3 Teachers might well find that a brief cloze test taken from the text of
  a given book and administered to the child before he reads the book
  itself would prevent a child experiencing failure through reading a book
  that is too difficult for him.
4 Cloze supplies a quick and easy way of checking important aspects of
  comprehension.
5 A battery of standardized cloze tests could simplify attainment testing
  in reading.

Preliminary report on a pilot study using cloze procedure in assessing the readability of a reading scheme

The purpose of this pilot study was simply to obtain evidence on the
possibility of using cloze procedure in the grading of books for children
in the early stages of reading. The Griffin and Dragon Books written by
S. K. McCullagh and published by E. J. Arnold were selected. These books
were chosen as they have proved popular with children and are well graded.
The only criticisms heard have been that the Griffins are heavily weighted
towards the interests of boys and that the scheme is rather steeply graded
at certain points.

Estimates of the difficulty of the books by teachers' committees have
varied somewhat. For example, *Griffin Book 1* has been given reading levels
varying from five to more than six years.

The Griffin Books present a single story in twelve parts which tell the
adventures of three pirates. The Dragon Books were added as supplementary
readers at a later date. Again there are twelve books but each presents a
complete story. Here the characters are more numerous and the content
would seem equally attractive to girls and boys.

Two passages of 100 words were selected from each of the twenty-four books, one beginning with the first complete sentence on the second page of the text and the other ending at the last complete sentence on next to the last page of the text. Structural deletion was employed and every tenth word was covered with masking tape.Children read the passages orally from the actual text and the actual responses were recorded though in fact only the authors' original words were counted as correct responses for the purposes of the analysis which follows. All the children were given a practice passage before they used the Griffins and Dragons and all read the page before the one containing the cloze test. The books were presented in the order suggested by the publishers and therefore practice in using the cloze technique may have reduced the discrimination of the tests between the early and later books.

Children from two schools varying in age from 6·0 years to 9 years 10 months were used as subjects. The schools were chosen to represent a wide range of ability and socioeconomic status. Ninety children were tested on the Schonell Graded Word Recognition Test and the Schonell Silent Reading Test R4B. Thirty-eight children were eventually selected for the evaluation of cloze results on the basis that the mean chronological age of each of the four age groups was equal to the mean reading age.

A further eighteen children were matched with the eight year old group and these children read the same passages without deletions. Their total reading errors were recorded.

A third measure was obtained by submitting the passages used for the cloze tests to analysis using the Fry (1968) Readability Graph. This computes a reading level from a combination of the number of syllables and the number of sentences per 100 words.

Results

Table 1
Reading age levels of Griffin Books 1 to 6 according to the Fry Readability Graph

Griffin Book	Reading age
1	6 yrs. 11 mths.
2	8 yrs. 10 mths.
3	8 yrs. 1 mth.
4	9 yrs. 8 mths.
5	7 yrs. 6 mths.
6	7 yrs. 5 mths.

Until applying this formula to the Griffin Books, I had found it to be reasonably reliable considering its simplicity. The weaknesses of assessing readability by sentence and syllable length are fully shown up here. One of the very strong points of McCullagh's writing is her ability to produce vivid description within the limits of a restricted vocabulary. However, descriptive writing usually employs long sentences and this explains in part the high reading levels given throughout. A second feature of course is the fact that American children start school, and usually therefore reading, later than British children.

The sudden jump of two years from Book 1 to Book 2 is interesting, for the passage selected in Book 2 consisted of the pirate's song. This has rythmic repetition and children usually read it easily. However, it has very long sentences and the name 'Acrooacre' occurs frequently. Thus the Fry score is raised considerably on both items which it measures. It will be noted that the cloze test did not suffer any distortion because of this passage.

Table 2
Results of cloze tests

Book	Average age	Percentage correct: closures				Total closures (possible 760)	Mean (possible 20
		9·6	8·6	7·6	6·6		
	N	5	17	11	5		
Griffin	1	76	74	55	53	503	13·24
	2	72	71	49	35	457	12·03
	3	70	68	39	25	412	10·84
	4	70	67	39	17	403	10·61
	5	64	51	23	9	337	8·86
	6	67	66	31	12	372	9·79
	7	64	54	26	9	313	8·24
	8	54	41	15	5	231	6·08
	9	50	39	14	8	223	5·87
	10	44	35	13	2	193	5·08
	11	39	30	8	0	160	4·21
	12	36	25	6	0	134	3·53
Dragon	A1	79	71	49	62	490	12·89
	A2	81	75	51	52	501	13·18
	A3	73	69	48	35	447	11·76
	B1	72	63	44	29	411	10·82
	B2	70	69	39	21	412	10·84
	B3	65	46	26	13	291	7·66
	C1	68	49	26	11	305	8·03
	C2	60	39	21	6	244	6·42
	C3	61	37	16	4	227	5·97
	D1	50	33	15	2	198	5·21
	D2	44	25	12	0	157	4·13
	D3	39	28	9	0	152	4·00

Table 3
Results of estimating difficulty by counting the number of errors made
in oral reading of the passages employed in the cloze tests of Griffin Books 1–6

Griffin Book	Average number of errors
1	3·7
2	4·9
3	5·1
4	6·2
5	9·9
6	9·6

*This table is based on the performance of 18 children – average
chronological and reading age 8 years 6 months.*

The results of the counting of errors method suggested by McLeod (1962)
is shown for the first six books of the Griffin series. It will be seen that the
grading of the books is identical in order to that given by the cloze procedure
results. All three measurements used in fact suggest that Book 5 is more
difficult than Book 6. Certainly teachers have often commented that Book
5 causes difficulty for children and it has been suggested that the high
literary quality of the language used to describe the storm involves sentence
constructions and figures of speech which are rather difficult at this reading
level.

The counting of errors procedure would seem to have two weaknesses
as a measure of readability. Firstly, it emphasizes reading accuracy rather
more than comprehension, and secondly it demands individual application
whereas the cloze procedure test can be given as a group test.

The cloze tests seem to suggest that with the exception of Book 5 the
Griffin scheme is extremely well graded.

Contrary to expectations the cloze tests did not show any difference in
readability levels between boys and girls. However one cannot rule out the
possibility of a cumulative effect where, on reading the whole series, boys
may eventually gain from the exercise because they find the subject matter
of the books more attractive.

The Griffin Books were written specifically for the retarded reader
in the junior school. It seems significant therefore that the only break in
the smooth gradient from book to book at all age levels and between the
age groups is shown in the difference between children in the 7 years
6 months and 8 years 6 months groups. The big jump in scores on the
cloze tests between two age groups is so marked that it could hardly
have occurred by chance. It could be that the concepts and language

used are more related to those of the older child. If this is so then there is a further argument for not using remedial readers in the infant school, no matter how attractive they may seem to the teacher.

As the Dragon Books are a series of supplementary readers and are individual stories grouped in sets of three, their precise positioning from a readability point of view is perhaps not quite so important within each set of three books.

Table 4
Griffin and Dragon Books in publisher's suggested order

Main scheme (Griffin)	Supplementary (Dragon)
Book 1	
Book 2	
Book 3	
	Book A1
	Book A2
	Book A3
Book 4	
Book 5	
Book 6	
	Book B1
	Book B2
	Book B3
Book 7	
Book 8	
Book 9	
	Book C1
	Book C2
	Book C3
Book 10	
Book 11	
Book 12	
	Book D1
	Book D2
	Book D3

The cloze tests suggest only minor modifications in the order planned by the publishers. On only one occasion, namely the case of B3 and C1, is there a suggestion that the presentation in groups of three is incorrect.

Table 5

Reordering of the scheme based on results of cloze procedure tests.

Griffin	Dragon
Book 1	
	Book A2
	Book A1
Book 2	
	Book A3
Book 3	
	Book B2
	Book B1
Book 4	
Book 5	
Book 6	
Book 7	
	Book C1
	Book B3
	Book C2
Book 8	Book C3
Book 9	
	Book D1
Book 10	
Book 11	Book D2
	Book D3
Book 12	

It should be noted that the reordering based on the results of the cloze tests is not a plan for action by teachers. To suggest for example that Griffin Book 5 should be read before Book 6 would make nonsense of the story content of the readers. Rather, the teacher should ensure that children have adequate help to overcome any difficulty they might experience with Book 5. In the case of the Dragon Books certain reordering in the placement could be made without any real damage to the scheme as a whole. However it must be remembered that the scheme has been constructed around a system of vocabulary control. Thus any change in order suggested by total readability must be weighed against a break in the sequence of vocabulary growth provided by the scheme.

Cloze procedure commends itself as an empirical measure of readability which would provide information complementary to the teacher's own subjective assessments of printed materials. There are however a number of aspects upon which we need further information:

1 What is the appropriate number of deletions for each age group?
2 Will deletion or omission have an effect upon results gained and might this vary as to whether the test is given orally or in group form?
3 What variables affect performance e.g. vocabulary, sentence completion or comprehension attainment, intelligence and socioeconomic status?
4 What effect on cloze scores is observed when there are heavy deletions of particular parts of speech?
5 Can a percentage score be suggested which can be equated with an individual's frustration or independent reading level?

Some work on the analysis of cloze procedure as a measure has been undertaken in the USA e.g. the factor analysis studies of Weaver and Kingston (1963) and Bormuth (1969). The writer hopes to report on some of the above questions in the near future as a result of work which is at present in hand.

References

Bormuth, J. R. 'Factor validity of cloze tests as measures of reading comprehension' *Reading Research Quarterly* volume IV, no. 3, 358-365
Fry, E. A. (1968) 'A readability formula that saves time' *Journal of Reading* volume 11, no. 7, 513-516
Lawson, K. S. (ed.) (1968) *Children's Reading* University of Leeds Institute of Education
McLeod, J. (1962) 'The estimation of readability of books of low difficulty' *British Journal of Educational Psychology* volume 32, 112-118
Pascoe, T. Q. (ed.) (1962) *A Second Survey of Books for Backward Readers* London: University of London Press
Rankin, E. F. (1959) 'The cloze procedure – its validity and utility' in *Eighth Yearbook of the National Reading Conference*, 131-144
Smith, H. P. and Dechant, E. (1961) *Psychology in teaching reading* Englewood Cliffs: Prentice-Hall
Taylor, W. L. (1953) 'Close procedure: A new tool for measuring readability' *Journalism Quarterly* volume 30, 415-438
Weaver, W. W. and Kingston, A. J. (1963) 'A factor analysis of the close procedure and other measures of reading and language ability' *Journal of Communication* volume 13, 252-261

An investigation into alternative methods of assessing the readability of books used in schools

S. Heatlie

Head of Remedial Department
Usworth Secondary School,
Usworth

E. Ramsay

Head of Remedial Department
Hermitage Secondary School,
Chester-le-Street

In presenting this report we are concerned to consolidate our research on the use of cloze procedure as a measure of readability.

The sequence of presentation will demonstrate the practical application of the AOSTMTEC routine outlined earlier by John Merritt.

We shall begin by reminding you of the headings referred to by these initial letters. The meanings of each heading and subheading will become clear as we progress systematically through the report.

The initials stand for the following terms: aims; objectives; strategies; tactics; method; technique; evaluation; consolidation. Each of these headings contains the following subheadings: modules; media; mode. The meanings of these three terms will also become clear, or so we hope, as you observe how they are used.

Aims

The aims in this context are the research aims. As class teachers we are faced with many day to day problems in the selection of suitable educational materials. We are expressly concerned here with reading materials and the problem of matching children to texts which are neither too difficult nor too easy.

Modules

The modules are the children with their varying levels of ability and interest. It is the teacher's job to cater for these variations.

Media

The media are the texts of various readability levels from which the teacher may select.

Mode

The mode is the procedures adopted by the teacher to ensure that modules and media are correctly matched, i.e. that the children are given books which are right for them in terms of readability.

Can teachers match books and children? And are children able to select books for themselves which are neither too difficult nor too easy? Evidence referred to in the previous papers suggests that the ability of the teacher to match book and child is less than perfect, and that children need guidance if they are to make an accurate selection of books for the purpose of independent reading. As one of our aims, therefore, we set out to test the hypothesis that both teachers and children have difficulty in assessing the readability of texts with an acceptable degree of accuracy.

As our second aim we chose to devise and test procedures which could be used by teachers to select texts of appropriate difficulty with reasonable accuracy and with no great inconvenience. A particular form of cloze procedure was adopted. Our second prediction, then, is that this form of cloze procedure would prove to be a satisfactory and convenient technique for assessing readability.

Having defined the aims we then proceeded to define specific objectives — again in terms of modules, media and mode.

Objectives
Modules
The modules were the specific estimates of readability to be made by teachers and children in two secondary schools.

Media
The media were the measures of readability derived from two forms of cloze procedure (see appendix A) and a standardized test of reading comprehension.

Mode
Two modes of relating the subjective estimates were selected:

1 Comparison of measures i.e. validation. This was to be achieved
    (i) by obtaining teachers' and children's subjective estimates of the degree of difficulty of the selected texts using a five-point scale, and comparing these measures with the scores obtained on the two different forms of the cloze texts
    (ii) by comparing the scores obtained on the two different forms of the cloze texts with scores on the test of reading comprehension.

2 Scaling of cloze scores against children's estimates. If the children's estimates proved to be a valid measure of readability the next step was to scale cloze scores against children's estimates in order to determine what percentage of correct responses represented an acceptable level of difficulty for independent reading.

Strategies
Modules
These were the samples of subjects involved in the pilot experiment and consisted of 1 pupil and 2 teachers

1 A year group of pupils was selected as it provided a sample of children of fairly equal ages as well as a wide spread of ability. First-year forms were selected simply because they proved to be most readily available.
2 The teachers were those who were responsible for selecting books to be used by first-year children.

Media
The media employed were (1) the texts and (2) the test.

1 The texts
The book selected was *Chang*, by Elizabeth Morse (Dent 1935). This is a 40,000 word tale of a jungle boy of Siam — a quite unexceptional work of fiction.

Criteria for selection of text
As this particular text was known to have been used with first-year pupils it was considered a realistic choice. It was also neutral in that it was not currently in use in the two schools involved in the experiment; nor did it seem likely to favour any particular social class or sex.

Selection of text samples
The search for a form of cloze procedure which would be simple and convenient for the average teacher to administer and interpret led to the adoption of a sample of only three pages. The smallness of a three-page sample made its validity as a representative sample of the whole book somewhat questionable, but it was undoubtedly more convenient than assessing every one of the book's pages. It was envisaged that a sample taken from the beginning, middle and end of the book would give a reasonable indication of the book's general readability. Pages were accordingly selected from the middle of the first third of the book, the middle of the central third and the middle of the final third of the book.

171

In future research it is intended to examine more fully the problems of sample-page selection.

Size of samples of text

Each of the three individual samples of text from the selected pages consisted of at least 200 words. The first 100 words were to be used by the children in making their subjective assessments of readability. This first passage also acted as a run-in to the second passage. The second 100 words, when read and completed as a cloze test, were to provide the objective assessments. It was therefore necessary for each of these passages to begin and end with a complete sentence.

Ideally the *same* passage should have been used for both the subjective and the objective assessments. Unfortunately this was not possible, as children could not, of course, make valid assessments of a passage from which certain words were missing. It was assumed that any differences between the two consecutive passages on any page would be minimal and would provide an adequate basis for the comparison of the subjective and objective assessments.

Treatment of sample texts

There are two basic methods for selecting words for deletion from a text: one is structural, the other lexical. Structural methods involve removal of a proportion of the textual words selected at random or according to a particular ratio; lexical methods involve removal of selected parts of speech. For this particular cloze procedure it was decided to use structural removals because they have been shown to correlate more highly with reading comprehension and vocabulary scores than do the lexical removals. (See previous paper by Moyle.)

Smith and Dechant, cited by Moyle in the symposium, suggest that for young children, one word in ten should be removed if a structural method of removal is adopted. Bloomer (1962) and Schneyer (1965) also adopted tenth word removals. It was decided, therefore, to follow these precedents.

One of the objectives of this research was to compare two forms of cloze procedure, whose basic differences lay in their respective systems of word removal. In one text, words were removed by omitting them entirely and in the other, the words were deleted (see appendix A). Therefore Group A cloze tests had tenth words omitted, whereas Group B's contained tenth-word deletions.

The advantage of the deletion procedure is that it can be applied

172

to the pages of an actual book. The disadvantage is that the children cannot insert their answers in the actual text as they can when words are omitted.

In order to keep both of these cloze texts as near as possible to the original text while still retaining the elements of a test, the initial letters of the removal words were provided. As the use of single letter cue in this way entails the use of what Merritt (1970) has termed 'intermediate skills' below the level of the individual word, the provision of initial letters was felt to be justified. However, this does introduce a slight phonetic ambiguity where there is not a one-to-one grapheme/phoneme relationship, as with such letters as 'c' in such words as 'come', 'chit', 'chic', 'city', and 'p' in 'phone', 'ptosis', 'psalm', 'prune'.

Group A cloze tests (i.e. the tests from which words were omitted) contained structural cues in the form of dots, each of which indicated one missing letter, and which were double-spaced to enable the children to write in their answers.

As may be seen in the example, Group B version brought the cloze test as near 'real reading' of continuous prose as was practically possible, short of giving actual letters or of laboriously disguising individual letters. The tenth-word deletions were carried out so as to leave visible the initial letters and certain configuration cues, namely the ascenders and descenders. This in fact approximates very closely to the problem a child faces when he encounters a new word – one he has not previously encountered in print, or one whose meaning he does not understand. It has the additional advantage of virtually eliminating the writing-in of synonyms and should therefore improve validity.

When dealing with deleted words, the children in Group B had to write their answers somewhere other than in the text itself. One fairly common method of catering for this is to number the deleted words and to number correspondingly the columnar spaces alongside the test passage. However, it was felt that numbers squeezed alongside a deleted word complicated rather than simplified the problem for the child. With only ten deletions involved, it was decided to give no numbers at all as there should be little chance of mistakes occuring in a child's recording of this small number of answers, especially when initial letters and structural cues (dots) are provided.

Certain arbitrary conventions were necessary in the preparation of materials for both groups: in Group A the words 'I' and 'A' were omitted altogether, and in Group B they were shown thus: ▮ and ▲.

Format of sample texts

For the sake of production convenience all of the texts were duplicated typewritten versions. Using this technique it was not possible to make the format of the copy match that of the original. The discrepancies between the spacing and the type size adopted and those of the original text meant that, in order to maintain the same numbers of words per line as the original, it was necessary to have only the left side of each typewritten text justified.

Photocopying or using the actual printed page would appear to eliminate almost all of these discrepancies. If both forms of the text are equally valid, deletion of words on the pages of the actual book will be adopted in the next stage of the research, for if both are equally valid, deletion from the actual book should presumably be more valid than either.

Scoring of texts

Bormuth (1965) demonstrated that the acceptance of synonyms answers to cloze tests did not significantly increase the validities of the scores. Accordingly, it was decided to accept only correct answers (including those misspelt), as it is much more convenient to mark tests on a simple right/wrong basis than to attempt to discriminate between the acceptable and the unacceptable synonym. One mark was to be awarded for each correct answer, so that a score of ten was the maximum for each page of text and a score of thirty was therefore the maximum that a child could record for the three passages.

Practice test

In order to familiarize both teachers and pupils with the experimental procedures it was decided to administer a practice test. A shorter and simpler form of the cloze tests was devised and administered (see appendix B).

The test was adapted to make it exceptionally easy to read in order to enable the children to concentrate as fully as possible on mastering the techniques of selecting and recording their answers. It consisted of a 50 word minimum run-in, followed by a cloze test of similar length. It was constructed so that the five tenth-word omissions or deletions provided a mixture of parts of speech in order to avoid the children developing a set towards seeking one particular part of speech. It also contained an example of one of the arbitrary conventions listed earlier.

Subjective evaluation scales

One of the aims of the research was to evaluate the ability of those concerned – the teachers and the pupils – to make accurate subjective assessments of the readability of the texts they use.

In the experiment, the children were asked to rate the difficulty of the run-in preceding each of the cloze tests. The teachers, on the other hand, were each presented with a copy of *Chang* and asked to assess it in any way they wished and to record their judgments on the rating scales provided. This technique could also have been adopted with the pupils but this was not attempted for practical reasons.

Scoring of subjective evaluations

The children's and teachers' estimates of difficulty were to be recorded on a five-point scale. For the children's assessments the scores ranged from one mark (for 'Too hard') to five marks (for 'Too easy'). As the children were required to assess each of the three pages the maximum number of assessment points was fifteen. The teachers, on the other hand, assessed the whole book – again on a five-point scale. To permit comparison between children's assessments and the teachers' assessments therefore it was necessary for the teachers' assessments to be weighted by a factor of three.

2   The test

We are still concerned with strategies and, specifically, with media. The second type of medium used was a reading test which was used to establish the RQ's of the pupils.

Selection of test

The group test selected was the NFER *Secondary Reading Test 1 (Vocabulary)*. This is a multiple choice sentence completion test and it was chosen because of its similarities to cloze tests, and the comparative ease with which it could be administered and its results converted.

Scoring of test

Standard NFER procedures were followed and transmuted scores from the tables provided reading quotients (RQ's).

Mode

The mode represents the interaction of modules with media, i.e. the pupils and teachers with the texts and tests, and this interaction will be reflected in the statistical analysis.

Administration

The pupil population of each of the two schools participating
in the research was treated separately. The children in the sample
were ranked according to RQ and arranged in matched pairs.
Matched members of each pair were then randomly allocated to
one of the two groups — Group A, whose texts involved tenth-word
omissions, and Group B, whose texts contained tenth-word deletions.

The administration necessitated knowing approximately how long
it would take the children to complete each text. The timing was
estimated and tried out with a class which was not directly involved
in the research. As a result of this trial, the following times were
deemed to be adequate for the completion of each text, although no
time limit was to be imposed:

	practice test	*tests 1 – 3*
run-in and recorded assessments	2 mins	3 mins
cloze text and recorded assessments	4 mins	10 mins

Some of the problems involved in this type of research concern
interference and practice effects. Absenteeism during test periods also
bring considerable difficulties. It was decided to try to minimize the
effects of these factors by administering the children's cloze practice,
cloze texts and subjective assessments all in one session. This made
rather a long test session for the children, but it did contain frequent
changes of task and it also allowed for brief periods of rest.

To keep differences in test administration to the minimum,
information and instructions to be used by the experimenters were
typewritten and duplicated.

Treatment of results

Our first objective was to validate the teachers' and the children's
subjective estimates by comparing their respective means with the
means of the children's scores on the two different forms of cloze text.
This analysis was to be carried out on a form basis.

Next, we were to assess the validity of the two forms of cloze by
correlating the children's scores on each of these two forms with the
RQs obtained from the NFER test SR1. A high correlation between
cloze scores and RQs would support the hypothesis that the cloze
scores provided a valid index of the comprehension of the passages.
If, as anticipated, the correlations between each of the two forms of cloze
and RQ did not differ appreciably from each other, this would justify
the selection of whichever form was more convenient when undertaking
further research in this field.

Tactics

Modules

Here the modules were (1) the schools and (2) the teachers

One of the schools, School 1, does not provide a complete cross-section of the population of the area as a number of children are creamed off to what was previously the local grammar school, although there remain at School 1 sufficient children to form two GCE forms in each group. All five first-year forms took part in the experiment.

School 2, a comprehensive school some six miles distant, does provide a fuller sample with its eleven-form entry. Administration difficulties within the experiment prevented the participation of all of the eleven first-year classes. Seven representative classes were eventually selected. The sizes of the final groups were as follows:

	Group A	Group B
School 1	59	59
School 2	89	89

The smallness of the samples was due less to the size of the classes than to absenteeism, as each pupil absent from one group automatically excluded his or her opposite number in the other matched group.

2 Teachers

Eighteen teachers took part in the experiments in School 1 and twenty-four in School 2. At both schools the subject teachers who were currently teaching the first-year classes participated. Heads of department also participated although some did not teach the children concerned. However, they were responsible for ordering books for these children. Differences within the sample of teachers, e.g. sex, length of service etc, were not considered as separate factors in the recording and treatment of results.

Media

The tactical media were the researchers and the subject teachers who helped to administer the tests. So far as was possible the tests were administered by the two researchers in order to minimize the experimental variable of teacher/researcher differences.

Mode

The mode was the testing procedures employed. Standardized procedures were adhered to. At both schools all tests were carried out during English lessons and as far as possible during periods of good attendance.

Method

As no implementation problems of any significance were encountered it is unnecessary to divide 'Method' into its three components. No methods were involved which could not be regarded as part of the normal repertoire of the average teacher.

Technique

Here again there were no implementation problems, other than occasional unavoidable interruptions during test administration, e.g. urgent messages being delivered to the researcher. No practical snags arose which could not be overcome by dint of routine techniques.

Evaluation

By defining precisely the modules, media and mode of evaluations it will become clear that the evaluation component of the AOSTMTEC routine is, in this report, concerned not merely with evaluation of results alone, but must in fact answer the questions — How valid was the total exercise? Has what we have done really been worthwhile?

Throughout this report we have used the term modules to represent relatively homogeneous units with which we are primarily concerned at any given level of operating, e.g. at the level of aims, objectives etc. The media have been the means or the resources which could be used to satisfy the needs at each level. Mode was the manner in which the media were used in order to satisfy the needs. What then are the modules and media to be identified in order to carry out evaluation?

Modules

These are the two elements of the research:
1 The product is the objective criteria in the form of statistical results.
2 The process and the subjective judgments of readers and researchers.

The product.
This divides into (i) teachers' and children's estimates and (ii) the correlations of cloze scores and children's estimates with SR1.

The process.
In addition to evaluating the research in terms of the product, it was necessary to look at it in terms of the process involved, namely the AOSTMTEC routine.

Media

The corresponding evaluation media are (1) the objective statistical tables and (2) the subjective educational evaluations by readers and researchers.

178

1 The statistical tables

Table 1
Scores and estimates for individual schools and classes

School 1

class	group	Children's mean cloze score	mean difficulty estimates	Teachers' mean estimates	mean RQ
	A	22·33	10·17		
1SB				9·33	103·71
	B	23·2	9·2		
	A	22·53	8·13		
1SG				9·33	101·3
	B	24·8	8·47		
	A	19·77	9·31		
1AB				6·00	96·84
	B	20·33	8·17		
	A	17·83	8·92		
1AG				6·00	91·63
	B	20·83	9·91		
	A	13·67	8·5		
1B				3·33	81·78
	B	17·67	8·5		

School 2

class	group	Children's mean cloze score	mean difficulty estimates	Teachers mean estimates	mean RQ
	A	25·42	9·15		
1X				10·17	116·43
	B	27·2	9·67		
	A	24·0	8·18		
$1S_1$				9·87	107·28
	B	25·13	9·2		
	A	24·5	8·5		
$1N_2$				8·37	105·55
	B	25·72	8·18		
	A	23·4	9·73		
$1S_3$				6·62	106·00
	B	23·33	9·5		
	A	19·15	7·62		
$1N_4$				4·37	91·18
	B	21·23	8·77		
	A	16·7	8·23		
$1N_5$	B	18·8	8·5	3·125	84·84
	A	13·21	8·79		
$1S_5$				3·125	81·62
	B	18·46	9·77		

Table 2
Correlations

Schools 1 and 2 combined

Group A	SR1	cloze scores	children's estimates
SR_1	—	0·74	0·199
children's scores		—	0·218

Group B	SR1	cloze scores	children's estimates
SR_1	—	0·687	0·112
children's scores		—	0·225

Table 3
Cloze procedure mean scores

Chang A	page 1	page 2	page 3
school 1	5·86	8·37	5·06
school 2	6·38	8·01	6·26

Chang B	page 1	page 2	page 3
school 1	6·99	8·71	6·41
school 2	7·29	8·77	7·11

1 Note the low correlation between actual reading ability and the assessment of book difficulty. There is no evidence of pupil ability to appraise texts accurately, i.e. good readers do not consistently assess the text as being easy and poor readers do not consistently assess the text as being hard. Similarly high cloze scores are not consistently accompanied by an 'easy' assessment or vice versa.

2 The correlations in Table 2 are of the same order of magnitude and suggest that the two forms of cloze procedure are comparable. The problem of page sampling was not intended to be an important feature in this research but the above figures show that this problem needs more attention in future research of this kind.

2 *The subjective evaluations*
Readers' evaluations
As there is no feedback to this written form, the prejudice of the researchers will continue to go uncorrected for the remainder of

this report although every effort has been made to reduce these prejudices by the application of the continuous process of evaluation.

A certain amount of feedback was obtained at the UKRA Congress presentation.

Researchers' evaluations
Having followed a hierarchial sequence, i.e. AOSTMTEC, culminating in the above results, it seemed to us that the evaluation carried out in the reverse order, i.e. TMTSOA, would bring us back to a final evaluation *vis a vis* our research aims. The validation of aims depends upon the results obtained. However, it is essential to evaluate the variables at each stage of the routine in order to assess the validity of each stage of the process.

Mode
Technique and method evaluation
There were no apparent problems at the implementation level and as a matter of judgment we feel that our methods and techniques were satisfactory. This can only be checked by the replication of this experiment by other researchers. We have presented this report in considerable detail in order to facilitate such replications.

Strategy and tactics evaluation
Our tactics also appear to have been satisfactory. So far as strategies media is concerned, it may be seen in Table 2 that the correlation between Text A and SR1 was minimally different from that between Text B and SR1. We may conclude therefore that omission and deletion techniques are equally valid and that we may use either for studies of this kind. Text B is easier to prepare as it simply entails deleting parts of words from existing texts or from photocopies of texts. This is preferable to preparing fresh copies as these would normally have to be typed and would therefore differ appreciably from the original text format. For both of these reasons the deletion procedure is clearly superior and is particularly convenient for teachers. This deletion procedure will, in fact, be used in our next research when we shall use original text material.

Objectives evaluation
Were the objectives sensible in the light of our aims? Table 2 shows low correlations between children's scores and their estimates on both forms of cloze. The problem presented in objectives mode 2, i.e. scaling of cloze scores, is therefore not resolved. In the future a check will be made to

see if better readers or brighter children can be selected as better predictors of readability.

Table 1 indicates that teachers also have difficulty in assessing books. There seems to be a tendency for teachers to underestimate the reading ability of children in the lower streams. Conversely there is also a tendency to overestimate the ability of those in the higher streams.

Still at the strategies level, criticisms need to be made of the teachers' questionnaire and the choice of book. The instructions to the teachers regarding the use of the book may have been confusing; it was not explicit in the instructions whether the book was to be inspected as a class reader or as an individual reading book. The book used is normally used as class reader.

Aims evaluation

Were the aims realistic and worthwhile, and have we achieved them? We can claim that our predictions have been validated by the results presented:

1 that teachers and children have difficulty in estimating the readability of books
2 that the particular form of cloze procedure adopted provides a valid and convenient technique for assessing readability.

We are now confident that this research has practical application for teachers who are faced as we are with the problem of matching children to books. But our confidence has to be communicated to readers and our communication must do more than provide a gentle academic exercise for the reader. We must therefore complete the final stage of the AOSTMTEC routine.

Consolidation

It is customary to conclude a report at this point. The evaluation has been made, the conclusions have been drawn and recommendations have been made. On the other hand, it has been said that every research in the field of education is duplicated at least once every ten years. No doubt some research needs to be duplicated. Much research, however, is duplicated unnecessarily because of failure at the consolidation stage.

It is what is done at this consolidation stage which determines the usefulness of any report. If the information the report contains subsequently proves to be irretrievable then the report is useless, no matter how important the report or its contents might be.

We therefore end our report with a brief exhortation to the reader:

182

1 to establish a resource unit which will maximize the usefulness of its contents
2 to use AOSTMTEC as headings and subheadings for the resource unit categories
3 to store this particular report (after any errors and prejudices of the researchers have been corrected) in the category most relevant to the needs of the reader.

In determining what is entailed in consolidation it may help us once again to think in terms of modules, media and mode.

Modules

These are the relevant storage and retrieval categories. They may be considered as catering for both primary and secondary references.

In this instance, primary references are those which are directly related to this research. For our Reading Resource Unit this report will be primarily labelled 'Readability' and categorized thus:
Objectives in reading: Media – assessment of.

The secondary references arise when we consider how else readability could be categorized. Now, although we have been using cloze procedure as a means of testing reading materials, we have noticed that the procedure can also be used to test the child, i.e. as a measure of comprehension. Our second storage category therefore is:
Objectives in reading: Modules – testing children's comprehension ability.

Cloze material can also be used for teaching children to use context cues. A further storage category for this material, therefore, is:
Aims in reading: Media – development of intermediate skills.

It is well worth mentioning in passing that the use of cloze procedures in the development of intermediate reading skills within the practical classroom context appears to have been neglected up to now. Those interested would do well to refer to Schneyer (1965) and Merritt (1969).

Media

These are (i) the personal resource unit in its physical form (probably consisting of card index system and files) and (ii) this actual report.

Mode

After the distribution/dissemination of the report, *mode* refers to storage and retrieval procedure. The importance of mode is obvious when we consider that this or any other report is completely useless unless it remains accessible when required.

All too often, memory is employed as a long-term as well as a short-term resource unit. At best this is on its own a makeshift and unreliable system and something better is clearly required — hence our emphasis on the development by the teacher of his own resource unit.

Conclusion
In the first paragraph of this report we stated that we were concerned to consolidate our research on the use of cloze procedure as a measure of readability. This we have done. The AOSTMTEC routine has been used as a problem-solving tool in the planning and implementation stages of this routine and has been demonstrated as such in this the reporting stage.

We hope that its usefulness will be further evaluated and developed, especially by the teacher in the classroom, not only in connection with problem-solving but also with drawing-up effective and efficient resource unit categories.

Appendix A
Chang 1: Group A

I knew where he came down to the water to drink, for I had seen his spoor, and I climbed into the branches of a tree that overlooked his drinking hole. My plan was to spear him from above as he drank. It was not long before I saw him slip out of the jungle and advance to the waterhole. I heard him lapping the water like a great cat, and held my spear poised ready to throw. But, just at that moment, I heard a slight rustle in the tree beside me, and glancing out of the corner of my eye, I saw a great king cobra with his hood spread wide, ready to strike

A murmur went up from the group round the f . . . ; they well knew the danger of such a situation, f . . to be struck by the poisoned fangs of such a k . . . cobra meant almost instant death. Nye Chut enjoyed the s . . . . , and slowly wrapped himself a quid of betel-nut b . . . . . he continued. Even the women who had been sitting o. the outskirts of the group drew near, and Savat s . . the deaf old Kung put her hand behind her e . . to hear better.

I took one look at the c . . . . , Nye Chut went on, and leaped to the ground a . . . . . at the feet of the tiger.

Chang 1: Group B

I knew where he came down to the water to drink, for I had seen his spoor, and I climbed into the branches of a tree that overlooked his drinking hole. My plan was to spear him from

above as he drank. It was not long before I saw him slip out
of the jungle and advance to the waterhole. I heard him
lapping the water like a great cat, and held my spear poised,
ready to throw. But, just at that moment, I heard a slight
rustle in the tree beside me, and glancing out of the corner
of my eye, I saw a great king cobra with his hood spread wide,
ready to strike.

A murmur went up from the group round the f██; they well
knew the danger of such a situation, f██ to be struck by the
poisoned fangs of such a ki██ cobra meant almost instant
death. Nye Chut enjoyed the s██████, and slowly wrapped
himself a quid of betel-nut b█████ he continued. Even the women
who had been sitting o█ the outskirsts of the group drew near, and
Savat s██ the deaf old Kung put her hand behind her e██ to hear
better.
    'I took one look at the c█████,' Nye Chut went on, 'and leaped
to the ground a██████ at the feet of the tiger.'

Answers
f . . .
f . .
k . . .
s . . . .
b . . . . .
o .
s . .
e . .
c . . . .
a . . . . .

Appendix B
Group A: Rags and his medal

Sam and I went to the pond. His dog Rags was with us.
'There is a raft on the bank,' I said to Sam.
'Let us put it in the pond and sit on it.'
'Yes, yes,' said Sam.
We slid the raft from the bank into the pond.

Sam had just got a foot on the ʳ . . . when it sank. Sam fell in.
'Help! Help! Get ᵐ . out quick! '
But it was Rags who got him ᵒ . . With a bark Rags grabbed

Sam's coat and pulled.
    strong pull had Sam back on the bank. Rags § . . a medal,
but Sam just got wet.

Group B: Rags and his medal

Sam and I went to the pond. His dog Rags was with us.
'There is a raft on the bank,' I said to Sam.
'Let us put it in the pond and sit on it.'
'Yes, yes,' said Sam.
We slid the raft from the bank into the pond.

Sam had just got a foot on the r▄ when it sank. Sam fell in.
'Help! Help! Get m▄ out quick!'
But it was Rags who got him o▄. With a bark Rags grabbed
Sam's coat and pulled.
    ▄ strong pull had Sam back on the bank. Rags g▄ a
medal, but Sam just got wet.

Answers

r . . .
m .
o . .
.
g . .

Appendix C
The table below represents the five-point scale used to record
children's and teacher's estimates of difficulty.

How hard you think it is

Too hard	A bit hard	Just right	A bit easy	Too easy

Bibliography

Bormuth, John R. (1966) 'Designing correlational readability studies'

in *Research Designs in Reading* Newark, Delaware: International l
Reading Association

Bormuth, John, R. (1966) 'Readability: A new approach' *Reading Research Quarterly* 1, 79-132

Bloomer, Richard H. (1962) 'The cloze procedure as a remedial reading exercise' *Journal of Developmental Reading* volume V, 173-181

Dale, E. and Chall, J. S. (1948) 'A formula for predicting readability' *Educational Research Bulletin* 27, 11-20

Gilliland, J. (1968) 'The concept of readability' *Reading* volume 2 no. 2, 24-29

Gilliland, J. (1969) 'An examination of measures of readability' *Reading* volume 3 no. 1, 16-21

Klare, G. R. (1966) 'Comments on Bormuth's readability: a new approach' *Reading Research Quarterly* 1, 119-125

Lorge, I. (1959) 'The Lorge Formula for estimating difficulty of reading materials' Bureau of Publications, Teachers College, Columbia University, New York

Merrit, J. E. (1969) 'The intermediate skills' in Gardner, K. (ed.)) *Reading Skills: Theory and Practice* London: Ward Lock Educational

Morse, Elizabeth (1952) *Chang* London: Dent

Schneyer, W. J. (1965) 'Use of the cloze procedure for improving reading comprehension' *The Reading Teacher* volume 19, no. 3, 174-179.

Part five
Towards literacy

Severe reading disability – Some important correlates

Gilbert R. Gredler

Professor of Educational Psychology and Chairman of Department of
School of Psychology
Temple University, Philadelphia

Reading problems in children continue to be of concern to many different
groups of individuals: school personnel, parents, and researchers. Of
particular concern to all is the child who shows extreme difficulty in
learning how to read and with whom the usual remedial methods have been
unsuccessful.

The intent of this paper is to review the problem of severe reading
disability and to look at important correlates of this condition in order to
arrive at some valid conclusions concerning causal factors and remedial
programmes. However, first we must look at the overall state of the field
today.

Definition of the problem

Hundreds of articles are written each year describing this or that facet of
reading disability. Most of these articles proclaim that they have 'unearthed',
'discovered', or documented 'fully' that x factor is a definite correlate of
reading disability and therefore should be attended to. Investigations of
the reading process have become so plentiful that many professional
magazines regularly devote one issue a year to a review of all the studies
completed.

Causes of this tremendous outpouring of 'research' are multitudinous
and beyond the scope of this particular paper. However, some attention
must be given to this matter or else the individual seeking out important
correlates of reading disability can be easily overwhelmed by 'research'
showing this or that conclusion.

Too often scholarship is defined by one's ability to mount an empirical

188

investigation of a particular topic, carry it through, and have it accepted for publication.

Increasingly journals are founded to take care of a group of 'scholars' who are in agreement on a basic set of ideas. Reading the issues of the *Journal of Applied Behavior Analysis*, one would have to conclude that we have at last found *the* way to control behaviour in the classroom; that the use of behaviour modification methods will invariably mean reduction if not elimination of all behaviour problems. Reading an issue of the *American Journal of Psychoanalysis*, one will be impressed by the documentation therein that the use of psychoanalytic methods will invariably result in improvement of behaviour and reduction of problems for the individual who undergoes such therapy. Reading an issue of the *Journal of Learning Disabilities*, one would feel that if we can only attend to the 'perceptual' factors in reading that there would be no reading problems.

While we can be glad that a large number of adherents of these various points of view have found a way to get their research and ideas published, this is not the real need of the day. What is needed today is a scholarly approach to the specific topic to be investigated, and a recognition of the deep-seated emotional conditions which impel the university researcher to proclaim that he has discovered *the* correlate of a disturbed condition or that he has found *the* method of eliminating the problem.

Opposing points of view within the field of reading

The field of reading is no stranger to opposing points of view. In discussing severe reading disability we have Critchley (1964) emphasizing the neurological component of the disability while at the same time heaping scorn on those who would stress emotional conditions as a factor. Clements (1962) also puts the matter quite strongly when he says:

> In the majority of present day training centers and institutions
> charged with teaching our future clinicians, regarding malajusted
> children, most of the emphasis is given to one side of the story only —
> the psychogenic side. The course material is steeped in the
> traditional stereotypes of sibling rivalry, rejecting parents,
> repressed hostility, oedipal conflict, repressed sexuality and the like.
> These are presented as being the major causes of deviant behavior,
> with only casual reference to the spectrum of organic factors which
> are primary to all learning and behavior. It is very like a child's game
> of make believe and we are playing like nothing new has been learned
> about human behavior over the past fifty years.

Rubin (1964) takes a more reasoned point of view when he tries to point

out that both emotional factors as well as perceptual and neurological
dysfunction can play a role in reading disability:

> . . . our approach and findings suggest the need to view emotional
> maladjustment as arising from more than one source. We must be
> ready to accept the possibility — even likelihood — that behavioral
> maladjustment, either of a withdrawing or aggressive type, may arise
> as a secondary phenomenon, the result of a child with certain types
> of limitations failing to cope adequately with the demands for
> adaptation made upon him by his family, his peers, or his school.
> In many instances the school experience quite unwittingly may be
> the chief stressor. . . . Our results suggest that dysfunction in
> cognitive-motor skills may play a very significant role in creating
> an increased vulnerability to life stresses.

It is an accepted fact of life that professionals with different kinds of
training will consider different factors of importance in a reading disability
case. Such emphasis is reflective of their narrow professional background
and efforts certainly need to be made to broaden this training. Another
facet has been now added to the current controversy with an attack on the
importance of medical and psychological diagnosis and studying the
etiology of reading disability. It is stated that a 'diagnostic teacher' in the
classroom is all that is necessary. For example,

> We tend to sustain a dependency relationship upon professions who
> are far less qualified than we to handle these (classroom)
> responsibilities. They have produced diagnostic processes that
> yield no information useful in a classroom setting.
> . . . The diagnostic teacher observes and experimentally teaches the
> referred child until she evolves an educational prescription which
> she has proven to be successful. She communicates this program to
> the child's teacher and works with the teacher, (and child), . . . with
> a complete de-emphasis on etiology and traditional categorical
> labelling. (Vinogradoff 1969)

While all of us are in agreement that part of the diagnostic process as
currently practised by school psychologist and physician is irrelevant and
that labelling is to be avoided, to say that the major sins committed on
special education and children with reading disabilities can be effectively
cured by either adding another diagnostician to the school setting or having
special education teachers do all the diagnostics, is to believe in fairy tales.

The main reason for this digression from consideration of severe reading
disability is to attempt to show how emotional and sociological aspects of a

situation will in turn determine what is perceived. For example, are the findings of the diagnostic examination of the educational psychologist or school psychologist on a retarded child or a child with severe reading disability really irrelevant to the classroom? Will the kind of diagnostics practised by a 'diagnostic teacher' automatically give all the information the teacher needs to be able to answer all the questions the teacher asks?

A main aim of this paper is to look at some valid correlates of severe reading disability — to go beyond the narrow confines of a specific discipline and attempt to indicate important factors involved in reading disability and to integrate such factors into an overall assessment of the point our present knowledge has reached.

A definition of reading disability

In order to talk of a disability in reading there must be agreement as to what constitutes this disability. Unfortunately, there is little consensus on this point. In addition to this lack of agreement, different population samples have also been utilized with, of course, disparate conclusions as to what psychological processes are actually involved.

Given below are some definitions of reading disability to indicate the considerable variations found:

1 The reading problem group scored below their grade level on a standardized reading test and are also retarded in classroom reading performance. (Trieschman 1968)

2 Dyslexic children are those who were one standard deviation or more below grade level and non-dyslexics are those whose reading ranged from the mean to a plus one standard deviation. (Anthony 1968)

3 Poor readers are defined as those whose reading scores fell into the lower 27 percent of the distribution of reading scores obtained from a standardized test. (Connor 1966)

Eisenberg (1966) helps us to see quite clearly the complexity of the situation by describing the relationship between socioeconomic level and reading retardation in his survey of sixth grade students. He found 57 percent of the children retarded by more than one year in an inner city school system as opposed to 19 percent in a suburban school system. He also found a higher percentage of males retarded than females, and ethnic differences between whites and Negroes.

Any discussion of reading disability, therefore, must deal with the factors of socioeconomic class, ethnic group membership and sex grouping. Too often studies of reading disability cases fail to take into account these sociological factors. By carefully considering possible etiological factors, we can gain much useful knowledge about reading disability. Eisenberg states that we must know the source of a fever in a population in order to gain valid information as to the epidemiology of infections. The same logic applies to the study of reading disability. To say that perceptual lags, emotional maladjustment and handedness problems are major determiners of the 57 per cent reading disability rate in the inner city school system, is to ignore the several other factors which play an important part. Poor teaching is more likely to be prevalent in the inner city school (Eisenberg 1966). A recent study (Beez 1968) indicates that lowered expectation on the part of teachers actually leads the teacher not only to expect less from such a child but not to attempt to teach the child the same number of learning exercises in comparison with a child who is perceived more positively.

Other factors that are important can be categorized as deficiencies in cognitive stimulation and deficiency in motivation, which can in turn be linked to social pathology as well as psychopathology (Eisenberg 1966).

In severe reading disability we are concerned with children whose reading shows a significant discrepancy below their age and ability level and is also not in accord with the child's cultural and educational experience (Harris 1970).

Factors involved in reading disability: Some important studies

The major thrust of this paper is a consideration of concomitants of specific reading disability. We are concerned with the children who fail to learn to read, despite adequate classroom instruction, and where cultural adequacy of the home environment, degree of motivation, sensory mechanism, and level of intelligence are not *major* determiners of the disability (Eisenberg 1966).

Too often severe reading disability is still seen as being linked to one factor rather than to a host of causative factors. The writer is impressed with the regularity of the classroom teacher's comment that a child has reading problems due to reversals (e.g. was for saw). What is often forgotten is that the normal child in learning to read manifests the same errors; the important variable for the severe disability case is the *frequency* and *persistence* of these errors (Eisenberg 1966). For example, Schonell (1942) found that by the age of eight to nine, 60 percent of all children backward in reading were still showing reversals of such letters as b, d, p, q, w and m, while only 12 percent of a sample of normal children did so.

Resistance to a careful consideration of the many faceted problem of severe reading disability is commonplace. Spache (1969) writes satirically on the various diagnostic and remedial absurdities he finds in the field. Abrams (1969) is concerned lest we forget that in reality emotional considerations ('disturbances in ego functioning') must still be foremost in any discussion of severe reading disability.

Isom (1969) offers us important information in his study of children's referral for reading retardation. He states his findings thus:

It was found that almost all poor readers were deficient in the ability to process sequentially presented material, particularly via the auditory as opposed to the visual channel. This deficit is expressed in developmental terms. The poor readers lagged behind the average readers with regard to the age at which they could state their complete birthdate, the months of the year or days of the week. They also lagged in the acquisition of ability to write, with correct spelling, their name, residential address, phone number, and the letters of the alphabet. These are behaviors or tasks that are learned by most children without formal instruction or with very limited instruction. The poor readers were universally unable to acquire these skills at the same age as children with normal reading ability.

Isom gives us a more sophisticated approach in looking at reading retardation, saying in effect that the syndrome also includes deficiencies as regards the concept of time, quantity and number, as well as a memory factor.

Anthony (1968) also helps us to see the interrelationship of several factors in his study of cerebral dominance and reading disability. Looking at dyslexics (children with reading scores a minimum of one standard deviation below the mean at the pupils' grade level) and non-dyslexics (children with reading scores from grade level to one standard deviation above the mean) Anthony divided these pupils into mixed-dominant and dominant categories, based on their performance on the Harris Tests of Laterality. Then he studied the importance of such factors as perceptual-motor level, directionality, as well as sensory integration in these two groups. Anthony's subjects were composed of sixty children with a mean chronological age of 8 years 6 months and of normal intelligence. The basic hypothesis of this study was that children who are dyslexic and mixed-dominant will also show below average perceptual development, will show more indications of neurological impairment, will perform more poorly on a measure of directional differentiation, as well as having more difficulty with tasks of auditory-visual integration.

What Anthony is saying is that a severely retarded reader of normal intelligence will manifest disturbances on a number of important dimensions. When such disturbances are found in conjunction with a child of mixed dominance, it will invariably mean the child is a poor reader.

The results from Anthony's study would indicate that mixed dominance status *by itself* does not predict a child's reading performance. This study also has important implications for the school psychologist. The results indicate more precisely the kind of diagnostic information needed in order to come to meaningful conclusions concerning the nature of the child's learning disabilities.

Anthony favours a maturational lag theory saying that such a lag is a global stress factor in that it limits the subject's coping capacity and thus serves to make the subject more vulnerable to environmental pressure.

The importance of directionality and laterality

Such findings also show the need for us to understand the conceptual importance of the development of directionality in the child. Jastak (1965) states that the letters a child is required to perceive can only be processed accurately if attention is given to their space or directional value. He holds that children with severe reading disability have failed to develop the proper directional clues which are necessary in learning to read. Thus, 'when the development of directional differentiation is blocked, reading disability results'. Jastak speculates that 'children with reading disability may be normal in all respects except to the acquisition of symbols based on directional clues'.

Basic to the development of directionality in the child is the establishment of laterality. Laterality is conceived as the awareness *within* the body of left and right. Directionality is considered to be the projection of of laterality onto external objects; it would deal with left and right differentiation of external objects in space (Anthony 1968).

The laterality status of the child in turn is supposedly reflective of lack of dominance in hemisphere development. Zangwill (1962) states the problem thus:

> On balance, the evidence suggests that an appreciable proportion of dyslexic children show poorly developed laterality . . . . If poorly developed laterality can be linked with incomplete cerebral dominance, it might be said that these patterns of disability reflect faulty establishment of asymmetrical (i.e. normally lateralized) functions in two hemispheres . . . but we have also to consider why all ill-lateralized children do not exhibit backwardness in reading.

A number of studies do indicate that many retarded readers show lack of lateralization of function or inconsistency of preference of hand, foot, and eye functions (Monroe 1932; Vernon 1957). Other investigations indicate that problems of measurement affect the result obtained. Silver (1963) questions whether peripheral dominance (i.e. eye, hand, foot, preference) reflects true cerebral dominance. Stephens *et al* (1967) in looking at eye/hand preferences and reading readiness of first grade children, question the importance of such preferences. They found no relationship between mixed eye/hand preferences, reading readiness, and performance on visual-motor tests.

They also state that their negative results indicate that neurological impairment or minimal brain dysfunction is not a factor in reading performance of first grade children. However one would question applying a label of neurological impairment to children showing only a mixed hand/eye performance pattern. Bond and Tinker (1967) cite a number of studies which indicate that there is no relationship between laterality and reading disability. In one such study (Karen Tinker 1965) no such relationship was found in a group of pupils from grades two, four and six. Here is where the difficulty arises, for the study is then quoted as further valid evidence that we should expect no relationship. The conclusion would be better stated that no relationship was found in children of superior ability, for only children whose mean IQ ranged from 126 to 131 were studied. Koos (1964) found a relationship between reading ability and mixed dominance but only for children below the median IQ of her sample. Similarly Trieschman (1968) found no relationship between mixed dominance and reading ability. In her sample only those children whose IQ was below 125 showed a reading retardation which was linked with mixed dominance of the subject.

In addition to raising questions about the influence of ability level, we need to question once again the attempt to find one causal factor which will explain the severity of the reading disability. Trieschman also makes the important point that differences in outcomes of studies as to important factors linked with reading disability are partially a function of how the sample of children is chosen. Children retarded in reading and chosen randomly from a school population such as Tinker's might show fewer disabling facets of their disability than children referred to some type of clinic for diagnosis and treatment.

Anthony's study mentioned previously is also important because it attempts to show how *one* factor such as mixed dominance *cannot* be utilized to explain all reading disability cases. But it does show very adequately how a number of factors taken together (i.e. mixed dominance status, poor perceptual development, below average directionality, inadequate intersensory performance) can all combine to limit the child's ability to learn to read.

The importance of perceptual factors in severe reading disability
A number of authorities have emphasized the importance of perceptual processes in learning to read. DeHirsch (1957) states how adequate

perceptual development is necessary or letters and words will remain undifferentiated and diffuse. Adequate development of spatial relationships is important or the child cannot cope with a pattern (i.e. words) which is laid out in space. Figure/ground relationships are important or the child will not be able to differentiate letters (figures) from the page (background). There must be adequate awareness of a L/R direction or the child cannot proceed with correctly understanding the symbol sequence of words.

Thus we might expect disturbance of the perceptual function to be one facet of a reading disability syndrome. And this often proves to be the case. In the study previously mentioned (Trieschman 1968) boys between seven and nine were studied to determine various factors which were present in those who were severely disabled readers. Children were presented with symbol material which reflected in part some of the features found in letters of the alphabet (i.e. straight lines, curved lines, angles etc). Results indicate that poor readers made many more perceptual errors than normal readers.

In this study perceptual competency was measured by the child's ability to match the standard stimulus with comparison stimuli. The results reinforce Jastak's (1965) ideas wherein he emphasizes that accurate performance in the reading process involves attention to the space and directional aspect of the letters. Thus children who have severe reading problems frequently will have failed to develop the proper directional clues which are necessary in learning to read. Adequate directional differentiation can be measured in part by performance on perceptual tasks such as those used by Trieschman.

In another study which dealt with boys aged 8 years 10 months to 10 years 11 months, and who were all two to three years below expected grade level, the subjects were consistently below age expectations on a test of visual-motor performance. Yet all these children showed additional dysfunctions, i.e. performance scale in excess of verbal on an ability scale; conceptual difficulties in space, time and directional areas, and articulatory difficulties (Haworth 1970).

Gredler (1969) cites the importance of visual perception in reading disability. He stresses, as does Benton (1962), that the development of visual perceptual abilities is of special importance when the young child is learning to read. Here is where adequate perceptual abilities will aid the child in perceiving the similarities and differences of letters and words. Adequate development of spatial relationships will aid the child to successfully perceive the pattern of letters which are laid out in space. Adequate visual perceptual development will result in the child being able to note the differences in two dimensional visual symbols. (Gofman 1966) Lovell's (1964) work can also be cited wherein he found perceptual dysfunction in a group of backward readers. It was Lovell's thesis that some cortical or subcortical dysfunction disturbs visual perception and in turn results in limited progress in reading.

Gibson (1966) emphasizes that learning to differentiate the graphic symbols is *one* important element in learning to read. She adds that there are several different aspects of the reading process which are important: receiving communication, decoding graphic symbols and relating them to speech and getting meaning from the printed word. Gibson states that once the child progresses from spoken language to written language there are three stages of learning tasks which must be looked at: (i) learning to perceive differences in graphic symbols; (ii) learning to associate letters with sounds; (iii) learning to use progressively more complicated units of structure as typified by spelling patterns. It is therefore logical to expect some disturbance of the visual perceptual process in disabled readers if we concede that learning to perceive differences in graphic symbols is one important aspect of the reading process.

In one study, Gibson (1963) investigated the perception of graphic symbols which were similar to letters. The task involved perceiving differences between the standard stimulus and transformation of that stimulus. The subject was required to match the standard stimulus with an identical form. Gibson found a decrease in number of errors made from age four to eight years and also found a high relationship between such errors and errors made with transformation of real letters.

Some of this material was used in Trieschman's work which has been previously cited. In another study Gibson and Gibson (1955) investigated the relationship between a standard stimulus figure and variants of that standard stimulus. Their rationale was that perceptual development will reflect increase in specificity of response. Drawings similar to scribbles were used as standard stimuli. Other cards were presented which differed from the original drawing on three dimensions: (a) the number of coils present; (b) the degree of compression or stretching; (c) the orientation of the figure (two kinds). In addition other cards were made up which contained stimuli quite different from the standard stimulus cards and thus were easily distinguishable. Results indicated that the younger the child the less the specificity reacted to by the subject.

In one of the few experiments done using the Gibson material, Whipple and Kodman (1969) investigated perceptual learning of fourth and fifth graders of normal intelligence and whose reading level ranged from eight to twenty-four months below their grade placement level. The results indicate that the perceptual level abilities of the child retarded in reading were distinctively inferior to those of the normal reader with the same IQ. Checking the norms of this task it was found that the perceptual ability of the ten year olds was similar to the perceptual ability level of the normal six to eight year olds used in the Gibson and Gibson study.

Gibson states that perceptual development reflects both maturation and learning. She contends that performance on the perceptual level tasks mentioned above reflect both the influence of age and changes which occur as the results of practice. For her the child's perceptual development (or his reduction in stimulus dependency) is tied in with attentional ability. (Gibson 1963). With an adequate attentional level the child has learned to select the critical aspects of the stimuli present to him. Vernon (1970) puts the issue somewhat differently:

> . . . it would seem that any increase in the extent and accuracy of form perception through learning is doubtful. Where there is some improvement, it probably results from improvement in the capacity to direct attention towards particular aspects or details of the forms presented which facilitates their discrimination and identification.

How improvement in perceptual development can come about and can be planned for cannot be considered in detail at this time. But we can state briefly the important features of perceptual development. Gibson says that criteria of perceptual learning include an increase in specificity of discrimination which is also called an increase in correspondence with the stimulus offered. In perceptual learning the capacity of ascertaining the distinctive features of objects and learning invariant relationships is acquired. For Gibson adequate spatial orientation would mean that an object in space is seen the same regardless of how it is oriented. However a child learning to read must supplant the law of object constancy (Money 1966) as defined above with the law of directional constancy wherein an alphabetic letter cannot change its position without changing its name or meaning (e.g. h and y). In addition the law of form constancy (Money 1966) means that a letter can be changed only within certain limits before it is considered a different letter (e.g. c and e). But other differences are tolerated and the letter will be the same regardless of these differences (e.g. g and G). Money also adds that there can be difficulty with conceptual discrimination in such words as their − there, to − too.

Goins (1958) investigated the role of visual perception in the reading achievement of young children. Her work indicates the importance of being able to hold a gestalt in mind against distraction. Obviously competence in this task involves being able to note details of the perceptual figure. For Goins a successful performance on a perceptual test requires manipulating parts of the whole with the whole pattern acting as a distractor. On a perceptual test of reversals, successful performance requires ability to keep in mind a figure against the distraction and confusion of figure and ground (i.e. the reversed and non-reversed figures). Success on these tasks indicates that the child shows adequate strength of closure.

198

Of course strength of closure reflects ability to deal with the specificity of the stimulus figure as outlined by Gibson. For Vernon (1970) adequate performance on such perceptual tasks as incomplete patterns and reversal figures would also reflect successful scanning and search efforts on the part of the child.

The controversy concerning the role of visual perception

It would seem from the foregoing discussion that there would be some consensus as to the importance of visual perception in the development of reading and in reading disability, but Vernon (1958) states:

> It seems possible that the childish tendency to overlook the orientation and order of shapes and letters is prolonged in the backward reader, partly as the result of continued immaturity, but partly also because of his general cognitive confusion.

Vernon also emphasizes that the children may show poor visual memory:

> Memorization of shapes, or the names given to shapes, may be defective.

She continues:

> It appears that some cases of severe reading retardation, but not all, do show a poor ability to relate shapes and details of shapes and to reason about them. We cannot assume, however, that the inability to read is due to this deficiency. It is possible . . . that it is a sign of lack of maturation. The normal reader may grow out of this immature type of behavior. But backward readers may fail to do so because they have not developed habits of orderly and systematic analysis of shapes into their essential constituents. This deficiency then is the result rather than the cause of the reading disability; or both may be produced by some other defect. (Vernon 1958)

Thus for Vernon, the emphasis on defects in visual perceptual development have been overstressed. She would emphasize the failure of the disabled reader in analyzing, abstraction and generalization, all of which can be subsumed under the overall label of cognitive difficulties.

Wolf is also quite concerned lest we overemphasize visual perception as an important factor in reading disability. He states:

> One variable that has received considerable attention in the literature as related to specific dyslexia is visual perception. With the exception of the suggested difficulties in visual imagery and visual memory,

controlled studies have failed to substantiate that visual imperception is relevant to specific dyslexia. (Wolf 1968)

Benton (1962) also inveighs against assigning too much influence to the role of visual perception in reading disability. He states:

My conclusion is that deficiency in visual form perception is not an important correlate of developmental dyslexia.

However Benton states that a certain level of visual perceptive development is obviously necessary in learning how to read. He mentions that retardation in this area will affect the child's progress in acquiring reading skills.

But this factor accounts . . . for only a very small proportion of cases of developmental dyslexia in older school children (i.e. above the age of ten).

Critchley (1970) concurs with Benton's approach to the problem. Much of the controversy as to the relative influence of visual perception in reading disability is reminiscent of the argument concerning the role of eye movements in reading disability. Faulty eye movements were once held responsible for poor reading. (Hildreth 1936) However Critchley maintains, as do other authorities, that faulty eye movements may be better considered as an outcome of difficulty in reading. This is the same thesis used in arguing against the primacy of visual perceptual development. Instead the child with poor development in visual perception is seen as showing an 'immature' type of behaviour due to lack of development of habits of systematic analysis of shapes. For Vernon the defect in visual perception is a result rather than a cause of reading disability.

However, if we follow Gibson's thesis we would need to consider seriously the idea that a child with severe reading disability is often an individual whose perceptual learning has not kept pace with other children. Thus special attention would need to be given to this area.

For Vernon it is 'cognitive incapacity' of some kind or other that needs to be ascertained. Discussion of cause and effect here is important for the programming implications involved. In the USA much importance is attached today to visual perceptive training. Frostig, in contrast to Benton and Vernon, places major emphasis on perceptual development:

The development of visual perceptive processes is the major function of the growing child between the ages of three and seven and . . . at this age level perceptual development becomes a most sensitive

indicator of the developmental status of the child as a whole.
(Frostig 1963)

Kessler (1970) reacts somewhat negatively to the emphasis on visual perception:

On the face of it, it seems reasonable to say that a child does not 'perceive' the 'gestalt' of letters or words and cannot read, but there is a danger of circular reasoning, that is, giving the phenomenon of failure to read another fancier name.

Kessler feels the perceptual proponents have not precisely stated their theoretical assumptions:

The explanation as to why a given child should have the perceptual deficit is vaguely given as a function left behind in successive waves of maturation.

Kessler also questions Frostig's emphasis on the development of perceptual processes in the child of five to seven and suggests that cognitive development within that age period might influence perceptual development. (Kessler 1970)

Perhaps some of the difficulties of ferreting out the exact role of visual perception in the reading process is that researchers tend to be victims of a stereotypy of thinking that a factor must have an all or none influence. We must be prepared to understand that cognitive variables, as well as perceptual and personality variables, may also be specifically involved in severe reading disability. To say that one particular factor *must* predominate is to underestimate the complexity of psychological processes which operate within any individual. It would appear that there is no one persuasive factor which can be held accountable for severe reading disability whether it be perceptual, cognitive or motivational in nature.

An example of two factors (perceptual and cognitive) which combine to affect performance is seen on the letter recognition test. In this test a child is exposed to a line of letters and asked to find and circle a certain letter. Many of the letters used are those commonly confused by children with severe reading disability. The score is the number of seconds required for the child to locate all the letters. Dyslexic children do quite poorly on this kind of test. (Wolf 1968) We would postulate that this would be so if we follow perceptual theories of directional and form constancy. (Money 1962) However Wolf points out that the identity of a letter is more than a perceptual act; it also involves cognition. Vernon would probably emphasize that performance on the letter recognition test reflects the degree of competency of search procedures on the part of the child.

In this study of dyslexic readers at the third and fourth grade level Wolf categorized the children into subgroups based on variables with the highest factor loadings. He found three different syndrome patterns containing fourteen variables which differentiated three groups of dyslexics from each other and from normal reading groups. It is interesting to note that one dyslexic subgroup was quite low in the letter recognition subtest, one performed at an average level and one above average. Yet the subgroup that performed best on the letter recognition test performed most poorly on the verbal scale of the IQ test, and the subgroup that performed best on the verbal scale performed most poorly on the letter recognition subtest.

If, as has been suggested, the letter recognition test is perceptual-conceptual in nature then we might have expected, based on prior reasoning, that those children with the higher verbal IQ might have done better. That they did not suggests the need for measures such as the letter recognition test in order to tease out all the specific processes involved in the dyslexic's difficulties.

Also popular as a measure of perceptual development is the Bender-Gestalt. Results of several studies have shown its sensitivity to perceptual development in retarded and normal readers. Bean (1967) found a significant difference in performance on the Bender with retarded and normal readers from grades seven, eight and nine. Connor's (1968) study of Bender performance of good and poor readers however, indicates some of the pitfalls of interpretation in trying to assess the importance of the perceptual performance in reading.

Connor (1968) investigated perceptual test performance in good and poor reading groups at the first grade level. He found, as was to be expected, that poor readers make more errors on the Bender-Gestalt. Numbers of distortion errors were also found significantly more often in the poor reading group. Connor went one step further and asked if significant group differences also meant that we could predict reading performance of individuals from their Bender scores.

When comparing Bender scores of good and poor readers, he found no difference as to number above or below the mean Bender scores for the chronological age of the group. Connor concludes that 'such test performance should be used with extreme caution in predicting or diagnosing poor reading performance'.

Perhaps it would be more accurate to state that when significant differences are found between groups on any test, such differences will not necessarily mean that the test can be used to predict accurately the performance of specific individuals.

Connor defined his sample by taking the upper and lower 27 percent of the second group population as representatives of good and poor readers. Poor readers thus defined would probably have different characteristics than a sample drawn from a clinic population.

In a monumental study by Doehring (1968), patterns of impairments in severe reading disabilities were also investigated. Results indicated that a wide variety of skills were impaired and that retarded readers had the most difficulty with visual or verbal tasks which required sequential processing of material. Doehring rejects the theory that immaturity of gestalt functioning as reported on perceptual tests was of primary importance. However, most of his perceptual measures were measures of perceptual speed which would be only one aspect of visual perceptual development. On one perceptual test (Thurstone Reversals) retarded readers performed significantly more poorly. Doehring considers such a test more of a measure of directionality, while other investigators (Goins 1958) have cited it as one important aspect of overall perceptual development. It is important to note that while Doehring found sequential processing skills poorly developed in his retarded readers aged ten to fourteen, Weiner (1970) found no difference in the sequential processing skill of her sample of good and poor readers of fourth grade level. Weiner makes the same statement that Benton makes about the role of visual perception in reading, namely that serial-order ability may be a more important variable in the reading performance of young children.

Recent research on visual perception

The importance of visual perception in the academic process is seen in a study of first graders matched as to IQ but separated into high and low groups on the basis of a perceptual measure. (Ferguson 1967)

Results indicated that those children with perceptual quotients of below 90 on the Frostig will be below grade level in reading and arithmetic at the end of first grade. In a followup study of these children it was found that the differences between the high and low perceptual groups persisted up to and throughout the second grade. (Fullwood 1968) While such studies dramatically illustrate the importance of the visual perceptive factor we must express caution in drawing conclusions.

While the groups were equated on the major variable of intelligence through the use of the Stanford Binet, we must ask if there were not other factors of major importance which could help to account for the differences at the end of the first grade and second grade. To explain adequately the differential functioning of these two groups, specific study of such processes as directionality, intersensory integration and personality functioning should be directly assessed. For example, 14 percent of the high perceptual group did not achieve up to the level predicted at the end of the second grade, which suggests that other factors were operating which need to be investigated.

It is our thesis that a number of factors are involved in the successful accomplishment of the act of reading. The principles of perceptual learning are indeed specific enough, so that when these principles are inadequately incorporated into the repertoire of the developing child he will have difficulty in learning to read. For the older child with severe reading disability, there is sufficient perceptual disability found that for many of such children inadequate progress in the perceptual area would be a major contributor to the reading disability.

Because successful academic achievement involves a level of maturity of several cognitive processes, auditory and visual perceptual maturity, adequate motivational level and a certain minimum level of emotional adjustment, attention must also be given to these factors in any study of reading disability.

A study by Lovell and Gorton (1968) provides us with further insight into factors involved in severe reading disability. Fifty backward readers, nine to ten in chronological age and with normal intelligence, were studied in an effort to ascertain the various psychological factors involved in the syndrome. A control group of fifty normal readers was also utilized.

Six components were extracted in the factor analysis; these components accounted for 86 percent of the variance of the scores in the retarded group and 77 percent of the variance in the normal group. Most important of the factors extracted was one labelled by Lovell and Gorton as reflecting a neurological integrity-impairment syndrome which accounted for 48 percent of the variance. Included in this component were measures of auditory-visual integration, figure rotation, spatial orientation, left/right discrimination, and motor performance.

This investigation can be considered a more sophisticated approach to ascertaining important attributes of reading disability. The authors have recognized that a number of factors have to be considered as being involved with the poor reading performance of children.

Theories of causation

The label given to a specific condition often determines future attitudes about the individual involved. Educators often inveigh against the use of the word dyslexia because they feel it implies that little can be done to help the child. Bender (1958) postulates that maturational lag in gestalt formation or an undifferentiated abstractedness is the prime factor involved in language and reading difficulties. But Vernon (1958) gets quite upset when such theories are expounded saying:

> All theories which attribute reading disability to some general lack
> of maturation are unsatisfactory in that they give no explanation as
> to why reading alone should be affected, and no other cognitive
> activities.

If we will concede that the term 'maturational lag' is but an indication of cortical immaturity or degree of neurological integration, then we can perhaps consider it to have a primary role in reading disability. The results of Lovell and Gorton's study certainly indicate that there is a neurological component which is important in reading achievement. Impairment in this area will result in reading retardation.

However, the term 'immaturity' is to be avoided at all costs. This word has such negative connotations that little will be done for a child so labelled. A typical American response to a young child who is doing poorly in reading is to say that he is 'immature' and that he should have stayed at home another year or repeated kindergarten so that he would then be mature enough to start the reading process. A study by Gold (1966) indicates that the favourite term to diagnose reading difficulties of children referred to a dyslexic centre was that they were 'immature'.

It is also important to avoid this term because it tends to absolve school personnel of any responsibility to help the child. The term 'immaturity' is so non-specific and nebulous in scope that it offers no real clue as to what is wrong with the child, and why he cannot cope with the reading process successfully.

Ascribing reading difficulty to a developmental lag or to cortical immaturity is but a small step for many teachers to an acceptance of a generalized concept of overall immaturity as *the* reason for poor reading. In all time-oriented systems, a time for starting school must be selected (Cohen 1970). American children start to go to school between 5 years 9 months and 6 years 5 months old; British children start school a year before. Yet many teachers in both systems ascribe a child's failure to the fact that he is 'immature' and needs another year to grow up and then all will be well. The importance of being more precise is self-evident. How we can effectively programme for the child is the important question.

Theoretical positions on reading disability: A summary

It is evident that a number of researchers can be identified as having a particular bias concerning causal factors which will 'explain' disability in reading. Unfortunately, many investigations of severe reading retardation are nothing more than a thinly disguised treatise in championing a particular viewpoint. Modern statistical techniques are used to 'prove' conclusively that such and such a factor is important. While there is no substitute for sound research and statistical design, there *is* a great need for an objective appraisal of the point we have reached in our total understanding of the severely disabled reader.

We know that there still exists a school of thought which emphasizes that reading retardation is primarily tied in with the neurotic defences of the individual. While definite attention has to be given to the status of ego controls of the reader, we also agree with Clements that too many reading cases have been dismissed as reflective only of neurotic symptoms. Others have been guilty in overvaluing the importance of a single index such as mental ability, forgetting that wide differences in reading performance are found in children of the same ability level.

Then there is a school of thought which has emphasized the neurological component in the child's reading difficulty. This school has progressed from being concerned only with organic brain damage to a consideration of minimal brain dysfunction to the current emphasis on central processing dysfunctions as the important factor in reading disability. Also included in this neurological school are those who think that ascertaining cerebral dominance or laterality in the child is a sufficient explanatory concept of reading disability. At present there are those who champion the perceptual factor as being *the* most important.

The concept of 'maturational lag' or immaturity of a specific function is preferable to an overall indictment of the child as 'immature'. For Money (1966) rotation errors are indicative of 'developmental dyslexia with arrest at an immature level'. He talks of maturational lag showing itself in a variety of ways — by slow language development or delayed maturation of intersensory transfer. He also mentions that such lag may be due to neurological deficits. This latter concept is similar to Rabinovitch's delineation of primary reading retardation in which there is a 'disturbed pattern of neurologic organization' (1962).

Bender (1966) speaks of maturational lag as 'slow differentiation in an established pattern'. For Bender, children with dyslexia show 'neurologic patterns (which) remain immature and poorly differentiated and the longitudinal course shows lags in maturation. Global primitiveness and plasticity in all the perceptual experiences with immature perceptual motor gestalten involve the child's own self-awareness, body image, identification, time, and space orientation and object and interpersonal relationships . . . .'

Bender poses an interesting point when she questions whether a child who is of borderline impairment as regards congential immaturities and motivational problems may 'compensate and never manifest a clinical problem in the absence of exogenous strains'.

Two recent studies help to further clarify the concept of 'immaturity'. Hyatt (1968) found that first grade children referred as 'immature' by their teachers showed deficits in several areas of psycholinguistic functioning and remained at these deficit levels up to and including their second year at school. Those children who had deficits in visual-motor sequencing and auditory-vocal sequencing Hyatt called poor in 'active listening and seeing'. She states:

The child must be able to think and interpret as he listens and sees and maintain this activity over long periods of time to keep up with ongoing developments in the classroom.

Hyatt suggests that the children found to be seriously deficient in the above sequencing skills be placed with highly trained specialists who would follow a very carefully worked out programme with them. Her proposals are important to note for this marks the appearance of an attempt to redefine the reading difficulties and resultant school failure of the young child on grounds other than overall emotional immaturity or being 'too young'.

Others also argue for redirection of our work with children who have learning disabilities. Santostefano (1969) suggests that the dyslexic child may scan printed material in a passive manner and take in only small bits of information at a time. He, therefore, would attempt to programme for the child in order to increase the amount and rate of information with which he can deal. His interest is in rehabilitating the cognitive controls the child is utilizing.

While we may rightly be concerned with the mechanistic aspects of the behaviour modification school and of the central processing deficit model, nevertheless proponents of these approaches are attempting to pinpoint factors important in the child's learning problems. This approach is to be preferred to categorizing a child as emotionally immature or ascribing his difficulties to the fact that he came to school too young.

Currently popular among some researchers is the 'expectation bias' phenomenon (Beez 1968) as an explanatory concept of why some children do not do well in learning tasks. This school of thought is a reflection of the importance of the attitudinal structure when attempting to explain lack of learning.

A school psychologist or educational psychologist called upon to diagnose the reading problems of an elementary school child will certainly need to understand as fully as possible the various theoretical positions on severe reading disability. For each such case he will want to look at the following:

1 Personality structure so as to be able to make valid statements about the child's motivation.
2 The cognitive structure of the child.
3 The central processing mechanisms and their level of operation.
4 The environment of the school which means not only the quality of the interaction going on in the classroom, but the quality of the teaching.

Bibliography

Abrams, J. C. (1969) 'Further considerations of the ego-functioning of the dyslexic child — A psychiatric viewpoint' in Spache, G. D. (ed.) *Reading*

Disability and Perception Newark, Delaware: International Reading Association

Anthony, G. (1968) *Cerebral dominance as an etiological factor in dyslexia* Unpublished doctoral dissertation, New York University

Bean, W. J. (1967) *The isolation of some psychometric indices of severe reading disabilities* Unpublished doctoral dissertation, Texas Technological College

Beez, W. V. (1968) *Influence of biased psychological reports on teacher behavior and pupil performance* Proceedings, 76th Annual Convention American Psychological Association, 605-606

Bender, L. (1968) 'Neuropsychiatric disturbances' in Keeney, A. H. and Keeney, V. T. (eds.) *Dyslexia: Diagnosis and treatment of reading disorders* St Louis: C. V. Mosby

Benton, A. L. (1962) 'Dyslexia in relation to form perception and directional sense' in Money, J. (ed.) *Reading disability and progress and research needs in dyslexia* Baltimore, Maryland: John Hopkins Press

Bond, G. L. and Tinker, M. A. (1967) *Reading difficulties: Their diagnosis and correction* New York: Appleton-Century-Crofts

Clements, S. and Peters, S. J. (1962) 'Minimal brain dysfunction in the school age child' *Archives of general psychiatry* 6, 185-197

Cohen, R. (1970) 'The role of immaturity in reading disabilities' *Journal of learning disabilities* 3, no. 2, 73-74

Connor, J. P. (1966) *The relationship of Bender visual motor gestalt test performance to differential reading performance of second grade children* Unpublished doctoral dissertation, Kent State University

Critchley, Mac D. (1964) *Developmental dyslexia* London: Heinemann

Critchley, Mac D. (1970) *The Dyslexic Child* Springfield, Illinois: C. C. Thomas

DeHirsch, K. (1957) 'Tests designed to discover potential reading difficulties at the six year old level' *American Journal of Orthopsychology* 27, 566-576

Doehring, D. G. (1968) *Patterns of impairment in specific reading disability* Bloomington: Indiana University Press

Eisenberg, L. (1966) 'The epidemiology of reading retardation and a program for preventive intervention' in Money, J. (ed.) *The disabled reader* Baltimore, Maryland: John Hopkins Press

Ferguson, N. U. (1967) *The Frostig – An instrument for predicting total academic readiness and reading and arithmetical achievement in the first grade* Unpublished doctoral dissertation, University of Oklahoma

Fullwood, H. L. (1968) *A followup study of children selected by the Frostig developmental test of visual perception in relation to their success or failure in reading and arithmetic at the end of second grade* Unpublished doctoral dissertation, University of Oklahoma

Gibson, J. J. and Gibson, E. G. (1955) 'Perceptual learning: Differentiation or enrichment' *Psychological Review* 62, 33-40

Gibson, E. J. (1963) 'Perceptual development' in Stevenson, H. W. (ed.) *62nd yearbook of the national society for the study of education* Chicago: University of Chicago Press

Gibson, E. J. (1966) 'Experimental psychology of learning and reading' in Money, J. (ed.) *The disabled reader* Baltimore, Maryland: John Hopkins Press

Gibson, E. J. (1968) *Trends in perceptual development* Paper presented at meeting of Eastern Psychological Association, Washington DC

Gofman, H. T. (1966) 'The training of the physician in evaluation and management of the educationally handicapped child' in Hellnuth, J. (ed.) *Educational therapy* volume 1 Seattle: Special Child Publications

Goins, J. T. (1958) 'Visual perceptual abilities and early reading progress' *Supplement Educational Monograph* no. 87 Chicago: University of Chicago Press

Gold, L., Heubner, F. M. and Bice, M. O. (1968) 'Characteristics of pupils who attend a regional learning center for treatment of developmental dyslexia' data cited in Harris, A. J. (1970) *How to increase reading ability* New York: David McKay

Gredler, G. R. (1968) 'Performance on a perceptual test with children from a culturally deprived background' in Smith, H. K. (ed.) *Perception and reading* Newark, Delaware: International Reading Association

Gredler, G. R. (1969) 'A study of factors in childhood dyslexia' in Arena, J. I. (ed.) *Selected papers on learning disabilities* Pittsburgh Association for Children with Learning Disabilities

Gredler, G. R. (1969) 'Factors in severe reading disability: The psychological test correlates' in *Selected Convention Papers* Washington DC Council for Exceptional Children

Haworth, M. R. (1970) *The primary visual motor test* New York: Grune and Stratton

Hildreth, G. (1936) *Learning the three Rs* Minneapolis: Minneapolis Education Publications

Hildreth, G. (1950) 'Development and training of hand dominance: IV Developmental problems associated with handedness' in *Journal of Genetic Psychology* 76, 39-100

Hyatt, G. (1968) *Some psycholinguistic characteristics of first graders who have reading problems at the end of second grade* Unpublished doctoral dissertation, University of Oregon

Jastak, J. and Jastak, S. (1965) *Wide Range Achievement Manual* Wilmington: Delaware Guidance Associates

Isom, J. B. (1969) 'An interpretation of dyslexia: A medical viewpoint' in Spache, G. D. (ed.) *Reading disability and perception* Newark, Delaware: International Reading Association

Kessler, J. (1970) 'Contributions of the mentally retarded toward a theory of cognitive development' in Hellmuth, J. (ed.) *Cognitive studies*, 1 New York: Brunner/Mazel

Koos, E. (1964) 'Manifestations of cerebral dominance and reading retardation in primary grade children' in *Journal of Genetic Psychology* 104, 155-165

Lovell, K. (1964) 'A study of some cognitive and other disabilities in backward readers of average intelligence as assessed by a non-verbal test *British Journal of Educational Psychology* 34, 58-64

Lovell, K. and Gordon, A. (1968) 'A study of some differences between backward readers of average intelligence as assessed by a non-verbal test *Educational Psychology* 38 Part 3, 240-248

Money, J. (1962) 'Dyslexia: A postconference review' in Money, J. (ed.) *Reading disability: Progress and research needs in dyslexia* Baltimore, Maryland: John Hopkins Press

Money, J. (1966) 'On learning and not learning to read' in Money, J. (ed.) *The disabled reader* Baltimore, Maryland: John Hopkins Press

Rubin, E. Z. (1964) *Secondary emotional disorders in children with perceptual motor dysfunction* Paper presented at annual meeting, American Orthopsychiatric Association, Chicago, Illinois

Santostefano, S. (1969) 'Cognitive controls vs. cognitive styles: An approach to diagnosing and treating cognitive disability in children' *Seminars in Psychiatry* 1 no. 3, 291-317

Silver, A. A. (1963) 'Diagnostic considerations in children with reading disability' *Bulletin of the Orton Society* XIII

Spache, G. D. (1969) 'Diagnosis and remediation in 1980' in Spache, G. D. (ed.) *Reading disability and perception* Newark, Delaware: International Reading Association

Stephens, W. E., Cunningham, E. S. and Stigler, B. J. (1967) 'Reading readiness and eye/hand reference patterns in first grade children' *Exceptional Children* 33, 7, 441-576

Stillwell, R. J., Artuso, A. A., Hewett, F. M., and Taylor, F. D. (1970) 'An educational solution' *Focus on Children* 2, no. 1, 1-15

Tinker, K. J. (1965) 'The role of laterality in reading disability' in Figurel, J. A. (ed.) *Reading and enquiry* Newark, Delaware: International Reading Association

Trieschman, R. B. (1968) 'Undifferentiated handedness and perceptual development in children with reading problems' *Perceptual and Motor Skills* 27, 1123-1134

Vinogradoff, V. (1969) *The role and function of the diagnostic teacher* Paper presented at annual meeting of Council for Exceptional Children, Denver, Colorado

Vernon, M. D. (1958) *Backwardness in reading* Cambridge: Cambridge University Press

Vernon, M. D. (1970) *Perception through experience* London: Methuen

Weiner, J., Barnsley, R. H. and Rabinovitch, M. S. (1970) 'Serial order ability in good and poor readers' *Canadian Journal of Behavioral Science* 2, 116-123

Whipple, C. I. and Kodman, F. Jr. (1969) 'A study of discrimination and perceptual learning with retarded readers' *Journal of Educational Psychology* 60, no. 1, 1-5

Wolf, C. W. (1969) 'Psychoneurological and educational characteristics of specific dyslexia' in Knowlton, D. and Kratoville, B. (eds.) *Ideas for action* Proceedings of the 14th convention of the Texas Association for Children with Learning Disabilities Houston, Texas: ACLD

Zangwill, O. L. (1962) 'Dyslexia in relation to cerebral dominance' in Money, J. (ed.) *Reading disability progress and research needs in dyslexia* Baltimore, Maryland: John Hopkins Press

The Flying Start early education kit: Rationale and description

D. H. Stott

Chairman of the Centre for Educational Disability and Professor of
Psychology
University of Guelph, Ontario

Reading failure is diagnosed in terms of cultural disadvantage, emotional
block, perceptual handicap, minimal brain damage, word blindness, crossed
laterality, immaturity — but implicitly the favourite has simply been low
intelligence. Many studies of the causes of reading disability cut out
children of so called low intelligence from the experimental sample as having
a self-evident cognitive disability. Consequently little of value to the
teacher is discovered about such children although they make up the
majority of disabled readers.

If a child cannot learn by the methods we are using to teach him, it is
comforting to be able to say 'He only has an IQ of so and so'. The
danger of such fatalistic explanations is that they tempt us to give up trying.
Why, after all, hit one's head against a brick wall? Some people even go
so far as to get worried about trying to teach a child to read until he has
reached a certain mental age, as if it were a form of cruelty.

I am going to describe quite a different way of approaching reading
failure that has been the foundation of our research in the Centre for
Educational Disabilities at the University of Guelph in Ontario. A child's
style of learning is seen as an aspect of his general style of behaviour
or the way in which he copes with life.

Any teacher with special school experience will have known children
with such severe behavioural handicaps that it is impossible even to begin
to teach them to read or to teach them anything else. They may never be
in the same place for more than a minute or two, or be so unresponsive
that one can make no headway at all. Many such are found in schools for
the severely retarded. We cannot discover what their mental potential is
because we cannot get through the behavioural barrier. As we find
them they are, in a formal sense, ineducable. Parents give instances of
their 'intelligence' but no one takes any notice of these awkward, isolated
contradictions.

It is tempting to conclude that, but for their behaviour problems,
these children could be of normal intelligence. But to put it thus would be
confusing the issue. Our concept of intelligence is compounded of the
quality and complexity of the behaviour that a person can put forth.
Being intelligent is doing intelligent things and being stupid is doing
stupid things. It is all a matter of behaviour.

Our new approach consisted in studying learning disabilities in behavioural terms or — if you like — of faults in the way a child copes with life. It is instructive to observe the spontaneous ways in which a representative group of five year old children tackle tasks. Some set about learning in an admirable way, without needing to be taught how to do so. Others, in varying degrees, do not know how to learn. Whatever intelligence they possess is not being used properly. In effect, those who of their own accord use good learning strategies come to be looked upon as the intelligent children, and the others as the not so intelligent. But this way of looking at individual differences is both unhelpful and unprogressive. If instead we train ourselves to observe the different learning styles that children adopt, we naturally begin to ask ourselves whether we can improve these styles, that is to say, teach them how to learn and make them what is ordinarily called more intelligent.

The essence of our approach was thus to identify common faults of learning style and to invent means of correcting them. These faults correspond to certain well known types of temperament. I can show what I mean by briefly describing two main types which account for perhaps eighty or ninety percent of our poor readers.

First there is what we call the 'unforthcoming' child. He decides in advance that learning is too difficult for him. He is frightened by anything which appears strange or complex. He becomes petrified when you try to make him give an answer and you can hardly get a word out of him. At best he will half give an answer and watch for encouraging signs from the teacher. It is a general attitude to life, he is timid like a little mouse. Learning is a real anxiety. But one thing he does learn; if he can't do a task the adult helps him. If the teacher thinks he hasn't the ability, she won't make demands upon him, so he takes refuge in dullness. His retreat into incompetence saves him from being pestered by people who try to make him face up to what seem to him difficult problems. So he gets relief from his anxiety. And the teacher's off the hook too. By accepting his dullness at its face value her professional competence is saved. In extreme cases the school calls in the psychologist and he's fooled too.

The truth is that his dullness is a false adjustment to life which, with his handicap of temperament, brings him rewards. In a sense we have trained him to be dull. But we can't just call his bluff. He is suffering from a real handicap. He needs special help to give him the confidence to use his mind.

At the opposite extreme is the 'inconsequential' child. He is willing to try anything — too willing. He cuts out an essential preparatory stage of behaviour i.e. thinking what the consequences will be. He rushes into everything, guesses, doesn't use his eyes as we say. He suffers from a general maladjustment or handicap of temperament which is seen as distractibility, impulsiveness, inattention. In recent years he has come in for quite a lot of professional name calling, often being diagnosed as minimally brain damaged or perceptually handicapped. There may indeed be some neurological damage, but the handicap we can observe is one of behaviour, of the way he sets about or doesn't set about learning. He acts without giving himself time to think things out. We may say that he short circuits his intelligence.

The same can be said about his perceptual ability. If he doesn't give himself time to look properly he doesn't get the information needed for learning and solving problems. He may or may not be perceptually handicapped in a physiological or neurological sense. Just as we cannot tell what intelligence potential the unforthcoming child has because he is not using it, so we cannot assess the perceptual ability of the inconsequential because he doesn't attend to the tasks.

Nor for that matter is the inconsequential child fully using his intelligence. When he guesses rather than thinks he cuts the higher parts of his brain out of the operation. Unfortunately for him only the very simplest tasks can be solved by guessing. The result is that he gets discouraged and becomes an avoider. Instead of getting on with his work he looks around for something else to interest him, something that will be fun, something to get him out of the classroom or out of work, such as being tired or going to the washroom. We all know the type!

It was observations such as these which prompted our new approach to teaching. After diagnosing these sorts of learning disability, the natural thing is to try to think of means of counteracting them. One difficulty is that they appear at quite an early age, probably springing from constitutional origins. Astonishingly early also, we can observe the secondary disabilities developing — the unforthcoming child retreating into dullness or retardation and the inconsequential retreating into hyperactivity, distractibility and nuisance. The moral is to start the corrective work early, above all to prevent the development of these secondary handicaps.

The ideal age at which to begin to train a child in good thinking strategies is probably well below that of starting school. But only a few children attend nursery classes and the detection of those who are likely later to show learning problems is complicated by widely differing milestones of development. In practice, therefore, first year infants, or kindergarten as we call it, is a good age to launch a detection and prevention programme and our experimental work at Guelph has confirmed this.

The Flying Start programme, which is the result of our efforts, is presented in three phases. The first is the Learning to Learn Kit. This teaches the child to examine a task closely. It gives him an expectation

214

of success by starting with very easy tasks and training him how to set about them. The tasks are graded by small steps so that he never becomes discouraged. The aim is to change his attitude from one of 'I can't do it' to one of 'I can do it'. It shows the impulsive child that there are better ways than guessing. For all types of children it results in their making the best use of their perceptual and mental abilities.

The second and third phases are Learning about Reading and Learning about Number. These do not aim at measurable attainment so much as developing the concepts which act as springboards for future progress.

However the Flying Start is not merely a compensatory programme for the learning disabled. If we leave children to develop their own learning styles in a so called free permissive educational environment, we end up with a wide range of scholastic ability. The intelligent — let us rather say those who spontaneously practise good strategies — forge ahead. Apart from the learning handicapped that I have described, there is the mass of average and somewhat subaverage children who get by, but are not making optimum use of their abilities. They also need to be shown how to learn if they are not to relapse into a second best performance. The Flying Start can thus be maximally effective in a preventive sense by general class use during the first year of school. Concurrent testing of the materials in a Surrey infants class shows that it fits well into a group work setting.

The materials are carefully programmed in that they are graded into a planned sequence of activities. The learning style a child uses and the degree of success he has are recorded day by day on a Progress Card. At the beginning some children will be reluctant to try. Even at the tender age of five many have decided to opt out of learning if they are allowed to do so. But once they can be induced to participate they are carried along by the appeal of the activities. These are entirely in the form of games. Some are individual, some are played with one other child, some are group games. We don't *tell* children that they have to attend, to use their brains, to have a try. Such nagging at best will be ineffectual, at worst it can force a child to strengthen his defences against being taught. They learn productive learning styles by experience. They find that looking closely, thinking things out, having a good try, bring success.

As soon as the children have learnt to organize their learning behaviour and to cooperate with others, the teacher leaves them so far as possible to play the games by themselves. All the activities are self-correcting either by the individual child, or by his partner or his group. There is plenty of room for initiative. The children can go and get a game and pack it up again without the intervention of the teacher. The teacher will always be needed to help those who haven't reached this stage, but at least she is free to help them rather than be forced to let them drift.

The Flying Start programme is not yet a finished product. Indeed it never will be because its use constantly reveals new needs and generates new ideas.However we have satisfied ourselves that in its present form it does achieve results. Among a sample of children referred by their kindergarten teachers as likely to have learning problems in Grade 1, all benefited from it, and the approach to learning of many was completely restyled. Moreover they enjoyed it, thus seeing that learning could be fun.

The illustrations show some representative items of the first Learning to Learn section, and how it merges into the Learning about Reading section.

Four-piece picture puzzles

As can be seen, there are no shapes and colours to act as a guide to fitting the pieces together . The child has to make sense of the picture. There is a premium on attention. The puzzles provide something that the child can do quickly and easily if he sets about it the right way.

Two-piece puzzles

Even the four-piece puzzles are too frightening for some children. If they have already learnt to avoid problems or to take refuge in dullness, they will respond only to something that they can see immediately how to do. But having done the very easy two-piece they can quickly be persuaded to do the four-piece puzzle. And from that stage success reinforces success.

Merry-go-rounds

When the Programmed Reading Kit was tried some years ago with culturally disadvantaged children in New York, the research team said it was useless to expect them to cooperate in any organized game. Again the behavioural barrier! With young inconsequential children one finds likewise that they snatch and play out of turn. So we invented the merry-go-rounds as a means of training this type of child to have the patience to play with other children.

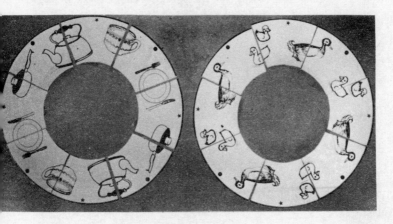

One child has the star segments and the other the dot segments, and since these are arranged alternately, neither can do any fitting alone. They learn by experience that they have to cooperate and to take turns.

In the simplest circle, the four pieces dealt to each player are identical. He can succeed merely by placing his pieces in turn.

In the second circle, two of the four are the same, so that a further simple act of attention is required.

In the third and fourth merry-go-rounds, all the four pieces dealt to each player are different. Progressively more attention and discrimination are required.

Post boxes

In the post box game the child has to post the letters in the right box. Easy enough if you take the time to look and compare but the inconsequential child often doesn't.

This is a self-correcting game. Another player checks the posting by matching the black half-discs on the backs of the cards with the other halves on the floor of the box. Thus each correct posting is reinforced straightaway. If the child gets careless he has the card returned by the other player with the word 'Wrong'. The wrong response is, psychologically speaking, punished not by an adult but by losing face in a game.

217

The blue post boxes contain the directionally confusing letters. If the child persists in getting them wrong more concentrated practice can be given by covering up the other letters.

The matcher's game

This conditions the child to withhold the impulsive response and to think ahead, i.e. to rehearse a solution mentally in advance. The task is to find the matching card from the set of six. There are always two criteria, one of which is subdivided into left and right alternatives.

This is the pirate set. The child has to note one difference (hat or no hat), hold it stored in his mind, then study the next difference (two legs or wooden left or right leg). Guessing means a low probability of success.

In this game the checking is by the number of lines on the backs of the cards.

Each child puts his set of six cards in a holder. Another child gives him the card to be matched.

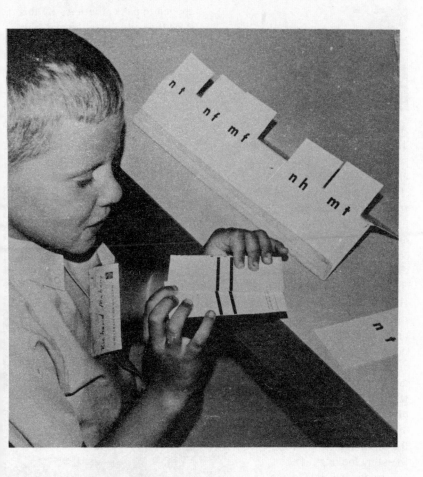

The child checks his choice by seeing if the bars tally.

In the later sets considerable discrimination is needed. An adult coming fresh to one of these sets has to spend some little time on it, and may make mistakes. But many five year olds or borderline mentally retarded manage quite well when they have had practice with the easier sets.

The principle of right and and left and of direction is then applied to pairs of letters. By this stage the child doing the matching has learnt to move the card systematically along the row. He has become conditioned to use a good strategy involving attention and forethought.

Animal puzzles

These animal puzzles are designed so as to make careful attention and understanding more effective as a strategy than the trial and error used by impulsive children in doing ordinary jigsaws. There are no colour differences and all the shapes are similar, so that the child has to look at the picture. He makes the puzzle by taking the pieces in a prescribed order, as given by the numbers on the backs. These are arranged so that he can always see, if he looks attentively, where the piece fits. The placing of each piece is a task of only limited complexity, the solution of which can be found by looking . The unforthcoming child learns not to be afraid to try.

There is a progression from six to eight to ten pieces. Animals have always had a great emotional appeal to children. They also have the advantage of being shapes that are easily recognized.

By the time the children have been through the Learning to Learn programme they have the right learning styles for making a start on the Programmed Reading Kit. These are some of the kindergarten (first year infants) referred to our Centre by their teachers as slow learners, working with the Giant Touch Cards. The great majority of them got through the Learning to Learn Kit of the Flying Start in seven to eight weeks, attending the Centre twice a week for an hour or so.

Here they are later using First-Letter Cards. We aim at getting them to learn to hear initial sounds and to generalize the letter/sound associations on a variety of words.

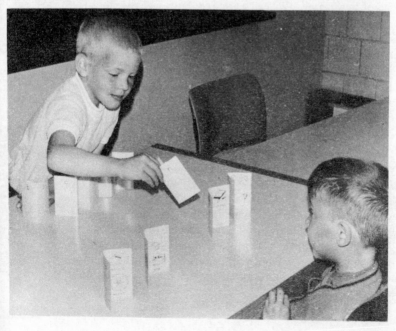

Conclusion

The rationale of the Flying Start Early Education Kit can be summed up in the following propositions:

1 Only a certain number of children make the best use of their abilities by spontaneously adopting good learning strategies. Probably the great majority of children fail to do so.
2 Learning ability is more a matter of the style of learning a child adopts than any hypothetical 'intelligence'. Even so called intelligence tests are chiefly measures of learning styles.
3 Learning styles are themselves aspects of the general behavioural or coping strategies which a child uses. Learning disability is thus best diagnosed in terms of behavioural or temperamental handicaps.
4 If the above propositions are extended to cover the severe learning disability of the retarded, and means can be found of correcting their poor strategies, much mental retardation and educational subnormality which has hitherto been accepted fatalistically may be curable.
5 It is important to initiate such a compensatory programme as early as possible, preferably during the first year at school, while a child can still be taught to adopt alternative learning styles and before secondary defences against learning have developed.

The new Programmed Reading Kit

During the years 1967-9 we subjected the Programmed Reading Kit to a very intensive reappraisal, working with the most difficult types of slow learner. We had a group of boys aged ten and a half to thirteen years old who owing to their hyperactivity, nuisance and disruptiveness had been placed in a special class as perceptually handicapped. We had a further group of thirteen to fourteen year old boys who, as a result of using wrong learning strategies or for cultural reasons, had become completely discouraged about reading. We had another group of young, supposedly dull but really unforthcoming children; and we had a mixture of children with very severe behaviour problems or other handicaps.

The psychological and educational principles upon which the Kit was developed have remained unchanged. It promotes learning through experiences and discovery rather than by being told. The mastery of the most important concepts and facts of reading – the sound/symbol associations and the ability to deal with sound groupings as units of response – forms the core of the method.

The learner is motivated to get this information for himself (from suitably presented material) because he wants to keep his end up in a game or to complete some attractive task for his own satisfaction. He can see if he is right or wrong since the results of his choices are immediately fed back to him. He is in an optimal learning situation. Good choices — which mean that he is using good learning strategies — are rewarded. Poor choices — resulting from poor strategies such as guessing or trying to pick up cues from the teacher — are penalized. The steps are finely graded so that every child becomes conditioned to expect to succeed, which means that he learns to try rather than to avoid.

In our work with the experimental groups of children, the regular procedure of the research team was to meet at the end of each day and ask themselves: Did anything not go as well as it might? Is anything else needed ? Was the level of motivation being maintained ? Is any pupil sticking at any point?

The result of this process was a thoroughgoing revision of the Programmed Reading Kit.

In the early part — where the learner has to learn to make the letter sound associations by listening to initial sounds — we decided that provision must be made for those who need more practice, in order to make the associations automatic, than could be provided by the Touch and Morris Cards and the written exercises. This applied particularly to the perceptually handicapped, better termed inconsequentials, who are alert and on the look out for novelty. A totally different form of activity was needed at this learning stage. This applied also to our work with the groups of slow-learning five year olds who had progressed from the Flying Start Programme to the beginnings of reading. We were able to observe the growth of the ability to generalize the sound values of letters on to all words. This conception did not come in a flash. There was no moment when the child suddenly appreciated that a letter stood for a certain sound whatever the word was. And having got this idea for one letter it was not immediately transferred to others. It had to be expanded from a particular observation to a general principle. So a great deal of experience has to be provided, especially for the young learner. It is not a question of their not being ready. They get there, even if, as with those we worked with, their learning styles are initially inefficient.

We developed the new First-Letter Bingo game to meet this need for experience of the general applicability of the letter/sound associations. Each word on any line begins with a different letter so that a correct choice depends only on being able to pair the initial sound and the initial letter. The demands of the game are such that the learning soon becomes habit in an unselfconscious way, rather like learning to be at ease in water by playing waterpolo.

We used the same strategy in building the phonic/sight habits of initial consonants and vowels. In the Pattern Bingo game all five words in any line begin with the same consonant, but the vowels are different. In a bingo game there is no time for a laborious building up 'm-a', 'm-e', 'm-i', 'm-o', 'm-u'. The first two letters have to be grasped as perceptual units without going through the slow and artificial building up process. This of course is the key to the effective use of the phonic code — coding by larger and larger units until the reader is responding to whole words at a glance.

The Half-Moon cards confirmed their value as a means of giving the idea of dealing with what is traditionally called fusing or blending. The point to emphasize here is that the process is a rapid unconscious one that deliberate building up can interfere with.

The next significant change was the division of the simple word building into two Brick Walls. The first deals with three-letter words only, the second with the two and three-letter consonant groupings such as 'bra', 'st', 'str'. Each Brick Wall has a boldly printed check card and a scoring card. Players move counters along a street of houses as they add the correct bricks.

In the latter part of the Kit there are important additions for dealing with the phonic conventions. The Tricky Bits are now called the Colour Sound Cards. The *name* of the colour acts as a reminder of the sound. 'Green' deals with the 'ee' sounds, 'White' with the long 'i', 'Brown' the 'ow', 'Blue' the 'oo' and so on. The long vowels associated with the 'lazy e' are also introduced here. For example the 'Gold' card has words like 'hole' and 'bone' as well as 'boat' and 'show'.

Then for each Colour Sound Card there is a Snakes Game following the same arrangement. The head of the snake bears the name of the colour, and the segments with which the snake is built up contain all the vowel conventions by which the sound is spelt. There is also a Check and Score Card as for the Brick Wall.

The Sentence Families with their Noun, Sentence and Sense and Nonsense remain, as do the Long-Word Jigsaws, but the Cinema Seats have been dispensed with in the UK edition in view of the use of bingo-type games at the earlier stages.

Breakthrough to Literacy
David Mackay

Warden
Centre for Language in Primary Education

The materials

The Breakthrough to Literacy materials do not claim to be entirely new; they make use of ideas and techniques which are a new departure in the teaching of literacy as well as using those that have been used before. They do, however, change the emphasis from *reading* to *composing* and as a result they dispense with the need for simplified texts on which to start children reading. They use our traditional orthography.

The pre-reading materials, the magnet board and accompanying figurines are intended as a means of encouraging talk, discussion, and story telling in children who have had too little of such experience of language. Some written language may be incorporated with this material at an appropriate stage.

The crux of the Breakthrough to Literacy is the Sentence Maker. The teachers' version is an enlarged version of the children's and is used to establish basic understanding of the English writing system, to train the children in the use of the materials and to enable them to learn how to use about fifteen to twenty words *of their own choice* to make sentences *of their own choice.*

The words are printed on white cards and these are contained in pockets attached to a sheet of stout card. Each word card has its own place in the word store. To make a sentence, the selected cards are placed in a plastic stand which grips them and holds them in position. Then, when the sentence has been read, the cards are removed from the stand and replaced in the word store, each word card being matched against the word printed behind the pocket. When children think of a sentence which requires a word not included in the store, the teacher supplies this by writing it out on specially prepared blank card.

The Word Store is a collection of 132 items arranged approximately in groups of nouns, adjectives, pronouns, verbs, prepositions. Word endings ('s', 'ed', 'ing') and punctuation (. ?) are included. Roughly half the items are grammatical items (words like 'and', 'when', 'of', 'am') and the remainder are lexical (words like 'school', 'dad', 'paint'). All the words included were found to be those mostt frequently asked for by children of five to six years old who used the materials during two years of trials.

The child's Sentence Maker is a triptych which stands in front of the child. The first two pages (as in the teachers' model) are printed with the entire word store, and children transfer to this personal model with the words they have learned to use with the teacher. The third page is blank in order to provide each child with items which are chosen personally. In this way each Sentence Maker has a common, shared store and a personal store which is likely to vary considerably from child to child.

When a child has made a sentence in the small plastic stand, it is taken to the teacher and read to her. She then records this in a special book, thus preserving a perfect record of the sentence. She goes on doing this until the child's skill in handwriting is sufficiently advanced to allow him to do so for himself. Thus, long before many children have mastered handwriting, they are able to compose with the written language. In short, they are writing their own books.

Breakthrough to Literacy exploits children's ability to compose in this way by including twenty-four printed books with texts of the kind children produce for themselves. These are accompanied by vivid and imaginative colour illustrations by many artists. These books are intended to be used as any other children's books might be used, for reading to children and discussing with them, and for children to read themselves. In many cases the simple text is supplemented by pictures rich in detail so that children may make their own uses of the stories to produce books of their own, tell stories from their own experiences, and take up suggestions for dramatic play.

The thinking behind the materials

Becoming literate is a process that takes many years. Few of us achieve full literacy; we give up when we reach point at which the demands made upon us are easily met and in most of us reading ability surpasses ability to write.

Breakthrough to Literacy is about the initial stages in learning to read and write. It introduces children to written language in order to provide an extension of their ability to use language by means of a second language medium. It proposes that the initial stages should be the same *in quality* as the more advanced stages, the only necesaary difference being in *the depth of understanding* with which the child begins, compared with that which he reaches on becoming fluent.

Breakthrough is intended for use as soon or as late as children are

226

ready to begin using written language. It has been found successful with all kinds of learners: children in a training centre (Brinkworth and Collins 1969) children in an ESN junior school, children in a partially hearing unit, children in a range of remedial situations (both primary and secondary), and over 7,000 five year old children in infants schools.

As materials and as a theory or set of theories, Breakthrough is not committed to particular ages or aptitudes. Having been used in a very wide range of both, it can truthfully be said that it is quite neutral to such aspects of the learner's situation. However it was devised as infant school material and it is in this role that it will be discussed here.

It is necessary to begin with the child as a successful language learner. The problem is, how can we enable him to succeed in using language in a second medium? It is complicated by the fact that we know all too little about children as language learners. We know much about what we as teachers ask them to do (and assertions here are not, to say the least, modest). We do not know what the child is in fact doing when we say 'Do this' or 'Do that'.

Breakthrough to Literacy begins with the child – the illiterate child – and provides a hypothesis about language learning which is exemplified by the materials . The materials are themselves inert. They are acted upon by the child. The teacher interacts with the child by talking about what he and she do, by showing how she does it and by helping the child to do it himself.

Thus in the beginning there is talk – talk that takes place when books are read in the classroom and talk that takes place when the teacher writes publicly in the classroom. Both kinds of talk are essential. In reading stories to the children the teacher is giving direct experience of what it means to read books which give pleasure to the listener. In talking about what she is doing she begins to use a metalanguage to describe in general terms what reading is as an activity. She mentions black marks, letters, words. She shows how she passes her eyes across a line of print. She points out the way lines of print follow one another. She shows how her finger can represent what her eyes do – more or less (leaving eye span and fixations on one side). She lets children show her and explain to her, so that they can put into their own language what they are learning. For only when they have done this will they be independent of the teacher, supported by their ability to understand complex and abstract matters related to the nature of the writing system. They learn the special use of words like begin, beginning, middle, end, direction, left and right, print, handwriting, letter, shape, sound, space. These are talked about and the teacher shows how, when *she* writes, she also arranges the marks the way the printer did. Telling and reading are differentiated — making up stories from pictures is differentiated from reading what is printed under the pictures. Children are learning to distinguish the ways in which these symbolic systems differ in how they represent reality. Learning of this kind may well begin in the nursery school and be encouraged to take place at home also.

Children are curious about their whole environment and are concerned to start mastering what they see adults able to do, especially when this is seen to have positive gain for the individual and the approval of everyone around the child. The child's motives for becoming like interested, patient, affectionate adults in the interests they have and the skills they command, are very great. Children work hard at this as soon as they understand what it is they are aiming for and they sustain their efforts while they have success in their achievement.

In any class there are likely to be many different departure times which represent readiness to become concerned with written language . The starting point chosen by the teacher will make a marked difference in the ability of the child to handle the ideas involved. It is for this reason that we begin with general notions about the written language that can be gained not just by reading and telling stories and by writing notices in the classroom, but by talking about it and giving children demonstrations of how we do it. So when the teacher writes 'The morning glory climbs up the window' she sees to it that children can watch her. She talks about where she starts her writing, about letter shapes, about words, word spaces and so on. She shows all this without expecting children to copy her. She is doing something quite different: she is explaining some of the fundamental notions behind what she is doing and showing how she operates with these notions. It is these fundamental aspects that we believe must be understood first. The details — the many complex details — come gradually and come later.

The teacher may continue for half a term or a term providing her children with the opportunity to talk with her in this way and to watch her do what she calls reading and writing. She is not waiting for readiness to happen, she is drawing children nearer and nearer to the point at which they wish to participate. By illustrating the same general points with a wide variety of examples, many stories, many pieces of writing, she presents the children with general ideas. Of course, stories are read and reread, and ideas about the stories are discussed, incidents retold and painted and acted. Rhymes are constantly used and the children get used to the variety of uses to which writing is put. During this time children begin to see written language consciously whereas before they ignored it and they begin to extend this interest beyond the classroom to the home, to television captions and printed programme notices, to the street, to shop fronts, street names, advertisements. Once awakened, children's interests widen all the time.

This attitude to readiness involves ideas, talking about them and demonstrations of the results of ideas in action. When children themselves begin to participate, what they most often choose to do is recognize words with special significance for them — these may not be what we expect, the range may be from Double Diamond to Chitty Chitty Bang Bang, Snow White, SS Northumbria and Concorde. They are also likely to ask to write, to make letter shapes and will attempt to write their own names. They will also begin to notice similarities — Celia notices her name begins in the same way as Cinderella — and contrasts and differences — it does not begin the same way as Patrick, it is smaller than Cinderella. These are the beginnings of useful strategies which will come to be used frequently, with many other strategies, later in their progress towards literacy.

The way in which children learn their mother tongue has many interesting features which contribute to their success:

1. There is interaction between adults and children.

2. There is interaction between receiving and producing language (between listening and speaking).

3. From the start the child has productive and receptive skills to use as befits his state of development. The receptive skill (listening) is more advanced than the productive skill, in the early stages.

4. Very early the child has ideas about the role of language. (See Halliday 1969) He uses the language for many purposes and in varying contexts.

5. His ideas about language change radically over the whole period of his childhood as his language skill comes nearer and nearer to matching that of the people around him.

6. This is not done in an *orderly* fashion like the schema of a grammar book, but in a way which is the outcome of interactions between people, events, objects, experiences, feelings, emotional states, social and psychological situations and so on. Thus each child discovers his own way of creating a model of the world, internalizing linguistic processes, social and cultural processes, psychological processes and modifying these in the course of time.

7   One feature in the child's learning is, in the light of the way
     teaching operates, remarkable: errors in the way he uses language
     are natural to him and to all children. Most of the time these
     are overlooked by the adults around them.

8   These errors are signs of strategies in use. Their disappearance
     may be taken to indicate that more workable linguistic hypotheses
     have been reached by the child.

9   In so doing the child's practice is a search for patterns and an
     understanding of how and where these occur. Searching for
     patterns and their power to symbolize experience are thus more
     important than repetition. For much of what the child hears
     is new in the sense that the speakers around him create very
     large numbers of sentences, many of which are being said for the
     first time, but which will at the same time be very like other
     sentences that have been created previously.

10   Many of the utterances the child hears will be partial and will
     contain false starts, repetitions, hesitations, mistakes. It is from
     such imperfect data that the child internalizes his systems of
     phonology, grammar, lexis and meaning.

11   The child's search for patterns in the spoken language lead him
     through familiarity to hold expectations of what is likely to
     happen. In time he uses these expectations and the redundancy built
     into the language to predict what is going to be said, to anticipate lexis,
     grammar and semantic features of discourse, and thus to speed up the act
     of communication.

Our major hypothesis was that most of these essential features of
learning to speak and listen were important for the way children should
come to use the written language to read and compose. Examination
of current and past practice in the classroom, along with the provision
of published manuals for the teacher and other materials for children's
use, does not support this view of the learner and the learning situation,
although the work of gifted and intuitive teachers does. It is interesting
to note some of the chief features of these practices about which some
teachers are now puzzled and confused.

1 The child is placed in a learning situation which demands the use of
the receptive skill of reading. He has to become a reader — exclusively
at first. However, the pedagogical material he is given to read uses
language in a way that is unique to material of this kind. In 1908 Huey
commented:

The most striking thing about most of them (primers) is the
inanity and disjointedness of their reading content, especially

in the earlier parts. No trouble has been taken to write what
the child would naturally say about the subject in hand, nor
indeed, usually, to say anything connectedly or continuously...

2 Teachers, as well as some reading theorists, are not adequately trained
in linguistic matters. They are not aware of the nature of language. They *are*,
however, overwhelmingly conscious of words and anxious and uncertain
about the relationships between speech sounds and letters. This results in
concern for only *certain* aspects of what it is the child has to learn at the
expense of *all aspects together.*

Strickland (1962) sums up her investigations of reading primers and
studies of these prior to hers, by saying:

There is no evidence that such studies give attention to the
structure of sentences or to the familiarity of such structures
to the readers for whom the material is written.

We are all familiar with texts which are written with this lack of
awareness of the nature of language — sentences such as

See Jane run. Run, run, run.
Baby see mother.
Put the pin in the tin bin Min.
Vick's velvet vest.
Dick, this seat by you is for Jack.
I am as I am, not as I am not.

In contrast to these, let me give some examples of sentences composed by
five year old Manchester children using The Sentence Maker from
Breakthrough to Literacy:

Mummy went to the clinic instead of to school this morning.
We have all been to church to see the font.
We have got a new bath and washbowl and toilet.
Only me is going to Auntie Betty's house.
Diane and me were playing at monsters.

Such sentences show children making use of their own linguistic resources,
using the language the way they know the language works and dealing with a
wide range of personal interests.

Reid (1970) quotes Schonell as asserting that 'It is through early
reading experiences that young children develop their first language
patterns'. There is a certain effrontery in such ignorance: perhaps this was

231

unintentional. At the very least, however, it reveals one reading expert
as very muddled and very mistaken in his views; which may explain the arid
syntax and semantics of the sentence from *Happy Venture Book 2,*
'Dick, this seat by you is for Jack'.

Reid (1970) herself comments:

> The aptness of Huey's strictures was borne out, however,
> by the fact that all the work on vocabulary and readability
> undertaken since his time has not removed the grounds of
> his criticism.

In the Teacher's Manual to Breakthrough we have set out
the criteria on which our own books were based. We hope Huey would
have approved of them, for we set children's interests and experience of the
language high on our list of priorities. We were concerned to keep close
to the life styles of real children and to use language the way they use
language.

3 The lack of awareness of grammar, semantics and context is further
confounded by a belief that it is the medium which presents the problem in
learning to read. We believe this sidesteps the major issues and draws
attention away from the fact that neither the writing system nor the nature
of language are sufficiently well understood. Goodman (1969) summarizing
the findings of research he has undertaken in America writes:

> With alphabetical orthographies the regularity of correspondence
> rules for letter/sound relationships is not nearly as important as
> many people have believed. Readers are able to use syntactic and
> semantic cues to such a considerable extent that they need only
> minimal graphic cues in many cases. They can tolerate a great
> deal of irregularity, ambiguity and variability in orthographies
> without the reading process suffering . . . . in my research I have encountere
> many youngsters who are so busy matching letters to sounds and naming
> word shapes that they have no sense of the meaning of what they are readin
> Reading requires not so much skills as strategies that make it possible to
> select the most productive ones.

Traditional orthography has been so misunderstood over the years ,
so badly written about by some linguists and all reading experts, that
teachers, let alone children, have had little hope of coming to understand
how it works the simple way — by understanding the ideas it embodies
and by utilizing its positive attributes. The criticism that it contains

large numbers of irregularly spelt words is based not upon adequate linguistic description, but rather upon a longing for the relationship between sounds and marks to be simple. But it is complex in this respect and it does much more than just reflect the sound system of English.

> ...our present writing system ... is largely morphemic in
> nature and alphabetic in expression. It would clearly
> be unwise to abandon the alphabetic style of writing.
> It is most economical in terms of the number of characters
> needed (though a small number of letters could without
> danger be added to our present inventory); and, at the
> same time, it is flexible since, if there is no slavish adherence
> to a one phoneme - one letter principle, considerable
> complexity of linear patterning is possible. In any
> case, it becomes evident that if an efficient system of
> visual communication is to be achieved, linguistic
> considerations on a higher level than the phonological
> should be taken into account. (Gimson 1968)

Complexity is confused with irregularity. The major fault in phonics is that it is based on an inadequate, home made description of the orthography.

Until recently, no detailed information of a completely reliable kind has been available. But now there are two such sources which may be used in the coming years. The first, the result of several years research, is a transformational orthographic description of English spelling. The results were made public this year by Venezky (1970) of the University of Wisconsin, and published by Mouton. The second is a systematic description by my colleague K. Albrow (1970) at University College London, to be published later this year.

These criticisms of the nature of phonic information at present in use in our schools must not be taken to mean that we wish to dispense with information of this kind but rather that we would wish it to be superceded by something better. At the same time it is necessary to give the warning that this is only a small part of the job of which grammar and meaning are far more important, more complicated and more ignored.

4 Teacher ability varies greatly. Not all teachers do equally well with the same method or the same materials. But if they have to, the best materials will be those that support the weak, do not get in the way of the strong, and above all, *enable the child to operate with his own power as a language user.*

5 Some children do well on any method and with any materials. This proves nothing more than that some children *learn* successfully whether we *teach* successfully or not. And they would almost certainly do even better with better teaching and better materials. Dakin (1969) has commented that 'Research and theory in the past have concentrated on looking at the child from the angle of the materials and the teacher. But the child is precisely the variable we know least about. How does he approach the teacher and the materials? How does he learn?' It is just this point which emerges from the interviews Reid (1966) describes in 'Learning to think about reading'. This too is what we asked before Breakthrough to Literacy was conceived. And in our answer we were concerned to place the child at the centre and to give him a power he had been denied with other materials — the power to produce language in written form for himself without awaiting the development of the ability to handwrite or spell.

Our theory attempted to

1 Provide the child with a way of utilizing his power as a language user/native speaker which allows him to start from where he was and who he was. The child must operate productively and receptively with the written language from the start.

2 Provide for the fact that the language user is involved at several linguistic levels simultaneously and that all these must be represented in what the teacher does, in what the child does, in what the materials seek to do. Most teaching methods and materials stop at 'word' and are largely unaware of structures and their intricate links with meaning.

3 Provide for the need to put ideas about what he is doing into words and given the power of generalizations which are then exemplified by the way he uses the written language.

4 Provide for practice which is personal to each child as it always is when learning to talk. Furthermore it is more concerned with discovering and exploiting patterns than with repetition of the same pattern, whether this be a word or a sentence.

5 Provide for interaction through talk between writers, readers, adults and other children when written language is being used. Clues to the formation of strategies grow out of confident use of the language and out of talk about the language.

6 Ensure that the social and creative activities of learning to use the written language are clearly acknowledged.

7 Ensure that experiment, play, accident, intent and error are all part of the natural language learning process and are to be expected and accepted.

Thus, in our theory we were concerned with the nature of the language, the nature of the language learner and the uses to which the language is put by native speakers and writers.

Eventually language users must understand ideas about the language and its availability in two media. They will have to work with ideas and with strategies – and these alone. The final aim, as Reid (1970) points out, 'should be to produce materials and methods by means of which children's linguistic resources, in their strengths and their limitations, may be first matched and utilized, and then carefully extended in ways which not only follow the chronology of acquisition but are of maximum usefulness in all aspects of communication behaviour'.

It is to meet such aims as these that Breakthrough to Literacy was produced. And for this reason Breakthrough is *not* a reading scheme. The Sentence Maker and the Word Maker are the kernel of the materials. It is these which personalize a process which has been stereotyped and impersonal for far too long and in which both the teacher and the child have played uncertain roles. The Teacher's Manual to Breakthrough gives the teacher extensive support in practical and theoretical matters. It places upon her the firm responsibility for knowing about the language and the child – knowledge she may not choose to ignore. This represents the formal aspect of her work. It leaves her free, and indeed positively encourages her, to invent infinitely various ways of presenting these formal aspects. One hopes that initial training and in-service training will serve increasingly to help her in both these respects in the future. For in the last resort, as Dakin (1969) warns, 'success or failure depends on what is learnt, not on what the knowledge she may not choose to ignore in her role as teacher. This represents the formal aspect of her work. It leaves her free, and indeed positively encourages her, to invent infinitely various ways of using the *content* of children's sentences to present these formal aspects. One hopes that initial training and in-service training will serve increasingly to help her in both these respects in the future. But in the last resort, as Dakin (1969) warns, 'success or failure depends on what is learnt, not on what the teacher and the materials set out to teach.'

References

Albrow, K. H. (1970) *The English Writing System: Notes towards a description* Department of General Linguistics, University College, London
Brinkworth, Rex and Collins, Joseph (1969) *Improving Mongol Babies and Introducing Them to School* (foreword by Professor L. S. Penrose) Belfast:

National Society for Mentally Handicapped Children, Northern Ireland
Region, 47, 56-61

Collins, Joseph (1968) *Improving Your Babies' Intelligence* Belfast:
National Society for Mentally Handicapped Children, Northern Ireland
Region

Dakin, Julian (1969) 'The teaching of reading' in Fraser, H. and O'Donnell,
W. R. (eds.) *Applied Linguistics and the Teaching of English* London:
Longmans

Gimson, A. C. (1968) 'The transmission of English: Supplement 1'
in Quirk, Randolph (ed.) *The Use of English* London:Longmans

Goodman, Kenneth. S. (1969) *Psycholinguistic Universals in the Reading*
Applied Linguistics, Cambridge, England

Applied Linguistics, Cambridge, England, September

Halliday, M. A. K. (1969) 'Relevant models of language' in Wilkinson,
A. M. (ed.) 'The state of language' *Educational Review* University of
Birmingham volume 22 no. 1 November

Halliday, M. A. K. (1968) 'Language and experience' in 'The place of languag
Educational Review volume 20 no. 2 February

Huey, E. B. (1908) *The Psychology and Pedagogy of Reading* Cambridge,
Massachusetts: MIT Press

Mackay, David, Thompson, Brian, and Schaub, Pamela (1970) *Breakthrough
to Literacy Teacher's Manual* London: Longmans

Reid, Jessie, F. (1966) 'Learning to think about reading' in *Educational
Research* volume 9 no. 1

Reid, Jessie F. (1970) 'Sentence structure in reading primers' in *Research
in Education* no. 3, Manchester University Press

Strickland, Ruth G. (1962) *The Language of Elementary School
Children: Its Relationship to the Language of Reading Textbooks and
the Quality of Reading of Selected Children* Bulletin of the School
of Education, Indiana University volume 38, no. 4

Venezky, Richard L. (1970) *The Structure of English Orthography*
The Hague: Mouton

Adult illiteracy – The general position
N. Dean

Principal Lecturer in Education
Sunderland College of Education

Summary
The adult illiterate finds many ways of concealing his problem from his
fellow workers. Authorities are willing to help if specific requests are
made to them. But the extent of the need is not obvious and is usually
much underestimated. In 1968, of forty-seven LEAs in twelve
geographical counties of England, seventeen reported that they had no
arrangements of a permanent nature to deal with adult illiteracy. A
national survey in 1969 by the National Association of Remedial
Education found 199 tuition centres runs by LEAs and voluntary
organizations.

Identifying the adult illiterate
A man with a small farm and one employee sees a television programme
about a centre ten miles away which offers to teach adults to read
and write and since, though he can read a little, his writing is negligible,
he goes there. He meets his employee who has seen the same programme.
Till then neither knew the other had any problem. The employee could
not read at all which eased the embarassment! This is not a fictitious
account shaped to introduce a talk: it is a true story of 1970.

A quick-witted and verbally adroit miner attending classes over a
period of almost three years to learn to read and write boasts that
he is able to keep his handicap a secret from the men he knows and
works with.

The Education Department of a large city in the south is asked to
respond to a questionnaire about provision for adult illiterates and
answers: 'We have no demand here for such provision, but if we did
we would offer home tuition.' This is, of course, a true and fair
answer; there has been no expressed demand. But it is hard to believe
that in a city of say 200,000 people, there are no illiterates, no
needs, no demands, if demand were defined as the difference between
the complete functional literacy of all and the actual position.

If such situations can exist, then any set of figures that claims to
offer even approximate numbers of adult illiterates and
semi-literates in this country must be suspect. Many may experience
no difficulty in revealing that they do not know margarine from
butter, but who readily admits that he does not know a from b?

237

A pilot questionnaire in 1968

In 1968 the writer chose twelve geographical counties of England:

North: Northumberland, Durham, Yorkshire
East: Norfolk, Suffolk, Essex
Midlands: Warwickshire, Staffordshire, Northamptonshire
South: Sussex, Kent, Hampshire.

All the LEAs situated in those areas were approached for information
concerning teaching centres for the adult illiterate. Of the forty-nine
LEAs originally approached, forty-seven responded and seventeen
of these reported that they had no such current arrangements. Of
the seventeen, five said that if approached they would offer home
tuition, one would arrange private tuition and a further three were
considering establishing teaching centres. Although this was only two
years ago it is fair to say that the position has improved since then.

Within each area described above, the writer then approached the
centres listed in the returns as providing courses or arrangements for
tuition either for the functional illiterate or the backward reader. The
criterion adopted in selecting such centres was that they should be for
adults who needed substantial help in reading in order to prevent them
from being significantly handicapped in their own society.

Thirty-six centres which responded to the questionnaire included
seventeen which had been running for at least five years, and a newer
wave that must have begun about 1965 to 1966. Most centres were,
naturally, in adult or further education centres. Others arose from other
work with ESN children, hospitals and centres for the physically handicapped,
and penal establishments.

Most classes were small — twenty out of thirty-six had less than six in
mid-session — and the number of dropouts could often have a critical
effect on the continued existence of the centre. Authorities seemed ready
to help if approached with specific requests but did not, on the whole,
take the initiative.

There was much difference of opinion about whom the classes should be
for. There was the economic argument — take only those able to benefit —
and the welfare argument — take them even if ultimate achievement will be
negligible. This latter view came usually from centres linked with child
guidance clinics and educational psychologists.

Research in this area

The writer then approached within the same sample area fifty-seven colleges
of education and the education departments of thirteen universities, asking
for any information they could give of relevant literature, research being
conducted in their university/college and so on. This crop took little
garnering. If there was relevant research in the universities concerned, the

professors of education did not seem apprised of it at that time. A few colleges of education running special one year courses in remedial education gave the topic of adult illiteracy some attention, but to the majority of tutors in colleges and universities it seemed that adult illiteracy was a problem for others — not for them.

A national survey in 1969

In 1969 the National Association for Remedial Education conducted a questionnaire throughout England. For various administrative reasons such questionnaires do not all reach their destinations, and many are never returned. This one reached 166 LEAs. Twenty-seven did not reply. Of those who replied, 104 were making regular provision, and a further fourteen were making no regular provision. Twenty-one more made no regular provision but would offer individual tuition on request.

The survey found 199 centres run by LEAs and voluntary organizations. There were at least 1170 immigrants receiving tuition in classes other than those for immigrants only, and there were 2,765 non-immigrants in classes. These figures exclude those being helped in hospital, handicapped and penal centres and must be regarded as an underestimate of those receiving attention.

Material available

The NARE has prepared a list of teaching centres in reading and writing for adults in England. Copies of this list, and of the NARE survey, are sent to any inquirer who sends a stamped, addressed envelope. Up to date information is always welcome and should be sent to NARE.

The Association has also attempted, experimentally, to circulate a duplicated news sheet about adult illiteracy. The cost for postage and production in the initial year was 12½p. The first issue was circulated at Easter 1970 and the next will be due in November 1970. Inquiries about such materials should be sent to: Mr N. Dean, Sunderland College of Education, Ryhope Road, Sunderland SR2 7EE.

Some handicaps are obvious. Some had to be made so — the leper had his bell. Some are unseen. I can claim that you passed in the street, or talked with, or perhaps even welcomed to your home, at least one illiterate last week — could you deny this? Some illiterates are financially better placed than some of us who help them. But they are all people with a handicap. Because of it they hide, they are frustrated, they are dissatisfied, they are lonely, they are anxious, they are defensive. They can conceal it, they can seem to get away with it, they can seem to be better off than many of us, but they are the 'secret people'. They can find it a relief to come for help, to admit what they have hidden, and to find that there are others there too.

Adult illiteracy – The Sunderland project

H. Lofthouse

Senior Lecturer in Education
Sunderland College of Education

Introduction

The work at the Sunderland College of Education concerned
with teaching reading and writing to adult illiterates began in October
1967 in response to an enquiry by the mother of a seventeen
year old youth. During the first term there were four course
members taught by three college tutors. From January to
Easter 1968 an extra course member was added and a number of
student helpers were recruited.

Publicity in the local press and a report on Tyne-Tees Television
brought an influx of applicants. By Easter 1970 there had been
fifty-five clients taught by five tutors, five qualified teachers and
twenty students.

Initial development

The first group of clients consisted of three men and one woman
whose ages varied between seventeen and thirty-two years. These were
taught by three volunteers from the staff of the Education Department.
The first question to be asked is why should they come forward, for
in two instances it had been seventeen years since they left school.

Two of the men (I shall call them G and R) were employed as miners,
and in this area of England some mines were closing because they were
considered uneconomic. For these men, therefore, redundancy was a very
real threat and in all probability they would soon have to find other
employment. In G's case the approach was made by his mother, a widow,
who saw only too well the future for her only son when she died. For
R the approach was made by his wife who saw a family unit breaking
up owing to the feelings of insecurity associated with the father's
illiteracy. R's wife was worried because the children, now at secondary
school, were asking father to help them with their homework. He, being
unable to do so, often sent them to his wife and told them not to
interrupt him as he was far too busy. As far as the children were concerned,
R would always be busy for he feared the day when they would discover
that he could not read. B aged seventeen wanted to join the merchant
navy but because of his extremely low educational standard was not able
to do so, so his mother contacted the college centre. Finally P, an attractive

twenty-two year old woman, was encouraged to attend by her mother and sister. It can be seen in these initial cases that all wanted to read for very different reasons.

In order to have as much teaching and contact time as possible, it was agreed to hold meetings on two evenings per week. One tutor would attend two evenings to teach G who appeared to be very withdrawn and whose speech was quiet and indistinct. The other two tutors attended one evening each and taught B, R and P as a small group.

One immediate problem was that of attendance for not all could attend every week. R and G for example worked from 2 p.m. to 10 p.m. one week in every four. If we take into consideration college vacations then effectively they were going to have fifty-four hours teaching per year, i.e. the equivalent of eleven school days.

We could have increased the time by doing one more evening but could we expect the clients to attend three evenings per week? Obviously not. Twice weekly attendance was the most we could expect for they had other commitments.

To establish a starting point for the teaching, each individual was tested for reading age and knowledge of small letter sounds using Schonell's Graded Word Reading Test and Test R 5a. Results showed in all cases a complete lack of knowledge of letter sounds, and reading ages of five years.

In some instances the problem was inability to discriminate the shapes of letters. Initially therefore use was made of materials to provide training in discrimination. This consisted of pictures and geometric shapes, as well as letter shapes. Practice was also given in the letter sounds.

Running parallel with this work there was a need for quick success in 'reading' to give a sense of achievement and confidence.To establish this, use was made of work and home experience to build a word and sentence vocabulary by 'look-and-say' methods using pictures from magazines and newspapers. Again we omitted the use of capital letters as we considered the problem of learning the lower case letters was difficult enough.

After some time G was still having a real problem in discriminating letter shapes. R was unable as yet to retain and recall some of the limited vocaublary introduced. P and B were making rapid progress. Because of the varying needs of each client it was felt that individual tuition was essential.

By this time, more clients were coming forward. In order to develop a one-to-one teaching situation we asked for volunteers from the students in the college of education. Apart from the obvious benefit to the clients, we felt that this would be a worthwhile experience for the students as they would be gaining insight into the problems of teaching reading.

When the first students came as 'helpers', the importance of the social situation was stressed for this was not just an instructional session.Breaks

241

and conversation were important. Many of the customers liked to talk about their problems, their progress in reading and also about work, home and family. It soon became clear that we were doing more than teaching reading – we were providing a therapeutic situation of a much broader kind.

Some clients were now at the stage when books were becoming important because, as they saw the situation, you were not really reading unless you had a book. P and B were at this point and were ready for the introduction of word building. We decided to use the Ladybird Key Words Reading Scheme because of its phonic basis. One problem however was the content. We were not at all sure that our mature clients would take kindly to material designed for young children. However we found that unlike scondary school children, the adults were only interested in the 'reading' i.e. word recognition and word building . Only later (Books 8 and 9 in the Ladybird series) did we find partial rejection of the material. When R reached this stage he wrote the following to one of the tutors: 'I am sick of this book. I want a better one or else. I will fetch my own.' Progress indeed! We introduced him to the Nippers series.

This introductory survey of the development of the centre is important as it was during this time that we laid the basis for the organization, namely the goals and how to achieve them within the framework of teachers and teaching.

Organization of the centre 1970
Finance
The course is free to the clients as the teaching is entirely voluntary. Books and materials are paid for by the Sunderland LEA and we have free use of the Education Department's annexe for two evenings per week for two hours each evening.

Sessions
A social club atmosphere has developed and time is not all instructional. This we consider is of use to the client as it helps him appreciate that he is not alone with his handicap.

Teachers
All the teachers are volunteers and receive no monetary remuneration. In our terminology they are the helpers. We have twenty college students, five qualified teachers employed by the Sunderland LEA and five college tutors.

The clients
The problem here is how to make contact, bearing in mind the scheme

and embarassment of the clients, and of course the fact that they themselves cannot read advertisements or other literature. A number of channels have been developed:

1 Institutional contact e.g. an enquiry through the local education authority, probation service, health service etc. .
2 Press/TV reporting contact. Following such reports we often receive a telephone call or a letter written by someone on behalf of the client.
3 Word of mouth contact through friends.

In three years we have had fifty-five clients — fourty-two men and thirteen women. Their age distribution is as follows:

Age in years	Number of clients
15 – 19	12
20 – 24	7
25 – 29	5
30 – 34	4
35 – 39	10
40 – 44	8
45 – 49	5
50 plus	3

Dropouts tended to be highest in the 15 – 19 age group as these are the clients who have joined the course under some pressure from employers or parents.

Attainment on entry (using Schonell's Letter Sounds Analysis Test R5a) show the following:

Number of clients	Letter sounds not known on entry
31	q
25 – 30	b g l y
20 – 24	c d f i j
	n r u w x z
15 – 19	a e h k m
	o p s t v

For example, between twenty-five and thirty of the fifty-five clients did not know the letter sounds b g l y.

Reading on entry as measured by the Schonell Graded Word Reading Test was found to be as follows:

Reading age	Number of clients
5·0	19
5 plus	11
6 plus	3
7 plus	9
8 plus	3
9 plus	2
10 plus	8

Our clients tend to fall into two categories:

1 Those with a low reading age (5·0 – 7·0) who are mainly concerned with reading – leading eventually to writing.
2 Those who feel that they are competent in reading but wish to improve their written work and who are very much aware of the fact that they are poor spellers. They tend to have a reading age of 8·0 or even higher.

Clients give various reasons for their disability and these are found to be distributed as follows:

Reason	Number
bad teaching	2
absence from school e.g. truancy	8
absence from school e.g. illness, physical defects	20
school changes (frequent)	2
low personal ability	15
reasons not clear	6

The main reason given for joining the course varies:

Reason	Number
better job opportunities	9
jobs plus increased personal independence	10
jobs plus better social opportunities	5
social opportunities plus family reasons	10
arranged by parents	4
no apparent reason	5

Having joined, the course ends when the client feels confident that he has achieved his aim. How long do they stay with us? R and G are still attending, while at the other end of the scale, some clients attended for one evening only. The total number who have left over the three years is twenty-five. Of these there were twelve whom we would consider dropouts. Their reasons for leaving were as follows:

Reasons for leaving	Number
change of employment	3
pressure from friends	1
medical and domestic	1
non-starters	3
not known	4

Most of the remaining thirteen clients whom we regarded as successful achieved a reading age of 10·0 plus. They were mainly concerned with written expression.

Conclusion

After three years of running this course we are now in a much better position to see what our general aims should be and to set realistic objectives for ourselves and our clients. Our aim is that clients should leave us not only able to read and write, but with an increased confidence in themselves based on their achievements. This, we hope, will enable them to lead a fuller life — one in which they enjoy the benefits of literacy as well as the satisfaction of belonging to the literate community.

United Kingdom Reading Association

The aims of UKRA are
to encourage the study of reading problems at all educational levels
to stimulate and promote research in reading
to assist in the development of teacher-training programmes
to act as a clearing-house for information about reading
to publish the results of pertinent and significant investigations
and practices

The activities of UKRA include
an international conference held each year
an information service on reading matters
an extensive range of publications available to members, often at
reduced prices
the journal *Reading* published three times a year
encouragement and guidance to help members set up local councils for
regular meetings

Membership of UKRA is
open to everyone interested in the study and teaching of reading
inexpensive – individual membership £1.00; student membership
£0.50; institutional membership £2.00

Membership enquiries to
W. Glyn Williams, Edge Hill College, Ormskirk, Lancashire

General enquiries to
Kenneth W. Birks, 69 Mile End Lane, Stockport, Cheshire SK2 6BP